UNIVERSITY OF CALIFORNIA
BIBLIOGRAPHIC GUIDES

SERIAL MUSIC

A Classified Bibliography of Writings on Twelve-Tone and Electronic Music

by ANN PHILLIPS BASART

1961
UNIVERSITY OF CALIFORNIA PRESS
BERKELEY AND LOS ANGELES

University of California Press
Berkeley and Los Angeles, California

Cambridge University Press
London, England

© 1961 by The Regents of the University of California
Library of Congress Catalog Card Number: 61-7538

In Memoriam E.S.S.

PREFACE

The twelve-tone technique, once thought to be the private and unintelligible musical language of a small group of composers, is today one of the most important influences in European and American music. Although it still creates a great deal of controversy, and although it has not yet been widely accepted by the general public, dodecaphony has achieved a permanent status in the history of music.

"Schönberg is not yet in 'Grove' (1910), and the notices in other works of reference are infinitesimal," wrote Charles Maclean in an early article on Schoenberg. Today the situation has changed so much that not only is Schoenberg in Grove's Dictionary, but articles and books about him, the twelve-tone technique, and other composers who use the technique continue to be written at an ever-increasing rate.

Because of this great body of writing, it is difficult for anyone interested in serial music to know where to begin. A few related bibliographies have appeared to date, but none so far with the purpose and scope of the present work. The most extensive bibliographies on Schoenberg, Berg, and Webern have appeared in René Leibowitz's Schoenberg and his school (1949), Luigi Rognoni's Espressionismo e dodecafonia (1954), Josef Rufer's Composition with twelve notes (1954), and George Perle's dissertation, Serial composition and atonality (1956; revised edition, University of California Press, 1961). Rognoni and Rufer list unpublished writings by these composers on a variety of topics—important information that is outside the scope of the present work.

Donald Mitchell has compiled a selective bibliography that lists writings on twelve-tone music and composers (Hinrichsen's Musical yearbook, 1952), but he does not indicate the contents of these writings. Since his list is taken from secondary sources, the bibliographical information offered varies widely and is in many cases quite scanty. Helmut Kirchmeyer's book, Igor Strawinsky (1958), contains a lengthy bibliography on contemporary music which includes some entries on serial music and composers.

Appearing too late for inclusion in the present work is a bibliography of books and articles on experimental music, compiled by Célestin Deliège and printed in the Revue Belge de musicologie [Special issue on experimental music], 8:136-148 (1959). It is preceded (p. 132-136) by an excellent discussion of the writings of the most important authors in the field. The bibliography is alphabetically arranged within each of the following categories: "Ouvrages," "Articles," "Témoignages d'écrivains," "Divers," and "Ouvrages et articles relatifs à l'électroacoustique musicale." It is principally concerned with the European avant-garde.

Other lists have appeared from time to time in periodical articles and in chapters of specialized books. Most of these are quite brief, and none indicates contents.

The present work is an attempt to gather together a large number of the significant writings—philosophical, historical, and analytical—which have appeared on serial music, and to arrange them by subject. "Serial music" is used in a wide sense here, because this bibliography includes not only twelve-tone music and electronic music (a very recent development, growing out of serial techniques), but also touches upon such related fields as musical expressionism, pre-dodecaphonic atonality, musique concrète, and "chance" music.

The bibliography is arranged in a classified manner, with entries under each topic subarranged chronologically. There are an author index and a subject index. Almost every entry is followed by a brief annotation, indicating the contents, scope, and/or general idea of the book or article. The present work is not, however, a critical bibliography, and, although an attempt has been made to guide the reader by means of the annotations, the quality of the material listed varies rather widely.

Ann P. Basart

CONTENTS

	Page
Introduction	xi
Abbreviations	xiii

	Entry no.
I. TWELVE-TONE MUSIC	
Philosophy and criticism	1-73b
History	74-118b
Analysis and theory	119-221
Compositional techniques	119-175c
Introductory articles addressed to the layman	119-125
Technical and specialized works	126-175c
Harmony	176-204a
Melody	205-207
Rhythm	208
Counterpoint	209-215
Notation	217-221
II. ELECTRONIC MUSIC	
Philosophy and criticism	222-233
Description and history	234-272
Compositional techniques	273-283a
III. THE VIENNESE SCHOOL	
Arnold Schoenberg	284-490
General	284-306a
Philosophy and criticism	307-354
Biography	355-372
Correspondence	373-379
Compositional techniques	380-394
General descriptions of works	395-413
Individual works	414-490
Alban Berg	491-563
General	491-498a
Philosophy and criticism	499-505
Biography	506-510
Correspondence	511-514
General descriptions of works	515-519
Individual works	520-563

Anton Webern 564-601
    General 564-572
    Philosophy and criticism 573-579
    Biography 580
    Correspondence 581-582
    Compositional techniques 583-586
    General descriptions of works 587-592
    Individual works 593-601

IV. OTHER COMPOSERS

Milton Babbitt 602-604
Luciano Berio 605-609
Pierre Boulez 610-631
    General 610-616
    Compositional techniques 617-618
    Individual works 619-631
John Cage 632-637
Luigi Dallapiccola 638-674
    General 638-643
    General descriptions of works 644-654
    Individual works 655-674
Wolfgang Fortner 675-684a
Roberto Gerhard 685-692
Josef Matthias Hauer 693-702
Hans Werner Henze 703-710
Hanns Jelinek 711-715
Giselher Klebe 716-719
Ernst Krenek 720-747
    General 720-727
    General descriptions of works 728-739a
    Individual works 740-747
René Leibowitz 748
Bruno Maderna 749
Luigi Nono 750-752
Henri Pousseur 753-754
Humphrey Searle 755-758
Mátyás Seiber 759-767
Karlheinz Stockhausen 768-777
Igor Stravinsky 778-823
    General 778-788
    Serial works 789-823

                                                                                           Page

AUTHOR INDEX 129

SUBJECT INDEX 147

INTRODUCTION

ARRANGEMENT

The bibliography is divided into four main sections:

    1. Twelve-tone music
    2. Electronic music
    3. The Viennese school (Schoenberg, Berg, Webern)
These three sections have a classified arrangement.

    4. Other composers who use serial techniques
This section is arranged alphabetically by composer.

The topics into which each section is divided are listed in the table of contents. All the entries under each topic are arranged chronologically. Where books and periodicals have the same year of publication, the books are listed first and the periodicals follow by months. Each entry is given in full only once, under the topic it most closely fits. Cross-references refer the user to related entries under other topics; they are arranged chronologically in with the entries.

FORM OF ENTRY

Articles

Entry for an article in a periodical:

491   Mantelli, Alberto. "Note su Alban Berg," <u>Rass mus</u> 9:117-132 (Apr 1936). Mus.

    This article by Mantelli will be found in the periodical <u>Rassegna musicale</u> (see the list of abbreviations, p. xiii) in volume 9, pages 117-132, for April 1936. There are musical examples.

Entry for an article in a book:

296   Stefan, Paul. "Arnold Schoenberg" <u>in</u> Thompson, Oscar, ed. Great modern composers. New York, Dodd, Mead, 1941, p. 267-277.

    Stefan's article is one of several in Thompson's book, and will be found on pages 267-277.

Books

Monographs

448a Wörner, Karl H. Gotteswort und Magie: die Oper 'Moses und Aron' von Arnold Schönberg. Heidelberg, Lambert Schneider, 1959. 93 p. Mus., port.

Wörner's book, Gotteswort und Magie: die Oper 'Moses und Aron' von Arnold Schönberg, was published in Heidelberg by Schneider in 1959, has 93 pages and includes some musical examples and a portrait (of Schoenberg).

Collections

168 Junge Komponisten. Wien, Universal Edition [c1958]. 133 p. Diagrs., mus., tables. (Die Reihe: Information über serielle Musik, 4.)

The title of this book is Junge Komponisten, published in 1958 by Universal Edition in Vienna. It has 133 pages and contains diagrams, musical examples, and tables. It is the fourth publication in the series, Die Reihe. (Because all the articles in the collection are relevant to the subject of this bibliography, they are listed in detail after the entry, and also will be found in the author index.)

Cross-references

See no. 89 (Reich, Willi. "Versuch einer Geschichte der Zwölftonmusik" in Alte und neue Musik. 1952).

This particular cross-reference, found under the general works on Arnold Schoenberg, refers the user back to Reich's article, which is listed in full under the history of twelve-tone music. For a general explanation of the cross-reference system, see "Arrangement," above.

TO USE THE BIBLIOGRAPHY

If you wish to find all the writings on one topic:
  Consult the table of contents (p. ix-x) if the topic is a broad one (such as "history of twelve-tone music," "Boulez—compositional techniques," or "Schoenberg—biography").
  Consult the subject index (p. 147-151) if the topic is more specialized (e.g., "Italy—twelve-tone composition," "Indeterminacy in musical composition," "Marxist criticisms of twelve-tone music," "Permutation of serial elements," or "Combinatoriality").
If you wish to locate all the writings by one author that are included in this bibliography, use the author index (p. 129-146).
If you want analyses and discussions of a particular composition, look up the composer in the table of contents; his works will be listed in alphabetical order at the end of his section. Individual compositions are not included in the subject index.
If you know the title of a book that has no author (e.g., Der blaue Reiter), but do not know what subject to look under, use the author index; some title entries are included there.

Note: An asterisk (*) indicates an item not seen; bibliographical information for these items has been taken from the Union Catalog at the Library of the University of California, Berkeley.

ABBREVIATIONS

BAMS	American Musicological Society Bulletin
diagr.	diagram
Dt Univ Zt	Deutsche Universitätszeitung [Göttingen]
I.S.C.M.	International Society for Contemporary Music
JAMS	American Musicological Society Journal
l.	leaf, leaves (i.e., typewritten pages)
M & L	Music and letters
M.G.G.	Die Musik in Geschichte und Gegenwart
Mo mus rec	Monthly musical record
MQ	Musical quarterly
ms.	measure, measures
MT	Musical times
mus.	musical example(s) included in the text
Mus rev	The music review
Mus sur	Music survey
Notes	Music Library Association Notes
NZfM	Neue Zeitschrift für Musik [formerly ZfM]
ÖMZ	Oesterreichische Musik Zeitschrift
op.	opus, opera
p.	page, pages
PAMS	American Musicological Society Papers
port.	portrait
Rass mus	Rassegna musicale
Rev mus	Revue musicale
Riv mus ital	Rivista musicale italiana
RMA Proc	Royal Musical Association Proceedings
Schw MZ	Schweizerische Musikzeitung
Score	The score and I.M.A. magazine
v.	volume, volumes
ZfM	Zeitschrift für Musik [now NZfM]

I
TWELVE-TONE MUSIC

PHILOSOPHY AND CRITICISM

1   Busoni, Ferruccio Benvenuto. Entwurf einer neuen Ästhetik der Tonkunst. 2., erweiterte Ausg. Leipzig, Insel-verlag [1916]. 48 p.
    Post-Wagnerian aesthetics. Discussion of new subdivisions of the octave.

See no. 128 (Eimert, Herbert. Atonale Musiklehre, 1924).

2   Tiessen, Heinz. Zur Geschichte der jüngsten Musik (1913-1928). Mainz, Schotts Söhne [c1928]. 91 p.
    Partial contents: "Expressionismus," p. 39-42; "Schönberg," p. 44-46, et passim.
    Aesthetics of the music of 1913-1928.

3   Adorno, Theodor Wiesengrund. "Zur Zwölftontechnik," Anbruch 11: 290-294 (Sept/Oct 1929).
    General considerations of the twelve-tone technique: its audibility; whether it is mathematical. Largely a discussion of Schoenberg.

4   Berg, Alban. "What is atonality?" in Slonimsky, Nicolas. Music since 1900. 3d ed., rev. and enl. New York, Coleman-Ross, 1949, p. 671-677.
    A translation by M. D. H. Norton from a radio talk given by Berg on the Vienna Rundfunk, April 23, 1930.
    Italian translation in Rognoni, p. 290-303 (see no. 94).
    First published as "Was ist Atonal?" in 23, eine wiener Musikzeitschrift, no. 26/27 (June 8, 1936).

5   Pacque, Désiré. "L'atonalité, ou mode chromatique unique," Rev mus 11: 135-140 (Aug/Sept 1930).
    The nature of "atonality"; not a new concept.

6   Reich, Willi. "Grenzgebiete der neuen Töne," Die Musik 25:120-123 (Nov 1932).
    "Der Weg zur Komposition in zwölf Tönen," p. 122-123.

7   Sessions, Roger. "Music in crisis: some notes on recent music history," Modern music 10:63-78 (Jan/Feb 1933).
    Discussion of the aesthetics of the twelve-tone system, p. 70-73.
    Also appears in no. 295 (Armitage, ed., p. 9-39).

8   Lissa, Zofja. "Geschichtliche Vorform der Zwölftontechnik," Acta musicologica 7:15-21 (Jan/Mar 1935).
    Scriabine's music as a forerunner of 12-tone principles.

9   Gray, Cecil. "Atonalism" in his Predicaments: or music and the future. London, Oxford University Press, 1936, p. 168-195.
    General essay discussing Schoenberg, Berg, and Webern.

10 Krenek, Ernst. Über neue Musik: sechs Verlesungen zur Einführung in die theoretischen Grundlagen. Wien, Ringbuchhandlung, 1937. 108 p. Mus.
    Six lectures given by Krenek in Vienna in 1936. Partial contents: "Zwölftontechnik," p. 51-70; "Musik und Mathematik," p. 71-89 (discusses various types of rows, including all-interval rows).
    Important and lengthy review by Roger Sessions in Modern Music 15:123-128 (Jan/Feb 1938).

11 Krenek, Ernst. Music here and now. Tr. by Barthold Flees. New York, Norton [c1939]. 306 p.
    An English translation of no. 10, with added material. Tries to show that atonality and the twelve-tone technique were inevitable developments of Western music, and are the only "music of the future."

12 Sackville-West, Edward. "Atonalism: second thoughts," New statesman and nation [ser. 2] 23:192 (Mar 21, 1942).
    A re-evaluation of the importance of atonality and the twelve-tone technique.

See no. 317 (Taylor, Noel H. "Arnold Schoenberg," autumn 1944).

See no. 137 (Eschman, Karl. Changing forms in modern music, 1945).

13 Adorno, Theodor Wiesegrund. Philosophie der neuen Musik. Tübingen, J. C. B. Mohr, 1949, vii + 144 p.
    "Schönberg und der Fortschritt," p. 19-88.
    Discusses expressionism, form, rhythm, harmony, instrumentation, counterpoint in relation to the twelve-tone technique. Cites works of Berg, Schoenberg, and Webern. No musical examples. (See no. 342.)

14 Koechlin, Charles. "Quelques réflexions au sujet de la musique atonale," Music today [Journal of the I.S.C.M.] 1:26-33 (1949).
    Résumé in English, p. 33-35.
    Contrasts atonality, which he finds acceptable, with the twelve-tone technique, which he calls unmusical and academic.

See no. 84 (Leibowitz, René. Schoenberg and his school, 1949).

15 "Open forum: variations on a theme. Music's future: tonal or atonal?" Music today [Journal of the I.S.C.M.] 1:132-152 (1949).
    Statements answering "Why do you believe or not believe that atonal music will be the music of the future?" by Schoenberg, Berg, Milhaud, Poulenc, Leibowitz, Searle, and other composers.

See no. 325 (Salazar, Adolfo. "Arnold Schoenberg post-mortem," 1951).

See no. 86 (Stuckenschmidt, Hans Heinz. Neue Musik, 1951).

16 Burnier, Lucien. "Réflexions sur la dodécaphonie," Schw MZ 91:14-17 (Jan 1951). Mus.
    On dodecaphony as a means of composition rather than as an intellectual exercise.

17 Krenek, Ernst. "Die Zwölftonmusik als Lehre," **Melos** 18:141-143 (May 1951).
   A discussion of the literature on twelve-tone theory, particularly Eimert's Lehrbuch der Zwölftontechnik (see no. 142).

18 Eimert, Herbert. "Ist Zwölftonmusik lehrbar?" **Melos** 18:249-251 (Sept 1951).
   On the difficulties of teaching the twelve-tone technique.

19 Krüger, Walther. "Zwölftonmusik und Gegenwart," **Musica** 5:503-505 (Dec 1951).
   The twelve-tone technique as a positive phenomenon. Comments on Eimert's Lehrbuch (see no. 142).

20 Hall, Richard. "Twelve-tone music and tradition," **Hinrichsen's Musical yearbook** 7:128-134 (1952). Mus.
   General considerations of tonality and atonality. Dodecaphony as a primarily contrapuntal technique.

21 Schmidt-Garre, Helmut. "Zwölftonmusik—Ende einer Entwicklung, nicht Neubeginn," **Melos** 19:10-13 (Jan 1952). Mus.
   Twelve-tone technique seen as the end point of a development rather than as a new approach to music.

22 Vlad, Roman. "Poetica e tecnica della dodecafonia," **Rass mus** 22:23-31 (Jan 1952).
   Expanded version in his Modernità e tradizione (see no. 35).
   On the scope of dodecaphony. Current literature on twelve-tone theory discussed.

23 Chailley, Jacques. "Malentendus sur le mot 'atonalité' et quelques autres," **Vie musicale** 2:8 (Feb 1952).
   Toward a definition of the terms "atonality," "dodecaphony," and others.

See no. 221 (Köhler, Siegfried. "Was ist Zwölftonmusik?" Apr 1952).

24 Thomson, Virgil. "Reflections," **Score**, no. 6:11-14 (May 1952).
   Reworked from several articles _in his_ The art of judging music. New York, Knopf, 1948.
   General evaluation of the twelve-tone system; its contrapuntal nature and its attractiveness for composers.

25 Il diapason: rivista di musica contemporanea, v. 3, no. 7/8 (July/Aug 1952), 38 p. [Twelve-tone issue.]
   "Questo numero è dedicato alle implicazioni ideali e filosofiche della poetica dodecafonica."
   Partial contents: Résumés in French and English, p. 5-8; Mila, Massimo, "La dodecafonia e la sua offensiva," p. 9-15; Rondi, Brunello, "La dodecafonia e il messaggio dell'ordine nello spirito contemporaneo," p. 16-18; Kaefer, Johannes, "Essenza della dodecafonia," p. 19-21; Vlad, Roman, "Elementi metafisici nella poetica dodecafonia," p. 22-26 (reprinted in his Storia della dodecafonia; see no. 116); Magnani, Luigi, "Schönberg e il simbolismo," p. 27-32.

26 Engelmann, Hans Ulrich. "Dodekaphonie und Musikgeschichte," **Melos** 19:273-276 (Oct 1952).
   Twelve-tone technique and the philosophy of music history.

See no. 339 (Adorno, Theodor Wiesengrund. "Arnold Schönberg," 1953).

27 Pfrogner, Hermann. Die Zwölfordnung der Töne. Zürich, Amalthea [1953]. 280 p.
    Development of the twelve-tone technique not a result of growing chromaticism, but of individual psychological concepts, such as Schoenberg's idea of the unity of musical space, derived from Swedenborg and Balzac.

28 [Keller, Hans]. "First performances and their reviews," Mus rev 14:55-59 (Feb 1953). Mus.
    On the audibility of the twelve-tone technique. A diatribe against George Perle, Eric Blom, and others. Musical examples from Schoenberg's op. 33A and Searle's Shadow of Cain.

29 Goléa, Antoine. Esthétique de la musique contemporaine. Paris, Presses universitaires de France, 1954, xix +˙205 p.
    "Ce livre n'est pas une histoire de la musique, mais une considération esthétique des principaux courants de la musique contemporaine."
    Partial contents: "Le dodécaphonisme," p. 48-71; Alban Berg, p. 52-56, 66-71; Pierre Boulez, p. 176-189, 193; John Cage, p. 183-184; Luigi Dallapiccola, p. 143-147; René Leibowitz, p. 179-180; Bruno Maderna, p. 187; Luigi Nono, p. 186-189; Arnold Schoenberg, p. 48-52, 56-63; Humphrey Searle, p. 186; Karlheinz Stockhausen, p. 195; Anton Webern, p. 63-66.

30 La musique et ses problèmes contemporains. Paris, Julliard, 1954, 127 p. (Cahiers de la Compagnie Madeleine Renaud-Jean Louis Barrault. Année 2, Cah. 3.) Illus., mus.
    Contents: Barrault, Jean Louis, "Pierre Boulez," p. 3-6; Boulez, Pierre, ". . . Auprès et au loin," p. 7-24; Fano, Michel, "Pouvoirs transmis," p. 38-51; Philippot, Michel, "Musique et acoustique, ou à propos de l'art de combiner les sons," p. 52-65; Martenot, Maurice, "Lutherie électronique," p. 69-75; Pousseur, Henri, "Domaines à venir," p. 76-80; Stockhausen, Karlheinz, "Une expérience électronique [his Composition 1953, no. 2]," p. 82-93; Goléa, Antoine, "Deux portraits: Luigi Nono-Karlheinz Stockhausen," p. 112-114.

31 Burkhard, Willy. "Versuch einer kritischen Auseinandersetzung mit der Zwölftontechnik," Schw MZ 94:85-93 (Mar 1954). Mus.
    Audibility of inversion, augmentation, and other contrapuntal devices in twelve-tone music. Examples from Krenek's Invention for flute and clarinet.

32 Turchi, Guido. "Critica, esegesi e dodecafonia," Riv mus ital 56:173-180 (Apr/Jun 1954).
    On the multiplicity and nature of critical writings on twelve-tone music. Contemporary culture and musical criticism.

33 Krenek, Ernst. "Ein Brief zur Zwölftontechnik," Schw MZ 94:173-174 (May 1954). Mus.
    A reply to Burkhard's article (see no. 31).

See no. 97 (Pannain, Guido. "Origine e significato," Sept 1954).

Philosophy and Criticism

34 Pizzetti, Ildebrando. "Internationale Musik?" ZfM 115:513-515 (Sept 1954).
  On whether the twelve-tone technique is an international style.

35 Vlad, Roman. Modernità e tradizione nella musica contemporanea. Milano, Einaudi, 1955. Mus.
  A collection of essays, mostly derived from earlier articles.
  Partial contents: "L'ultimo Schönberg," p. 158-173; "Note sulla dodecafonia," p. 174-184; "Elementi metafisici nella poetica schönberghiana," p. 185-196; "Dallapiccola," p. 197-211; "'Il Prigioniero' [di Dallapiccola]," p. 212-216.

36 Adorno, Theodor Wiesengrund. "Das Altern der neuen Musik," Der Monat 7:150-158 (May 1955).
  Italian translation, by Giacomo Manzoni: "Invecchiamento della musica nuova," Rass mus 27:1-22 (Mar 1957).
  Musical radicalism for its own sake no longer meaningful.

37 Adorno, Theodor Wiesengrund. "Zum Verständnis Schönbergs," Frankfurter Hefte 10:418-429 (Jun 1955).
  Schoenberg's development of the twelve-tone technique; its philosophical implications and its importance.

38 Boulez, Pierre. "Einsichten und Aussichten," Melos 22:161-164 (Jun 1955), tr. from the French by Hilde Strobel. Mus.
  A discussion of the esthetics of the "pointillist" school.

39 Xénakis, Yannis. "La crise de la musique sérielle," Gravesaner Blätter, Heft 1:2-4 (Jul 1955).
  Summaries are in German and English.
  Philosophy of "totally controlled" serial music.

40 Keller, Hans. "The audibility of serial technique," Mo mus rec 85:231-234 (Nov 1955).
  Serial music must be listened to with a "contrapuntal ear."

41 Keller, Hans. "Dodecaphoneys," Mus rev 16:323-329 (Nov 1955). Mus.
  Satirical article on "Twelve-tonesmanship" among the post-Webernites (see no. 44).

42 Myhill, John. "Musical theory and music practice," Journal of aesthetics and art criticism 14:191-200 (Dec 1955).
  Atonality, p. 191-194.
  Twelve-tone theory does not correspond with twelve-tone practice: cites as an example Krenek's Studies in counterpoint (see no. 209).

43 Rochberg, George. "Tradition and 12-tone music," Mandala [Philadelphia] 1:49-70 ([Dec 1955?]).
  Brief bibliography, p. 70.
  The relationship of musical form to the twelve-tone technique; the nature of twelve-tone material; hexachordal row techniques of Schoenberg and Webern.

44 Mason, Colin. "Dodecaphoneys: a reply," Mus rev 17:90-94 (Feb 1956).
  A reply to Hans Keller (see no. 41).

45 Milner, Anthony. "The vocal element in melody," MT 97:128-131 (Mar 1956). Mus.
  The "unvocal" character of melodic lines in some twelve-tone music.

46 Kelterborn, Rudolf. "Stilistisch gegensätzliche Entwicklungen auf der Basis der Zwölftontechnik," Schw MZ 96:162-166 (Apr 1956). Mus.
   Rhythmic problems in "pointillist" music; total and relative atonality; electronic music as a consequence of totally controlled serial music.

47 Thilman, Johannes Paul. "Die Kompositionsweise mit zwölf Tönen," Musik und Gesellschaft [E. Berlin] 6:247-251 (Jul 1956) and 6:288-292 (Aug 1956). Mus.
   Development of the twelve-tone technique. "Rules" of composition, as codified from Krenek and Jelinek; philosophical implications.

48 Sessions, Roger. "Song and pattern in music today," Score, no. 17:73-84 (Sept 1956).
   Consequences of total control in music.

49 Milner, Anthony. "The lunatic fringe combed," MT 97:516-518 (Oct 1956).
   Do "extreme" composers think musically? Audibility of serial techniques and effects on the audience.

50 Krenek, Ernst. "Alle spalle dei giovani," Incontri musicali 1:51-54 (Dec 1956).
   On the aesthetics of "totally controlled" serial music.
   English translation in Electronic music (Die Reihe, 1). (See no. 275.)

See no. 166 (Eimert, Herbert. "Von der Entscheidungsfreiheit des komponisten" in Musikalisches Handwerk [Die Reihe, 3]).

51 Goldbeck, Fred. "Séries et hérésies," Schw MZ 97:4-8 (Jan 1957). Mus.
   Discussion, in dialogue form, of the various styles of twelve-note music.

52 Rössler, Ernst Karl. "Zeitgenössische Kirchenmusik und christliche Gemeinde," Musik und Kirche 27:12-22 (Jan/Feb 1957).
   The religious music of Webern and Schoenberg is mentioned. Twelve-tone technique in church music. Appended is a brief review of Krenek's Lamentatio Jeremiae Prophetae.

53 Rostand, Claude. "Zwölfton-Manierismus," Melos 24:39-42 (Feb 1957), tr. from the French by Helga Böhme.
   On the Post-Webern, experimentalist school.

54 Dansk Musiktidsskrift [København], v. 32, no. 2 (May 1957). Mus., port.
   "Dette nummer . . . er hovedsagelig helliget tolvtone- og elektronmusik."
   Contents: Thybo, Leif, "Menneske-Maskine," p. 29-30; Krenek, Ernst, "Lydteorier: Betragtninger over electron-musik, p. 31-33 (Chapter 9 of his book, De rebus prius factis); Maegaard, Jan, "Dodekafoni—et resumé," p. 34-37 (mus.); Pade, Else Marie, "Lydprofetier?" p. 38-41 on electronic music; examples of scores by Messiaen and Stockhausen); Bentzon, Johan, "Musik er mere end musik," p. 42-43; also reviews of some twelve-tone and electronic recordings and scores.

Philosophy and Criticism

55 Santi, Piero. "Conseguenze e inconseguenze delle 'estreme conseguenze,'" Ricordiana 3:342-345 (Jul 1957).
On totally controlled serial music.

See no. 170 (Adorno, Theodor Wiesengrund. "Kritieren" in Darmstädter Beiträge, 1958, p. 7-16).

See no. 168 (Junge Komponisten, 1958; esp. articles by Metzger and Eimert).

56 Melichar, Alois. Musik in der Zwangsjacke: die deutsche Musik zwischen Orff und Schönberg. [Wien], Wancura [1958]. 280 p. Mus.
A lengthy attack on modern music, especially serial music; J. M. Hauer and Schoenberg are discussed at some length. The lack of a table of contents and an index makes this book difficult to use. For a commentary upon and extension of Melichar's viewpoint, see Korn, Peter Jena. Apropos Zwangsjacke: eine Analyse der Angriffstaktik gegen Alois Melichar. Wien, Wancura, 1959. 33 p.

57 Stadlen, Peter. "Serialism reconsidered," Score, no. 22:12-27 (Feb 1958). Mus.
German translation: "Kritik am Seriellen," Musica 13:89-98 (Feb 1959).
On the question of the audibility of serial technique. Basic fallacies of twelve-tone premises, such as the equivalence of octave transpositions. Performance problems of Webern's Piano variations, op. 27. [See nos. 59 (Gerhard), 61 (Sessions), 66 (Stadlen), and 69 (Perle).]

58 Castiglione, Niccolò. "Il valore del silenzio e della durata nel linguaggio musicale contemporaneo," Aut aut [Milano], no. 46:196-202 (Jul 1958).
The function of silence and durations in serial music.

59 Gerhard, Roberto. "Apropos Mr. Stadlen," Score, no. 23:50-57 (Jul 1958). Mus.
An answer to Stadlen's attacks on serialism; some discussion of Webern's Piano variations. [See nos. 57 (Stadlen), 61 (Sessions), 66 (Stadlen), and 69 (Perle).]

60 Piston, Walter. "More views on serialism," Score, no. 23:46-49 (July 1958).
Problems, e.g., that of harmonic rhythm, arising from the displacement of tonal means of organization by serial means.

61 Sessions, Roger. "To the editor," Score, no. 23:58-64 (July 1958).
A reply to Peter Stadlen's article (no. 57). [See also nos. 59 (Gerhard), 66 (Stadlen), and 69 (Perle).]

62 Smith, Robert. "Nichtsmusik," Mus rev 19:222-225 (Aug 1958).
A satire on pointillism.

63 Porena, Boris. "L'avanguardia musicale di Darmstadt," Rass mus 28:208-214 (Sept 1958).
Discusses particularly the works and aesthetics of Cage, Stockhausen, and Nono.

64. Walter, Franz. "A l'écoute des musiciens d'avant-garde," Schw MZ 98:342-345 (Sept 1958).
   General description of the aesthetics and techniques of the "experimental" group: Boulez, Stockhausen, Berio, etc.

65. Lang, Paul Henry. "Editorial," MQ 44:503-510 (Oct 1958).
   An evaluation of dodecaphony at mid-century.

66. Stadlen, Peter. "No real casualties?" Score, no. 24:65-68 (Nov 1958).
   A reply and self-justification. [See nos. 57 (Stadlen), 59 (Gerhard), 61 (Sessions), and 69 (Perle).]

67. Metzger, Heinz-Klaus. "Gescheiterte Begriffe in Theorie und Kritik der Musik" in Berichte/Analysen. Wien, Universal Edition [c1959], p. 41-49 (Die Reihe, 5).
   Terminology and (mis)conceptions in critical writings on new music.

See no. 775 (Scherchen, Hermann. "Stockhausen und die Zeit," 1959).

68. Middleton, Robert E. "Abt," Mus rev 20:52-55 (Feb 1959). Mus.
   A satire on totally controlled serial music.

69. Perle, George. "Theory and practice in twelve-tone music (Stadlen reconsidered)," Score, no. 25:58-64 (Jun 1959).
   Further comments on basic problems of serialism. Corrects some errors in previous analyses of Berg's Lulu and Lyric Suite, and of Schoenberg's Pierrot. [See nos. 57 (Stadlen), 59 (Gerhard), 61 (Sessions), and 66 (Stadlen).]

70. Ordini: studi sulla nuova musica [Roma], no. 1 (Jul 1959), 115 p. English translations by Robert W. Mann and William Weaver.
   Contents: Adorno, Theodor Wiesengrund, "Musica e tecnica oggi"/"Technique, Technology, and music today"; Macchi, Egisto, "Produzione e consumo della nuova musica"/"The composer, the listener, and the new music"; Guàccero, Domenico, "Problemi di sintassi musicale"/"Problems of musical syntax"; Titone, Antonio, "Ordine e quadridimensionalità"/"Order and quadridimensionality"; Evangelisti, Franco, "Verso una composizione elettronica"/"Towards electronic composition"; Masullo, Aldo, "La 'struttura' nell'evoluzione dei linguaggi scientifici" (not translated); Letture, corrispondenze.

71. Eco, Umberto. "L'opera in movimento e la coscienza dell'epoca," Incontri musicali, no. 3:32-54 (Aug 1959).
   Freedom of choice on the part of the interpreter in such recent works as Stockhausen's Klavierstücke XI, Berio's Sequenza per flauto solo, and Pousseur's Scambi. Problems of such compositionally "open" works.

72. Ruwet, Nicolas. "Contraddizioni del linguaggio seriale," Incontri musicali, no. 3:55-69 (Aug 1959), tr. by Umberto Eco. Mus.
   Contradictions between theory and practice in post-Webern serial music (see no. 73).

73. Pousseur, Henri. "Forma e pratica musicale," Incontri musicali, no. 3:70-91 (Aug 1959), tr. by Umberto Eco.
   A reply to Nicolas Ruwet's article (see no. 72).

73a Rochberg, George. "Indeterminacy in the new music," Score, no. 26:
9-19 (Jan 1960).
    The paradox created by the similarity between "totally controlled" serial music and "chance" music.

73b Nono, Luigi. "Gitterstäbe am Himmel der Freiheit," Melos 27:69-75 (Mar 1950). Port.
    Originally given as a speech at the 1959 Darmstadt Festival. Discusses the aesthetic problems raised by "chance" elements in music. English translation: "The historical reality of music today," Score, no. 27:41-45 (Jul 1960).

HISTORY

74 Der blaue Reiter. Hrsg. [Wassily] Kandinsky [und] Franz Marc. 2. Auflage. München, Piper, 1914. 140 p. Illus., mus.
    One of the chief expressionist manifestos.
    Partial contents: Schoenberg, Arnold, "Das Verhältnis zum Text," p. 27-32; Hartmann, Thomas von, "Über Anarchie in der Musik," p. 43-47; Kulbin, N., "Die freie Musik," p. 69-73; Kandinsky, Wassily, "Über die Formfrage," p. 74-102. The appendix contains a facsimile of the entire Herzgewächse of Schoenberg; Berg's song, op. 2, no. 4; and Webern's song, "Ihr tratet zu dem Herde."

75 Steinhard, Erich. "Bemerkungen zum Expressionismus," Die Musik 15:49-50 (Oct 1922).
    Brief description of expressionism in music.

See no. 128 (Eimert, Herbert. Atonale Musiklehre, 1924).

76 Schoenberg, Arnold. "Gesinnung oder Erkenntnis?" in 25 Jahre neue Musik; Jahrbuch 1926 der Universal-Edition. Wien, Universal Edition, 1926, p. 21-30.
    On tonality vs. atonality; summary of harmonic developments, 1900-1925.

See no. 7 (Sessions, Roger. "Music in crisis," Jan/Feb 1933).

77 Stuckenschmidt, Hans Heinz. "Das Zwölftonsystem," Die neue Rundschau 45:301-311 (Sept 1934).
    Changing concepts of harmony and tonality in Debussy, Reger, Strauss, Schoenberg, Berg, Hauer, and Krenek.

78 *Wind, Hans E. Die Endkrise der bürgerlichen Musik und die Rolle Arnold Schönbergs. Wien, Krystall-Verlag [1935]. 71 p.

See no. 386 (Hill, Richard S. "Schoenberg's tone-rows and the tonal system of the future," Jan 1936).

79 Magni Dufflocq, Enrico. La musica contemporanea. Milano, Società editrice libraria, 1937. Mus., port.
    Brief and popularized survey.
    Partial contents: "Politonalismo e atonalismo," p. 48-56; "Arnold

Schönberg," p. 142-147; "Anton von Webern," p. 148-149; "Ernest Krenek," p. 152-153; "Alban Berg," p. 156-157.

80 Fleischer, Herbert. La musica contemporanea. Milano, Hoepli, 1938. ["Tr. di A. Hermet in collaborazione con l'autore."]
Partial contents: "Schönberg," p. 111-134; "Dallapiccola," p. 218-222; "Anton Webern e Alban Berg," p. 224-229; "Krenek," p. 230-233.
All are surveys, except the Schoenberg article, which is more detailed; these articles discuss expressionism and the twelve-tone technique.

81 *Hijman, Julius. Nieuwe oostenrijkse musiek (Schönberg, Berg, Webern). Amsterdam, Bigot en van Rossum [1938]. 129 p. Illus., mus.
"Synchronologie: Schönberg, Alban Berg, andere componisten," p. 130-133; "Discographie," p. 134; "Litteratur," p. 135-136.

See no. 136 (Krenek, Ernst. "New developments of the twelve-tone technique," Feb 1943).

82 Salazar, Adolfo. Music in our time: trends in music since the romantic era. Tr. by Isabel Pope. New York, Norton [c1946]. Mus.
Partial contents: "The road towards atonality," p. 200-210; "Expressionism," p. 211-220; "Expressionism in the theatre," p. 221-230; "The twelve-tone technique: Berg, Webern, Krenek, Hauer," p. 231-247.
Discussion of some works with musical examples.

83 Schlee, Alfred. "Vienna since the Anschluss," Mod mus 23:95-99 (Spring 1946).
Primarily on Hauer and Webern.

84 Leibowitz, René. Schoenberg et son école: l'étape contemporaine du language musical. Paris, Janin, 1947.
_____. Schoenberg and his school: The contemporary stage of the language of music. Tr. by Dika Newlin. New York, Philosophical Library [c1949]. xxvi + 305 p. Mus.
Contents: "Prolegomena to contemporary music," p. 1-39; "Arnold Schoenberg," p. 41-134; "Alban Berg," p. 135-186; "Anton Webern," p. 187-255; "The structure of contemporary musical speech," p. 256-290; Bibliography and discography, p. 298-305.
The first important book on the history of the twelve-tone technique, this work suffers from bias and inadequate analyses, but nevertheless is helpful if used with care.
Lengthy reviews: Luigi Magnani in Rass mus 18:29-37 (Jan 1948); Milton Babbitt in JAMS 3:57-60 (1950).

See no. 484 (Leibowitz, René. Introduction à la musique de douze sons, 1949. Première partie).

See no. 142 (Eimert, Herbert. Lehrbuch der Zwölftontechnik, 1950).

85 Almeyda, Renato. "Atonalistas brasileños," Revista musicale Chilena 6:37-42 (Autumn 1950). Mus.
History of twelve-tone music in Brazil.

History   11

86 Stuckenschmidt, Hans Heinz. Neue Musik. [Berlin], Suhrkamp Verlag, 1951, 479 p. Mus. (Zwischen den beiden Kriegen, v. 2.)
    A collection of essays, with an appendix of writings by various composers and critics. Has an excellent index; extensive musical examples, p. 401-424; list of works of 21 20th-century composers, p. 425-434; bibliography, p. 435-437; discography, p. 438-460.
    Partial contents: "Der Radikalismus der Jüngeren," p. 13-38 (music in the first decades of the 20th century); "Das Jahrzehnt des Experimenten," p. 64-92 (Stravinsky, Schoenberg, Der blaue Reiter, Webern, etc.); "Zwölf-töne-technik," p. 144-163 (broad theoretical and historical discussion).

87 Thomson, Virgil. "Atonality today," Etude 69:18-19, 64 (Nov 1951). Mus. [Reprinted from his Music right and left. New York, Holt, 1951.]
    A general article, discussing the international situation in twelve-tone composition after Schoenberg's death.

88 Mitchell, Donald. "The emancipation of the dissonance: a selected bibliography of the writings of composers, theorists, and critics," Hinrichsen's musical yearbook 7:141-152 (1952).
    Lists of twelve-tone composers and of some of their works, and a bibliography of writings on atonality and the twelve-tone technique. The bibliographical information varies widely in style and coverage; evidently compiled from secondary sources.
    Contents: European composers, p. 142-143; British composers, p. 144; "Critics and theorists" (i.e., a bibliography of their writings), p. 144-152.

89 Reich, Willi. "Versuch einer Geschichte der Zwölftonmusik" in Alte und neue Musik: das Basler Kammerorchester . . . 1926-1951. Zürich, Atlantis [1952], p. 106-132.
    Bibliography, p. 131-132.
    History and theory: Hauer's twelve-tone technique and system of notation; Schoenberg, Berg, Webern, Krenek, and some younger composers.

90 Rostand, Claude. La musique française contemporaine. [Paris], Presses Universitaires de France, 1952, 126 p. Mus.
    "Les dodécaphonistes," p. 105-120: discusses basic serial technique. Pierre Boulez, p. 115-116.

    ———. French music today. Tr. by Henry Marx. New York, Merlin Press [1957]. 147 p.
    An abridged translation without musical examples. "The dodekaphonists" [sic], p. 127-141.

91 Mellers, Wilfred. "Recent trends in British music," MQ 38:198-199 (Apr 1952).
    Short article on British twelve-tone school.

See no. 123 (Seiber, Mátyás. "Composition with twelve notes," Jun 1952).

92 Ackere, Jules van. "Schönberg en de atonale school" in his Muziek van onze eeuw, 1900-1950: een inleiding tot de hedendaagse toonkunst. Antwerpen, De Sikkel, 1954, p. 163-194. Illus.
    A survey.

See no. 29 (Goléa, Antoine. Esthétique de la musique contemporaine, 1954).

93 Herzfeld, Friedrich. Musica nova: die Tonwelt unseres Jahrhunderts. [Berlin], Ullstein [c1954]. 334 p. Illus., mus.
"Angst . . . Angst . . . Angst" (chapter on the history of the twelve-tone technique), p. 51-102: "Arnold Schönbergs Frühwerke; die Luft von anderen Planeten; Wendung zur Atonalität; die Angst und das Es; das Gesetz der Zwölftontechnik; verschiedene Reihen; der schwere Weg zu Arnold Schönberg; von der Macht der Zahl; Anton von Webern und Alban Berg."

94 Rognoni, Luigi. Espressionismo e dodecafonia: in appendice scritti di Arnold Schönberg, Alban Berg, Wassily Kandinsky. [Torino], Einaudi, 1954, 395 p. Mus., port.
Schoenberg and his school, and their relation to the expressionist movement in art and music.
Appendix 1: writings of Schoenberg, p. 231-274; of Berg, p. 277-303; of Kandinsky, p. 307-311.
Appendix 2, part 1: bibliographies, lists of works, discographies.
Schoenberg, p. 315-335 (includes previously unpublished articles); Berg, p. 336-344; Webern, p. 345-351.
part 2: general bibliographies. Expressionism, p. 355-363; music, p. 367-384.
Extensive review by Massimo Mila in Rass mus 24:121-128 (Apr/Jun 1954).

See no. 153 (Searle, Humphrey. "Twelve note music" in Grove's Dictionary of music and musicians, 1954).

95 Wörner, Karl H. Neue Musik in der Entscheidung. Mainz, Schott [1954]. 347 p. Mus., port.
Partial contents: Bibliography, p. 311-329; "Reihenprinzip," p. 220-232 (twelve-tone theory); Alban Berg, p. 90-93; Pierre Boulez, p. 147; John Cage, p. 181; Luigi Dallapiccola, p. 153-154; Wolfgang Fortner, p. 101-104; Josef Hauer, p. 99; Hanns Jelinek, p. 101; Ernst Krenek, p. 99-100; René Leibowitz, p. 147; Luigi Nono, p. 155; Henri Pousseur, p. 147; Arnold Schoenberg, p. 56-67; Karlheinz Stockhausen, p. 107-108; Anton Webern, p. 94-98.

96 Wörner, Karl H. [and others]. "Expressionismus" in Die Musik in Geschichte und Gegenwart. Kassel, Bärenreiter, 1954, v. 3, col. 1655-1675. Mus.
A history of musical expressionism. Bibliography, col. 1762-1763.

97 Pannain, Guido. "Origine e significato della musica dodecafonica," Nuova antologia [Roma] 462:79-86 (Sept 1954).
A brief history of the development of the classical twelve-tone technique.

98 Myers, Rollo H. "Music in France in the post-war decade," RMA Proc 81:93-106 (1954/55).
The twelve-tone group, p. 97-100; electronic music, p. 102-104.

99 Neighbor, Oliver. "The evolution of twelve-note music," RMA Proc 81:49-61 (1954/55).
Concise and clearly written presentation of the history of the

twelve-tone technique: early dodecaphonic procedures in Hauer and Schoenberg; quasi-serial treatment in Bartók, Debussy, Stravinsky, and Scriabine; mention of the Russian twelve-tone composer, Lev Golyshev.

99a Chase, Gilbert. "Twelve-tone composers" in his America's music, from the Pilgrims to the present. New York, McGraw-Hill [c1955], p. 597-616.

Brief discussion of Schoenberg's and Krenek's American works, and of the compositions of Stefan Wolpe, Adolph Weiss, Wallingford Riegger, Kurt Liszt, George Perle, Milton Babbitt, Ben Weber, and other American serial composers.

100 Collaer, Paul. La musique moderne, 1905-1955. Paris, Elsevier, 1955, iv + 304 p. Mus., port.

"134 exemples musicaux sous plaquette séparée."
Partial contents: "Arnold Schoenberg, Anton Webern, Alban Berg, expressionisme, atonalité, dodécaphonisme," p. 35-77; John Cage, p. 287; Luigi Dallapiccola, p. 272-274; Ernst Krenek, p. 238; Bruno Maderna, p. 277; Karlheinz Stockhausen, p. 289.

101 Wiedman, Robert William. Expressionism in music; an interpretation and analysis of the expressionistic style in modern music. [Ann Arbor, Mich., University Microfilms], 1955, 487 p. (University microfilms, no. 12,248.) (Thesis, Ph.D., education, New York University.)

Not seen; abstract in Dissertation Abstracts 15:1189-1190 (Jul 1955).

102 Carsalade du Pont, Henri de. "La musique dodécaphoniste," Etudes [Paris], no. 287:363-365 (Dec 1955).

A history of the development of the twelve-tone school and of its most important composers.

103 Gottschalk, Nathan. Twelve note music as developed by Arnold Schoenberg, with an analysis of two representative works for violin. 68 l. Mus. (Thesis, D.M.A., Boston University, 1956.)

Partial contents: "The dissolution of the modal and tonal systems," p. 7-13; "The twelve note music of Schoenberg," p. 14-25; "Analysis of Tripartita of Richard Hoffmann," p. 26-32; "Analysis of Phantasy for violin with piano accompaniment, op. 47, by Arnold Schoenberg," p. 33-40; "Performance of contemporary music," p. 41-42; appendices (tone-row analyses); bibliography, p. 67-68.

The historical résumé seems to be patterned largely after Leibowitz (see no. 84); the analyses are primarily row and thematic analyses. Useful but somewhat superficial.

104 Smith Brindle, Reginald. "The origins of Italian dodecaphony," MT 97:75-76 (Feb 1956).

A brief history of the adoption of the twelve-tone technique in Italy.

105 Hartog, Howard, ed. European music in the twentieth century. London, Routledge and Kegan Paul [1957]. viii + 341 p.

Partial contents: Goehr, Walter, and Goehr, Alexander, "Arnold

Schoenberg's development towards the twelve-note system," p. 76-93; Hamilton, Iain, "Alban Berg and Anton Webern," p. 94-117; White, Eric Walter, "Stravinsky" (twelve-tone works), p. 54 et passim; Milner, Anthony, "English contemporary music" (Roberto Gerhard, p. 146; Mátyás Seiber, p. 146; Humphrey Searle, p. 146-147); Smith Brindle, Reginald, "Italian contemporary music" (Luigi Dallapiccola, p. 176-181; Bruno Maderna, p. 184, 185-186; Luigi Nono, p. 184, 186-187); Hartog, Howard, "German contemporary music" (Wolfgang Fortner, p. 197); Drew, David, "Modern French music" (Pierre Boulez, p. 292-294).

See no. 496 (Redlich, Hans Ferdinand. "The second Viennese school," in his Alban Berg, 1957, p. 13-18).

106 Pestalozza, Luigi. "I compositori milanesi del dopoguerra," Rass mus 27:27-43 (Mar 1957).
   The younger Milanese composers, including Luciano Berio and Bruno Maderna. Short biographical sketches, p. 41-43.

107 Stuckenschmidt, Hans Heinz. "German musical life: patterns of conservatism and experiment," Atlantic monthly 199:167-171 (Mar 1957).
   The German twelve-tone school, p. 170-171. A very general article.

108 Searle, Humphrey. "A new kind of music," Twentieth century [London] 161:480-483 (May 1957).
   The post-Webern composers; a brief summary.

See no. 614 (Hodier, Andre. "The young French music," May 25, 1957).

109 Rostand, Claude. "L'Italie musicale actuelle," Table ronde, no. 117:79 (Sept 1957).
   A very brief survey of Italian contemporary music, especially the serial composers: Dallapiccola, Peragallo, Maderna, Vlad, Nono, Berio, Prosperi, and others.

110 Schatz, Hilmar. "Theoretiker des Zufalls: junge Komponisten dozieren bei den Darmstädter Ferienkursen," Melos 24:298-300 (Oct 1957). Port. [of Luigi Nono].
   One of the better of the many articles written about the Darmstadt Summer School; clearly summarizes the general activities there and the trend of the post-Webern composers who participate.

111 Gradenwitz, Peter. "Reihenkomposition im Orient" in Bericht über den Internationalen Musikwissenschaftlichen Kongress, Wien; Mozartjahr 1956. Hrsg. von Erich Schenk. Graz, Hermann Böhlaus, 1958, p. 238-241.
   A brief résumé of twelve-tone activities in the Middle and Far East, especially in Israel and Japan.

See no. 786 (Kirchmeyer, Helmut. Igor Strawinsky, 1958).

112 Prieberg, Fred K. Lexikon der neuen Musik. Freiberg, Karl Alber, 1958, x + 495 p. Illus., mus.
   Entries related to serial music include: Hans Erich Apostel,

p. 10-11; Atonalität, p. 13-16; Henk Badings, p. 21-22; Alban Berg, p. 36-41; Luciano Berio, p. 42; Pierre Boulez, p. 53-55; John Cage, p. 67-68; Luigi Dallapiccola, p. 87-90; Hanns Eisler, p. 110-112; Elektronische Musik, p. 116-121; Hans Ulrich Engelmann, p. 122; Wolfgang Fortner, p. 139-142; Jef Golyschew [Lev Golyshev], p. 167; Josef Matthias Hauer, p. 185; Hans Werner Henze, p. 187-189; Hanns Jelinek, p. 221-222; Giselher Klebe, p. 228-229; Ernst Krenek, p. 234-238; René Leibowitz, p. 254-255; Elizabeth Lutyens, p. 262-263; Bruno Maderna, p. 263; Jan Maegaard, p. 263; Riccardo Malipiero, p. 268; Riccardo Nielsen, p. 318; Luigi Nono, p. 318-320; Mario Peragallo, p. 331-332; Henri Pousseur, p. 344-345; Wallingford Riegger, p. 365-366; Giacento Scelsi, p. 376; Arnold Schoenberg, p. 381-392; Humphrey Searle, p. 398-399; Mátyás Seiber, p. 399-401; Igor Strawinsky, p. 405-416; Camillo Togni, p. 429; Roman Vlad, p. 440; Anton Webern, p. 446-449; Zwölftonmusik, p. 458-462.

113   Searle, Humphrey. "Atonal and serial music" in Simpson, Robert Wilfred, ed. Guide to modern music on records (1958). [London], Anthony Blond [c1958], p. 151-172.
A general discussion of twelve-tone composers and of the recordings to date of twelve-tone and electronic music. List of records, p. 170-172.

114   Simbriger, Heinrich. "Die heutige Situation der Zwölftonmusik" in Bericht über den Internationalen Musikwissenschaftlichen Kongress, Wien; Mozartjahr 1956. Hrsg. von Erich Schenk. Graz, Hermann Böhlaus, 1958, p. 593-598.
Post-Schoenbergian concepts of serial technique.

115   Stuckenschmidt, Hans Heinz. Schöpfer der neuen Musik: Portraits und Studien. [Frankfort am Main], Suhrkamp Verlag, 1958. 301 p.
Biographical and stylistic discussions.
Partial contents: "Igor Strawinsky," p. 128-161; "Stil und Asthetik Schönbergs," p. 162-179 (from Schw MZ, Mar 1958; see no. 306); "Alban Berg," p. 180-191; "Anton von Webern," p. 192-203; "Luigi Dallapiccola," p. 228-240; "Hans Werner Henze," p. 290-301.

116   Vlad, Roman. Storia della dodecafonia. Milano, Suvini Zerboni [1958]. 395 p. Mus.
The most comprehensive history of the twelve-tone technique published to date; broad but rather superficial.
Contents: "Acquisizione dello spazio dei dodici suoni," p. 13-21; "Premesse dei nuovi principi strutturali," p. 23-32; "Applicazioni parziali del metodo dodecafonico," p. 45-58; "Prime musiche dodecafoniche per orchestra," p. 59-70; "Prime opere teatrali dodecafoniche," p. 71-84; "Aspetti metafisici della poetica dodecafonica," p. 85-94; "Ricupero di elementi tradizionali nell'ultimo periodo creativo di Schönberg," p. 95-114; "Berg e la libera articolazione della dodecafonia," p. 115-124; "I traguardi del radicalismo di Webern," p. 125-130; "Diffusione della dodecafonia," p. 131-160; "Strawinsky e la dodecafonia," p. 161-174; "Influsso della dodecafonia su compositori che non ne adottano integralmente il metodo," p. 175-192; "La dodecafonia in Italia," p. 193-254; "La

serialità integrale e la musica elettronica," p. 255-274; "Luigi Dallapiccola," p. 275-314; "Le opere postume di Schönberg," p. 315-328; "'Agon' di Strawinsky," p. 329-338.

See no. 393 (Wellesz, Egon. The origins of Schönberg's twelve-tone system; 1958).

117 Henderson, Robert L. "Schönberg and 'expressionism,'" Mus rev 19:125-129 (May 1958).
Discussion of the literature on Schoenberg and the Viennese school; thesis is that most writings ignore the social and cultural background of Vienna at the turn of the century.

118 Stuckenschmidt, Hans Heinz. "Sitten und Gebräuche der Neutöner," Der Monat 11:51-57 (Dec 1958).
A history of the I.S.C.M. and a discussion of the younger generation of composers.

See no. 306a (Adorno, Theodor Wiesengrund. "Zur Vorgeschichte der Reihenkomposition" in his Klangfiguren, 1959, p. 95-120).

See no. 174 (Cage, John. "Zur Geschichte der experimentellen Musik in der Vereinigten Staaten" in Darmstädter Beiträge, v. 2, 1959).

See no. 174 (Wörner, Karl H. "Neue Musik 1946-1958: Versuch eines historischen Überblicks" in Darmstädter Beiträge, v. 2, 1959).

118a Zillig, Winfried. Variationen über neue Musik. [München], Nymphenburger Verlagshandlung [c1959]. 283 p. Illus.
Partial contents: "Die Antipoden: Arnold Schönberg und Igor Strawinsky," p. 11-12; "Strawinsky und das Zwölftonsystem," p. 50-59; "Schönberg und sein Weg von der Tonalität zum Zwölftonsystem," p. 61-107; "Alban Berg und die Wiener Schule," p. 140-148; "Die Erneuerung der italienischen Musik von Malipiero bis Dallapiccola," p. 165-173; "Anton Webern, Aussenseiter und Vorbild," p. 181-190; "Die Jungen: Stockhausen, Boulez, Nono, Berio," p. 190-199; "Krenek, der Sucher," p. 236-239; "Neue Musik in Deutschland: Pepping, Genzmer, Fortner, Henze, Klebe," p. 254-263; "Zusammenfassung und Ausblick," p. 263-270; Literaturverzeichnis, p. 283.

118b Perle, George. "Atonality and the twelve-note system in the United States," Score, no. 27:51-66 (Jul 1960). Mus.
An historical survey.

ANALYSIS AND THEORY

COMPOSITIONAL TECHNIQUES

Introductory Articles Addressed to the Layman

119 Costarelli, Nicola. "Nota sulla dodecafonia," Rass mus 15:267-271 (Sept/Oct 1942). Mus.
A simple article on the principles of the twelve-tone technique.

120 Carner, Mosco. "Technique of twelve-note music," The Listener 41:1040 (June 16, 1949).
   A general and brief description of the use of the row.

121 Symkins, L. O. "Arnold Schoenberg's new world of dodecaphonic music," Etude 68:12-14 (Sept 1950). Illus., mus.
   Includes a very brief description of the row treatment in Schoenberg's piano piece, op. 33a.

See no. 325 (Salazar, Adolfo. "Arnold Schoenberg post-mortem," 1951).

122 Rostand, Claude. "Dodécaphonisme," Larousse mensuel 12:712-713 (Sept 1951). Mus.
   A simple explanation.

123 Seiber, Mátyás. "Composing with twelve notes," Mus sur 4:472-489 (Jun 1952). Mus.
   ". . . script . . . originally prepared for a 30-minutes' broadcast."
   A clear and excellent article for the layman. Examples from Schoenberg's 3rd and 4th Quartets, Berg's Violin Concerto, Webern's Three songs, op. 23, and other works.

See no. 301 (Rostand, Claude. "Note sommaire sur le système dodécaphonique et la méthode sérielle" in Stuckenschmidt, Hans Heinz, Arnold Schoenberg, 1956, p. 139-143).

124 Fiebig, Kurt. "Was ist Zwölftonmusik?" Der Kirchenchor [Kassel] 16:66-69 (Sept/Oct 1956). Mus.
   Somewhat more penetrating than most introductory articles.

125 Cecchi, César. "Qué es la dodecafonía," Revista musical Chilena 11:8-15 (Apr/May 1957).
   Elementary article on the theory of dodecaphony.

Technical and Specialized Works

126 *Hauer, Josef Matthias. Vom Wesen des Musikalischen: ein Lehrbuch der atonalen Musik. Berlin, Schlesinger [c1923]. 61 p. Diagrs., mus.
   An enlarged edition of his Über die Klangfarben, 1919.

127 Hauer, Josef Matthias. "Atonale Musik," Die Musik 16:103-106 (Nov 1923).
   Elaborate system of comparison of tonal and atonal music. Permutations of the arrangement of the twelve tones.

128 Eimert, Herbert. Atonale Musiklehre. Leipzig, Breitkopf und Härtel, 1924. iv + 36 p. Mus., tables.
   Part 1: theory and practice; atonality and the twelve-tone technique (melody, harmony, form, etc.).
   Part 2: historical and aesthetic discussions.
   One chapter from this book was published as "Zum Kapitel: atonale Musik," Die Musik 16:899-904 (Sept 1924).
   A comment on this chapter, by Josef Matthias Hauer: "Offener Brief [an Herbert Eimert]," Die Musik 17:157 (Nov 1924).

129 Hauer, Josef Matthias. Von Melos zur Pauke: eine Einführung in die Zwölftonmusik. Wien, Universal Edition [1925]. 21 p. (<u>His</u> Theoretische Schriften, Bd. 1.) Mus., tables.
    A little manual of twelve-tone technique, with brief discussions of harmony, melody, rhythm, etc. Tables of tropes.

130 *Hauer, Josef Matthias. Zwölftontechnik, die Lehre von den Tropen. Wien, New York, Universal Edition [1926]. xii + 23 p. (<u>His</u> Theoretische Schriften, Bd. 2.) Mus.

131 Mersmann, Hans. Die Tonsprache der neuen Musik. Mainz, Melosverlag/Schotts Söhne [c1928]. Mus.
    On theoretical problems of 20th-century music. Examples drawn from Schoenberg, Krenek, Berg, Webern.

<u>See no. 6</u> (Reich, Willi. "Grenzgebiete der neuen Töne," Nov 1932).

<u>See no. 10</u> (Krenek, Ernst. Über neue Musik, 1937).

<u>See no. 295</u> (Weiss, Adolph. "The twelve-tone series" <u>in</u> Armitage, Merle (ed.), Schoenberg, 1937, p. 75-77).

132 Nathan, Hans. "The Viennese Lied, 1910-37," <u>Modern music</u> 14:136-142 (Mar/Apr 1937). Mus.
    Technique of song composition, from Mahler to Schoenberg, Berg, Webern, and Hauer. Melody, rhythm, accompaniment, relation of text and music.

133 Slonimsky, Nicolas. "The plurality of melodic and harmonic systems," <u>PAMS</u> 3:16-24 (1938). Mus.
    "Twelve-tone system," p. 17-24.
    Principle of nonrepetition of tones; division of the row into hexachords.

134 Perle, George. "Evolution of the tone row: the twelve-tone modal system," <u>Mus rev</u> 2:273-287 (Nov 1941). Mus., tables.
    The nonmotivic function of the row: its modal application.

135 Krenek, Ernst. "Cadential formations in twelve-tone music," <u>BAMS</u>, no. 6:5 (Aug 1942).
    An abstract only.
    The modality concept of the row; three cadential types.

136 Krenek, Ernst. "New developments of the twelve-tone technique," <u>Mus rev</u> 4:81-97 (Feb 1943). Mus.
    Secondary series derivations; hexachords; modality.

137 Eschman, Karl. Changing forms in modern music. Boston, E. C. Schirmer [c1945]. xii + 180 p. Mus.
    The twelve-tone systems of Hauer and Schoenberg, p. 83-110.
    Discusses the changes that have occured in the 20th century in musical aesthetics and in the elements of music (phrase structure, harmony, variation technique, etc.).

138 Babbitt, Milton. The function of set structure in the twelve-tone system. [Unpublished MS. Princeton, N.J.? 1946.]
    Not seen. Undoubtedly highly technical. (Reference taken from Perle, no. 196.)

139 *Jachino, Carlo. Tecnica dodecafonica, trattato pratico. Milano, Curci [1948]. 19 p. Mus.

See no. 13 (Adorno, Theodor Wiesengrund. Philosophie der neuen Musik, 1949).

140 Heiss, Hermann. Elemente der musikalischen Komposition (Tonbewegungslehre). Heidelberg, Hochstein [1949]. 207 p. Mus.
Most of the musical examples seem to be from the author's own compositions.
Partial contents: "Der Zwölftonsatz," p. 145-205: "Abstrakte Darstellung," p. 145-153; "Die kompositorische Handhabung," p. 154-173; "Die Trope," p. 174-180; "Das Kontinuum (Formbildung)," p. 181-205.

See no. 484 (Leibowitz, René. Introduction à la musique de douze sons, 1949. Première partie).

141 Le système dodécaphonique. Paris, Richard-Masse [1949]. 83 p. Mus. (Polyphonie, cahier 4.)
Contents: "Résolution du premier Congrés international pour la musique dodécaphonique," p. 5-6; Schoenberg, Arnold, "La composition à douze sons," tr. by René Leibowitz, p. 7-31; Leibowitz, René, "Aspects récents de la technique de douze sons," p. 32-53; Saby, Bernard, "Un aspect des problèmes de la thématique sérielle," p. 54-63; Krenek, Ernst, "Technique de douze sons et classicisme," p. 64-67; Martin, Frank, "Schoenberg et nous," p. 68-71; Dallapiccola, Luigi, "A propos d'un trait 'expressionniste' de Mozart," p. 72-79; "Un musicien d'aujourd'hui: ené Leibowitz," p. 80-83 (portrait and list of works).
Review by Milton Babbitt in JAMS 3:264-267 (Fall 1950); primarily a discussion of Schoenberg's article, "La composition à douze sons" (see no. 143).

142 Eimert, Herbert. Lehrbuch der Zwölftontechnik. Wiesbaden, Breitkopf und Härtel, 1950, 61 p. Mus., tables.

* ———. 2. verm. Aufl. 1952. 64 p.

* ———. 3. Aufl. 1954 [c1952]. 64 p.

* ———. Manuale di tecnica dodecafonica. Prefazione e note di Luigi Rognoni. [Tr. di Mariangela Doná.] Milano, Carisch, 1954, 84 p.
Part 1: Theory of the twelve-tone technique, including intervallic inversions; tonal elements in twelve-tone music; row systems (e.g., all-interval rows); statistics.
Part 2: Form in twelve-tone music.
Part 3: History of the twelve-tone technique (see nos. 17, 19).

143 Schoenberg, Arnold. "Composition with twelve tones" in his Style and idea. New York, Philosophical Library [c1950], p. 102-143. Mus.
"Delivered as a lecture at U.C.L.A., March 26, 1941."
Schoenberg's exposition of his development and use of the twelve-tone technique. Use of the four forms of the row; manipulation of the basic set in composition.
French translation, as "La composition à douze sons," in no. 141.

Important reviews: Dean, Winton. "Schoenberg's ideas," M & L 31:295-304 (Oct 1950); Babbitt, Milton (see no. 141).

144 Brainard, Paul. A study of the twelve-tone technique. (Thesis, M.A., University of Rochester, 1951.) 74 l., mus.
Contents: Atonality and the development of the row; general characteristics; technique of the row; [Berg's] Lyric Suite; functions of the tone row; bibliography.

145 Chailley, Jacques. Traité historique d'analyse musicale. Paris, A. Leduc [1951]. v + 130 p. Mus.
"La musique atonale," p. 77-87 (includes serial music).
Definition of atonal and serial music; examples of "classical" serial techniques from Schoenberg and Webern.

See no. 86 (Stuckenschmidt, Hans Heinz. "Zwölf-töne-technik" in his Neue Musik, 1951, p. 144-163).

See no. 89 (Reich, Willi. "Versuch einer Geschichte der Zwölftonmusik," 1952).

146 Boulez, Pierre. "Eventuellement," Rev mus, no. 212:117-148 (Apr 1952). Diagrs., mus.
Technical article on serial organization of rhythm and other non-pitch elements. Future of "totally controlled" serial music.

See no. 392 (Perle, George. "Schönberg's late style," Nov 1952).

147 *Bentzon, Niels Viggo. Tolvtoneteknik. København, W. Hansen, 1953. 82 p. Illus.
Review in Nordisk Musikkultur 4:129-130 (Dec 1953).

148 [omitted]

149 Malipiero, Riccardo. "La dodecafonia come tecnica," Riv mus ital 55:277-300 (Jul/Sept 1953). Mus.
Questions discussed at the Primo Congresso per la Musica Dodecafonica, Milano, 1949.
Rather general article, dealing with tonality, atonality, and the characteristics of dodecaphony.

150 Krenek, Ernst. "Is the twelve-tone technique on the decline?" MQ 29:513-527 (Oct 1953). Mus.
A discussion of post-Schoenbergian dodecaphony; the use of hexachords, row permutation and rotation; "totally organized" serial music.

See no. 93 (Herzfeld, Friedrich. Musica nova, 1954).

151 Rufer, Josef. Composition with twelve notes related only to one another. Tr. by Humphrey Searle. London, Rockliff [c1954]. xiv + 218 p. Mus. (24 p. of musical examples inserted between p. 214-215.)
Appendix 1: "Contemporary composers on their experiences of composition with twelve notes": Boris Blacher, p. 177-178; Luigi Dallapiccola, p. 178-181; Wolfgang Fortner, p. 181-183; Roberto Gerhard, p. 183-185; Hans Werner Henze, p. 185; Richard Hoff-

Theory—Compositional Techniques

mann, p. 185-186; Hanns Jelinek, p. 186-188; Ernst Krenek, p. 188-191; Rolf Liebermann, p. 191-193; Humphrey Searle, p. 193-195; Mátyás Seiber, p. 196-198; Rudolf Wagner-Régeny, p. 198-200; Winfried Zillig, p. 200-201.
Appendix 2: "Arnold Schoenberg: sketch for a series of lectures [on composition]," p. 202-204; "Complete list of Arnold Schoenberg's musical and literary works," p. 205-214.
A textbook of twelve-tone composition, with Schoenberg as a model. Important review by Richard S. Hill in Notes 12:223-225 (Mar 1955).

152 Schoenberg, Arnold. "Apollonian evaluation of a Dionysian epoch" in his Structural functions of harmony. London, Williams and Norgate [1954], p. 192-196.
Brief description of the method of composing with twelve tones, and criticism of some compositional procedures in contemporary music.

153 Searle, Humphrey. "Twelve-note music" in Grove's Dictionary of music and musicians. 5th ed. London, Macmillan, 1954, v. 8:617-623. Mus.
Includes a short bibliography. Some examples of Hauer's system of notation.

See no. 95 (Wörner, Karl H. Neue Musik in der Entscheidung, 1954).

154 Erickson, Robert. The structure of music: a listener's guide; a study of music in terms of melody and counterpoint. New York, Noonday Press, 1955. xi + 208 p. Mus.
Many examples drawn from Schoenberg, Berg, and Webern.

155 Ogdon, Wilbur Lee. Series and structure: an investigation into the purpose of the twelve-note row in selected works of Schoenberg, Webern, Krenek and Leibowitz. [Ann Arbor, Mich., University Microfilms], 1955. 341 p., mus. (University microfilms, no. 14,663.) (Thesis, Ph.D., Indiana University.)
Primarily a row analysis of Schoenberg's Op. 33a, Webern's Variations for piano, Krenek's Symphonic elegy, Leibowitz's Third Quartet, and other works by these composers.

156 Rochberg, George. The hexachord and its relation to the twelve-tone row. Bryn Mawr, Pa., Presser [c1955]. viii + 40 p. Mus., tables.
A manual on symmetrical row construction: hexachords related by mirror inversion; interchangeable hexachords.
Important reviews by Richard S. Hill in Notes 12:223-225 (Mar 1955) and by George Perle in JAMS 10:55-59 (Spring 1957) [Discusses "combinatoriality"].

157 Babbitt, Milton. "Some aspects of twelve-tone composition," Score 12:53-61 (Jun 1955). Mus.
Highly technical and important article, on his theory of combinatoriality and on music totally controlled by serial principles. Discusses developments in the U.S.

158 Keller, Hans. "Strict serial technique in classical music," Tempo [ser. 2], no. 37:12-24 (Autumn 1955). Mus.

"The present essay . . . proposes to demonstrate that two great 18th-century composers [Beethoven and Mozart] did in fact [use] the method of composing with tone rows."

159 Ballif, Claude. Introduction à la métatonalité: vers une solution tonale et polymodale du problème atonal. Paris, Richard-Masse [c1956]. 116 p. Tables. (Polyphonie, cahier 11/12.)
"Tonalité et atonalité," a comparison of tonal and atonal melody, counterpoint, harmony, and form, p. 69-76; "Tonal analysis" of Schoenberg's Piano piece, op. 19, no. 25, p. 111.

See no. 103 (Gottschalk, Nathan. Twelve-note music as developed by Arnold Schoenberg, 1956).

160 Perle, George. Serial composition and atonality. [Ann Arbor, Mich. University Microfilms], 1956 [c1959]. 211 p. Mus. (Thesis, Ph.D., New York University, Graduate school of arts and sciences.)
Contents: "Tonality, atonality, dodecaphony," p. 1-12; "'Free' atonality," p. 13-48; "Non-dodecaphonic serial composition," p. 49-79; "Motivic functions of the set," p. 80-110; "Simultaneity," p. 111-160; "Structural functions of the set," p. 161-199; Index to basic definitions, p. 200; Bibliography, p. 201-211.
Includes a discussion of the technical procedures employed in the nonserial and atonal and in the twelve-tone compositions of Schoenberg, Berg, and Webern, and a description of non-dodecaphonic serial procedures in some of the works of Debussy, Scriabine, Roslavetz, Bartók, Stravinsky, and in Schoenberg's op. 23 and 24.

161 Smith Brindle, Reginald. "The lunatic fringe: III, computational composition," MT 97:354-356 (Jul 1956). Mus.
Serial organization of rhythmic and other non-tone elements; examples from Dallapiccola, Donatoni, Togni, and Maderna.

See no. 47 (Thilman, Johannes Paul. "Die Kompositionsweise mit zwölf Tönen," Jul 1956; Aug 1956).

162 Milhaud, Darius. "Konstruierte Musik," Gravesaner Blätter, Heft 5:14-15 (Aug 1956). Musical examples, p. 9-13.
A brief description of Milhaud's experience with the technique of total control.

163 Gerhard, Roberto. "Developments in twelve-tone technique," Score, no. 17:61-72 (Sept 1956).
Gerhard's use of the twelve-tone technique. Combinatoriality; derivation of rhythmic series from tone row.

164 Simbriger, Heinrich. "Die Situation der Zwölftonmusik," Musik und Kirche 26:209-223 (Sept/Oct 1956). Mus.
An explanation of Hauer's and Schoenberg's twelve-tone principles; the twelve-tone technique in church music.

165 Dallin, Leon. Techniques of twentieth century composition. Dubuque, Iowa, W. C. Brown [c1957]. xix + 223 p. Mus.
"The twelve-tone technique," p. 180-194.
A textbook which summarizes the techniques of contemporary

composition. Examples in this chapter are taken from Schoenberg and Krenek; Webern is relegated, along with the post-Webern composers, to a chapter on "special effects."

166 Musikalisches Handwerk. Wien, Universal Edition [c1957]. 88 p. Diagrs., mus. (Die Reihe: Information über serielle Musik, 3.)

Musical craftmanship. Bryn Mawr, Pa., Theodore Presser [c1959]. 88 p. Diagrs., mus. (Die Reihe: a periodical devoted to developments in contemporary music, 3.)
Contents of American edition: Eimert, Herbert, "The composer's freedom of choice," tr. by Leo Black, p. 1-9; Stockhausen, Karlheinz, ". . . how time passes . . .," tr. by Cornelius Cardew, p. 10-40; Cage, John, "To describe the process of composition used in 'Music for piano 21-52,'" p. 41-43; Pousseur, Henri, "Outline of a method: introduction [p. 44-47], Quintet in memory of Webern [p. 48-55], Impromptu [p. 56-63], Variations I [p. 64-81], Variations II [p. 82-88]," tr. by Leo Black.

See no. 496 (Redlich, Hans Ferdinand. "The problem of tonality" in his Alban Berg, 1957, p. 19-31).

166a Rufer, Josef. "Was ist Zwölftonmusik?" NZfM 118:11-13 (Jan 1957); 118:552-553 (Oct 1957); and 119:14-16 (Jan 1958). Mus.
The first two articles deal with the technique in general; the third shows its treatment in Schoenberg's Fourth Quartet.

See no. 110 (Schatz, Hilmar. "Theoretiker des Zufalls," Oct 1957).

167 Kelterborn, Rudolf. "Gegensätzliche Formprinzipien in der zeitgenössischen Musik," Schw MZ 97:472-474 (Dec 1957).
Permutational principle in serial music.

168 Junge Komponisten. Wien, Universal Edition [c1958]. 133 p. Diagrs., mus., tables. (Die Reihe: Information über serielle Musik, 4.)
Contents: Lewinsky, Wolf-Eberhard von, "Junge Komponisten," p. 5-8; Unger, Udo, "Luigi Nono," p. 9-17; Koenig, Gottfried Michael, "Henri Pousseur," p. 18-31; Stephan, Rudolf, "Hans Werner Henze," p. 32-37; Ligeti, György, "Pierre Boulez," p. 38-63; Metzger, Heinz-Klaus, "Intermezzo I: das Alten der Philosophie der neuen Musik," p. 64-80; [Eimert, Herbert], "Intermezzo II: Adorno und Kotschenreuther," p. 81-83; Koenig, Gottfried Michael, "Bo Nilsson," p. 85-88; Lewinsky, Wolf-Eberhard von, "Giselher Klebe," p. 89-97; Santi, Piero, "Luciano Berio," p. 98-102; Schubert, Reinhold, "Bernd Alois Zimmermann," p. 103-112; Manzoni, Giacomo, "Bruno Maderna," p. 113-118; Schnebel, Dieter, "Karlheinz Stockhausen," p. 119-133.

169 Reti, Rudolf Richard. Tonality, atonality, pantonality: a study of some trends in twentieth century music. London, Rockliff [c1958]. xii + 166 p. Mus.
Part two, atonality: Schoenberg's search for a new style, p. 33-41; Composition with twelve tones, p. 42-48; Twelve-tone technique in evolution, p. 49-55.

170 Steinecke, Wolfgang, ed. Darmstädter Beiträge zur neuen Musik. [V. 1.] Mainz, Schott [c1958]. 100 p. Diagrs., mus., ports.

Contents: Schoenberg, Arnold [a brief untitled article from his unpublished writings], p. 5-6; Adorno, Theodor Wiesengrund, "Kritieren," p. 7-16; Krenek, Ernst, "Bericht über Versuche in total determinierter Musik," p. 17-21; Fortner, Wolfgang, "Kranichsteiner Aspekte," p. 22-24; Nono, Luigi, "Die Entwicklung der Reihentechnik," tr. by Willi Reich, p. 25-37 (technical article, with analyses of row treatment in the theme of Schoenberg's Variations for Orchestra, op. 31, in Webern's Variations for Orchestra, op. 30, and in Boulez' Structures; Stockhausen's Komposition Nr. 2 für Sinustöne, and Zeitmasse are also discussed; describes and illustrated the technique of row permutation); Pousseur, Henri, "Webern und die Theorie," p. 38-43; Boulez, Pierre, "Alea," tr. by Heinz-Klaus Metzger, p. 44-56 [Italian tr. in Incontri musicali, no. 3:3-15 (Aug 1959); discusses function of chance in composition]; Stockhausen, Karlheinz, "Sprache und Musik," p. 57-81 (detailed discussion of the vocal and serial techniques in Boulez's Le marteau sans maître, Nono's Il canto sospeso, and Stockhausen's Gesang der Jünglinge); Henze, Hans Werner, "Wo stehen wir Heute?" p. 82-83; Kolisch, Rudolf, "Über die Krise der Streicher," p. 84-90; Stuckenschmidt, Hans Heinz, "Entwicklung oder Experiment?" p. 91-93; "Zwölf Jahre Kranichstein, Chronik 1946-1958," p. 94-100.

170a   Stephan, Rudolf. Neue Musik: Versuch einer kritischen Einführung. Göttingen, Vandenhoeck & Ruprecht [c1958]. 74 p. Mus.
       The compositional techniques of Schoenberg, Berg, Webern, and Stockhausen are discussed on p. 36-67.

171   Payne, Elsie. "The theme and variation in modern music," Mus rev 19:112-124 (May 1958). Mus.
       Variation technique in serial music, p. 115-117; examples from Schoenberg and Webern.

172   Krenek, Ernst. "Was ist Reihenmusik?" NZfM 119:278-281 (May 1958) and 119:428-430 (Aug 1958).
       The concepts of serialism and the twelve-tone technique; the serialization of non-pitch elements. An answer to questions raised by Rufer (see no. 166).

173   Kagel, Mauricio. "Ton-Cluster, Anschäge, Ubergänge" in Berichte/ Analysen. Wien, Universal Edition [c1959], p. 23-37. Diagrs. (Die Reihe: Information über serielle Musik, 5.)
       Tone clusters and similar procedures as compositional resources used in serial composition.

174   Steinecke, Wolfgang, ed. Darmstädter Beiträge zur neuen Musik. v. 2. Mainz, Schott [c1959]. 94 p.
       Contents: Wörner, Karl H., "Neue Musik 1946-1958: Versuch eines historischen Überblicks," p. 7-14; Pousseur, Henri, "Theorie und Praxis in der neuesten Musik," p. 15-29; Stockhausen, Karlheinz, "Musik im Raum," p. 30-35 (see no. 772); Berio, Luciano, "Musik und Dichtung: eine Erfahrung," p. 36-45 (see no. 609); Cage, John, "Zur Geschichte der experimentellen Musik in den Vereinigten Staaten," p. 46-53; Metzger, Heinz Klaus, "Hommage

à Edgard Varèse," p. 54-66; Nono, Luigi, "Vorword zum Kranichsteiner Kompositions-Studio 1958," p. 67-68; "Kranichsteiner Chronik, 1958," p. 69-74; "Neue Musik in Darmstadt 1946-1958," p. 75-94.

175 Clarke, Henry Leland. "The abuse of the semitone in twelve-tone music," MQ 45:295-301 (Jul 1959).
Tonal implications of the half-step. Suggests use of all-interval rows and other solutions.

*175a Spinner, Leopold. A short introduction to the technique of twelve-tone composition. New York, Boosey & Hawkes, 1960. 37 p. Mus.

175b Babbitt, Milton. "Twelve-tone invariants as compositional determinants," MQ [special issue on the Princeton Seminar in Advanced Musical Studies] 46:246-259 (Apr 1960). Diagrs.
Technical article on set structure.

See no. 739a (Krenek, Ernst. "Extents and limits of serial techniques," Apr 1960).

175c Walker, Alan. "Back to Schönberg," Mus rev 21:140-147 (May 1960). Mus.
Audibility of serial derivations, as determined by experiments with listeners.

HARMONY

176 Alaleona, Domenico. "I moderni orizzonti della tecnica musicale; teoria della divisione dell'ottava in parti ugali," Riv mus ital 18:382-420 ([Apr/Jun] 1911). Mus.
Pre-twelve-tone theories on the harmonic implications of the equal division of the octave into twelve parts. Purely theoretical article.

177 Alaleona, Domenico. "L'armonia modernissima: le tonalità neutre e l'arte di stupore," Riv mus ital 18:769-838 ([Oct/Dec] 1911). Mus.
Chromatic tonal harmony at the point of its change to atonality; a theory of musical expressionism. An important and little-known article.

178 Hauer, Josef Matthias. "Die Tropen und ihre Spannungen zum Dreiklang," Die Musik 17:257-258 (Jan 1925). Mus.
Resolutions of six-note chords (tropes) to triads.

179 Klein, Fritz Heinrich. "Die Grenze der Halbtonwelt," Die Musik 17:281-286 (Jan 1925). Mus., tables.
On atonal harmony: number of possible chords, etc.

180 Pisk, Paul. "The tonal era draws to a close," Modern music 3:3-7 (Mar/Apr 1926).
A summary of Hauer's and Schoenberg's new harmonic principles.

181 Erpf, Hermann Robert. Studien zur Harmonie- und Klangtechnik der neueren Musik. Leipzig, Breitkopf und Härtel, 1927. 235 p. Mus.

General discussion of twelve-tone music, p. 83-86; examples from works of Schoenberg.

182   Hábá, Alois. Neue Harmonielehre des diatonischen, chromatischen, viertel-, drittel-, sechstel- und zwölftel-Tonsystems. Leipzig, Kistner & Siegel, 1927. xviii + 251 p. Mus., tables.
      No index; difficult to use. A manual of all the possible chord combinations and scale patterns in each of these harmonic systems.

183   Deutsch, Leonhard. "Das Problem der Atonalität und des Zwölftonprinzip," Melos 6:108-118 (Mar 1927).
      "Tries to prove that all possible combinations of the twelve tones may be referred back to altered diatonic chords, therefore the twelve-tone system as such . . . has no justification" (Richard Hill, "Schoenberg's tone-rows and the tonal system of the future," p. 16-17). (See no. 386.)

184   Schoenberg, Arnold. "Problems of harmony," Modern music 11:167-187 (May/Jun 1934). Tr. by Adolph Weiss. Mus.
      "First presented as a lecture during Mr. Schoenberg's recent professorship at the Berlin Akademie der Künste." Also appears in Armitage, ed., Schoenberg. 1937 (see no. 295).
      Weakening of tonality by means of chromaticism; twelve-tone technique as another means of organizing music; new concepts of dissonance (see no. 192).

See no. 77 (Stuckenschmidt, Hans Heinz. "Das Zwölftonsystem," Sept 1934).

185   Schoenberg, Arnold. "Tonality and form," Pacific Coast musician [Los Angeles] 24:3 (May 4, 1935).
      A refutation of the concept that musical form is impossible without tonality.

186   Taylor, Noel Heath. "The Schoenberg concept," M & L 20:183-188 (Apr 1939).
      Schoenberg's theory of harmony.

187   Kessler, Hubert. "Some problems of tonality in relation to Schönberg's twelve-tone technique," JAMS 1:49-50 (Fall 1948).
      Abstract only.
      Does the twelve-tone technique exclude tonality? "Laws" of twelve-tone music related to those of tonal music.

188   *Brauner, Rudolph Franz. Vom Dreiklang zum Zwölftonakkord: ein Rückblick auf die Entwicklung des Tonsatzes von Bach bis Hindemith. Wien, Verlag für Jugend und Volk, 1949. 284 p. Mus., diagr.

189   Jelinek, Hanns. "Versuch über der Sinn der Verwendung von Zwölftonreihen," Melos 18:252-255 (Sept 1951). Port.
      Harmonic problems and overtone bases of the twelve-tone technique.

190   Jelinek, Hanns. Anleitung zur Zwölftonkomposition nebst allerlei Paralipomena. Appendix zu [Jelineks] "Zwölftonwerk," op. 15. Erster Teil: Allgemeiner und vertikale Dodekaphonik. Wien, Universal Edition, c1952. 106 p. Mus.

Theory—Harmony

_____. Anhang zu Anleitung zur Zwölftonkomposition. Tabellen und Kompositionsbeispiele von Schoenberg, Webern und Jelinek. [Wien] Universal Edition [1952]. Unpaged. Mus.

A manual of composition. This first part deals only with harmony; a second part treats of counterpoint (see no. 215); and a future third part is to cover "broken" dodecaphony. Almost all the examples are from the author's composition, "Zwölftonwerk." [See Roland Tenschert's article, "Hanns Jelinek: zu seinem 'Zwölftonwerk,' op. 15" (no. 715).]

An important review by Ernst Krenek is in MQ 40:250-256 (Apr 1954). (See no. 712.)

191 Gerhard, Roberto. "Tonality in twelve-tone music," Score, no. 6:23-35 (May 1952). Mus.

The twelve-note technique as a new principle of tonality. "Classical" row treatment and permutational treatment. Possible chords in dodecaphonic harmony.

192 Yasser, Joseph. "A letter from Arnold Schoenberg," JAMS 6:53-62 (Spring 1953). Mus.

A reply from Schoenberg to a letter from Yasser on Schoenberg's article in Modern music (see no. 184). Twelve-tone technique and problems of equal temperament; consonance and dissonance; small and large intervals.

193 Costère, Edmond. "Entre l'harmonie classique et les harmonies contemporaines, y a-t-il rupture, ou continuité?" Revue de musicologie 36:55-65 (Jul 1954). Mus.

"Nous examinerons successivement l'incidence des relations cardinales: 1° sur l'accord dit de septième de dominante; 2° sur l'échelonnement diatonique; 3° sur un example de musique dite primitive; 4° sur un exemple de musique sérielle; 5° sur un exemple de musique contemporaine par superpositions de sons fixes."

194 Perle, George. "The possible chords in twelve-tone music," Score, no. 9:54-58 (Sept 1954). Tables.

The number of different chord combinations possible in twelve-tone music. Corrects figures in Gerhard's article (see no. 191).

195 Gerhard, Roberto. "Reply to George Perle," Score, no. 9:59-60 (Sept 1954). Mus.

Further corrections of errors in chord tables in Gerhard's article of May, 1952 (see nos. 191, 194).

196 Perle, George. "The harmonic problem in twelve-tone music," Mus rev 15:257-267 (Nov 1954). Mus.

How the row governs the vertical ordering of sound. Discusses Babbitt's theory of combinatoriality (see no. 157).

197 *Neumann, Friedrich. Tonalität und Atonalität: Versuch einer Klärung. Landsberg a. Lech, H. Hohler, 1955. 30 p. Mus. (Beiträge zu Gegenwartsfragen der Musik, 1.)

198 Keller, Hans. "Serial octave transpositions," Mo mus rec 86:139-143 (Jul/Aug 1956); and 86:172-177 (Sept/Nov 1956). Mus.

Problems created by the identity of complementary intervals in "classical" twelve-tone music.

199 Gould, Glenn. "The dodecaphonist's dilemma," Canadian music journal 1:20-29 (Autumn 1956). Mus.
  Harmonic problems of the post-Webern composers; division of the row into hexachords and three-note groups.

200 Forneberg, Erich. Der Geist der neuen Musik: der neue Klang im Spiegel der traditionellen Harmonielehre. Würzburg, Triltsch, 1957, xxvi + 130 p.; Anhang [mus. and illus.] 42 p. (Literar-historisch-musikwissenschaftliche Abhandlungen, 15.)
  Contents: bibliography, p. xviii-xxvi; "Der Geist der neuen Musik," p. 22-78; "Das 'Neue' in der zeitgenössischen Musik," p. 79-113 ("Die Komposition mit zwölf Tönen," p. 98-113).

201 Prosperi, Carlo. L'atonalità nella musica contemporanea. Caltanissetta [Sicily], S. Sciascia [1957]. 47 p. Mus. (Lo Smeraldo, 7.)
  A brief general discussion.

202 Frid, Géza. "Twaalf contra twaalf," Mens en melodie 12:366-369 (Dec 1957). Mus.
  The author suggests another twelve-tone "system" (originated by a theorist named Ernö Landvai), based on functional tonal relations (see no. 203).

203 "Twaalf contra twaalf; standpunten inzake de dodecafonie," Mens en melodie 13:16-19 (Jan 1958).
  Articles by Hendrik Andriessen, Géza Frid, and Harry Mayer; further commentary on Frid's article (see no. 202).

204 Truscott, Harold. "The real atonalism," Chesterian 33:35-44 (Autumn 1958).
  "Atonality" only an extreme form of chromatic tonality; tonality "normal" but atonality "abnormal."

204a Rochberg, George. "The harmonic tendency of the hexachord," Journal of music theory 3:208-230 (Nov 1959). Mus.
  Serial structure based on symmetrically arranged hexachords produces a new type of harmonic order. Discusses Hauer's tropes and Babbitt's source sets. Hexachordal analysis of Schoenberg's op. 45 and 50b.

MELODY

205 Stuckenschmidt, Hans Heinz. "Vocal style in the twentieth century," Modern music 13:3-13 (Mar 1936). Mus.
  Schoenberg, Krenek, and Berg, p. 5-8; a brief discussion, not a melodic analysis.

See no. 388 (Jalowetz, Heinrich. "On the spontaneity of Schoenberg's music," Oct 1944).

See no. 141 (Saby, Bernard. "Un aspect des problèmes de la thématique serielle" in Le système dodécaphonique, 1949).

206 Johnson, Martha. A study of linear design in Gregorian chant and music written in the twelve-tone technique. Minneapolis, Burgess, 1954, p. 69-99. Mus. (Hamline studies in musicology, ed. by Ernst Krenek, v. 1.)
  Melodic analyses of Webern's String quartet, op. 28, Schoenberg's Fourth string quartet, and Krenek's Lamentatio Jeremiae.

207 Scriabine, Marina. "Athématisme et fonction thématique dans la musique contemporaine" in Inventaire des techniques rédactionnelles. Paris, Richard-Masse [1954], p. 35-46. (Polyphonie, $9^e/10^e$ cahier.)
  Résumé of the last chapters of a "work in preparation," Les perspectives de la musique contemporaine.
  So-called athematicism as an "ultra-thematicism"; the characteristics of themes.

See no. 154 (Erickson, Robert. The structure of music, 1955).

See no. 45 (Milner, Anthony. "The vocal element in melody," Mar 1956).

See no. 351 (Skrebkow, S. "Gegen die Atonalität Schönbergs," May 1957).

See no. 215 (Jelinke, Hanns. Anleitung zur Zwölftonkomposition. Zweiter Teil, 1958).

RHYTHM

208 Boulez, Pierre. "Propositions" in Le rythme musical. Paris, Richard-Masse [1948], p. 65-72. Mus. (Polyphonie, 2e cahier.)
  Rhythmic treatment in Stravinsky and Boulez.

See no. 146 (Boulez, Pierre. "Eventuellement," Apr 1952).

See no. 618 (Barraqué, Jean. "Rythme et développement," 1954).

See no. 157 (Babbitt, Milton. "Some aspects of twelve-tone composition," Jun 1955).

See no. 46 (Kelterborn, Rudolf. "Stilistisch gegensätzliche Entwicklungen auf der Basis der Zwölftontechnik," Apr 1956).

See no. 599 (Elston, Arnold. "Some rhythmic practices in contemporary music," Jul 1956).

See no. 161 (Smith Brindle, Reginald. "The lunatic fringe, III," Jul 1956).

See no. 163 (Gerhard, Roberto. "Developments in twelve-tone technique," Sept 1956).

See no. 58 (Castiglione, Niccolò. "Il valore del silenzio e della durata," Jul 1958).

See no. 166 (Stockhausen, Karlheinz. ". . . How time passes . . ." in Musical craftsmanship, 1959, p. 10-40).
  Detailed and technical analysis of his serial treatment of rhythmic elements; the relation of pitches to frequencies, and frequencies to tempi.

COUNTERPOINT

209 Krenek, Ernst. Studies in counterpoint based on the twelve-tone technique. New York, Schirmer [c1940]. ix + 37 p. Mus.

_____. Zwölfton-Kontrapunkt-Studien. Tr. by Heinz Klaus Metzger. Mainz, Schott, 1952. 51 p. Mus.
    Textbook of the twelve-tone technique approached through counterpoint (see no. 42).

210 Thilman, Johannes Paul. Problems der neuen Polyphonie. Dresden, Dresdener Verlagsgesellschaft [1949?]. 111 p.
    Contains much discussion of twelve-tone music. No music examples; no analyses; no index.
    Contents: "Einleitung," p. 7-18; "Melodik," p. 19-37; "Harmonik," p. 38-55; "Polyphonie," p. 56-75; "Form," p. 76-87; "Rhythmus," p. 88-98; "Klangverwirklichung," p. 99-102; "Sinn," p. 103-109.

See no. 20 (Hall, Richard. "Twelve-tone music and tradition," 1952).

See no. 24 (Thomson, Virgil. "Reflections," May 1952).

211 Searle, Humphrey. Twentieth century counterpoint. London, Williams and Norgate [1954]. ix + 158 p. Mus.
    Partial contents: "The development of chromatic counterpoint," p. 7-21; "Schoenberg and twelve-note composition," p. 71-117; "Postscript" (includes some comments on recent twelve-tone composers), p. 47-150.

See no. 31 (Burkhard, Willy. "Versuch einer kritischen Auseinandersetzung mit der Zwölftontechnik," Mar 1954).

See no. 154 (Erickson, Robert. The structure of music, 1955).

212 Herzfeld, Friedrich. "Der Reiz des Krebses: Bedeutungswandel einer Kompositionsform," NZfM 11:71-74 (Nov 1955). Mus.
    On the contrapuntal device of retrograde motion; some discussion of its use in serial music.

See no. 40 (Keller, Hans. "The audibility of serial technique," Nov 1955).

213 Unger, Udo. Die Klavierfuge im zwanzigsten Jahrhundert. Regensburg, Gustav Bosse, 1956. 147 p. Mus., tables. (Kölner Beiträge zur Musikforschung, 11.)
    Partial contents: "Fuge und Zwölftontechnik," p. 107; "Fuge und serielle Technik," p. 108; "Analyse von W[olfgang] Fortners Fuge aus 'Kammermusik,' komp. 1943," p. 91-92.

214 Adorno, Theodor Wiesengrund. Die Funktion des Kontrapunkts in der neuen Musik. [Berlin-Dahlem, Akademie der Künste, 1958]. [43 p.] (Anmerkungen zur Zeit, 4.)
    Counterpoint in contemporary music, especially in the twelve-tone school.

215 Jelinek, Hanns. Anleitung zur Zwölftonkomposition nebst allerlei Paralipomena; Appendix zu "Zwölftonwerk," op. 15. Zweiter Teil: Horizontal Dodekaphonik, Kombination und Abteilungen. Wien, Universal Edition [1958]. 107-239 p. + [110 p.] Mus.

Not seen; entry from M.L.A. Notes 16:576 (Sept 1959). (See no. 190.)

216 [omitted]

NOTATION

217 Wirtz, Warren. "The problem of notation in the twelve-tone technique," Mus rev 7:103-110 (May 1946). Mus.
    A new notational system.

218 Schnippering, H. "Atonalität und temperierte Stimmung," Melos 17:9-11 (Jan 1950). Mus.
    On the notation of atonal music.

219 Gindele, Father Corbinian. "Von cis nach c," Melos 17:169 (Jun 1950). Mus.
    A reply to Schnippering (see no. 218).

220 Schnippering, H. "Von der Logik der Zwölftonmusik," Melos 17:312-314 (Nov 1950). Mus.
    On the notation of atonal music, III (see nos. 218 and 219).

See no. 89 (Reich, Willi. "Versuch einer Geschichte der Zwölftonmusik" in Alte und neue Musik, 1952).

221 Köhler, Siegfried. "Was ist Zwölftonmusik? Eine kritische Wertung," Musica 6:142-144 (Apr 1952). Mus.
    Definition of twelve-note music; discussion of the problem of notation.

See no. 153 (Searle, Humphrey. "Twelve-note music" in Grove's Dictionary of music and musicians, 1954).

See no. 238 (Meyer-Eppler, Werner. "Elektronische Musik," Dec 6, 1954).

See no. 279 (Prieberg, Fred. "Erste elektronische Partitur," Apr 1957).

See no. 263 ("The progress of science," Jan 1958).

II
ELECTRONIC MUSIC

PHILOSOPHY AND CRITICISM

222 Beyer, Robert. "Die Klangwelt der elektronischen Musik," ZfM 113:74-79 (Feb 1952). Illus.
Composition of "Klangfarbenmusik"; implications of electronic music.

See no. 30 (La musique et ses problèmes contemporains, 1954).

223 Beyer, Robert. "Elektronische Musik," Melos 21:35-39 (Feb 1954).
Electronic music as a development of Klangfarbenmelodie; its problems and implications.

224 Beyer, Robert. "Zur Situation der elektronischen Musik," ZfM 116:452-456 (Aug/Sept 1955).
Electronic music as the beginning of a new era in music. Its relation to the serial music of Schoenberg and Webern. Klangfarbenmelodie.

225 Suder, Alexander L. "Die überflüssige Windmaschine; eine Betrachtung zur 'Elektronischen Musik,'" ZfM 116:456-459 (Aug/Sept 1955).
Fallacies of the assumptions and philosophy of electronic music.

226 Keller, Wilhelm. "Elektronische Musik und musique concrète," Merkur [Stuttgart] 9:877-881 (Sept 1955).
A definition and description of each; aesthetic implications.

227 Dahlhaus, Carl, and Stephan, Rudolf. "Eine 'dritte Epoche' der Musik? Kritische Bemerkungen zur elektronische Musik," Dt Univ Zt 10:14-17 (Sept 12, 1955).
Philosophical considerations; discussion of problems raised in Elektronische Musik (Technische Hausmitteilungen des Nordwestdeutscher Rundfunk, 1954) and Elektronische Musik (Die Reihe, 1). (For the latter, see no. 275.)

228 Rognoni, Luigi. "La musica 'elettronica' e il problema della tecnica," Aut aut, no. 36:450-461 (Nov 1956).
Drawn from two lectures given at Darmstadt in July 1956: "Musik der jungen Generation: Kompositions und Interpretations-Probleme" and "Die Frage der Technik in der elektronischen Musik."

See no. 54 (Dansk Musiktidsskrift, May 1957).

229 Metzger, Heinz-Klaus. "Nochmals 'Wider die Natur'; zur Frage der Verwendung der menschlichen Stimme in elektronischer Musik,"

NZfM 118:329-330 (May 1957).
On the use of voices in electronic music.

230 Berio, Luciano. "Sur la musique electronique," Schw MZ 97:265 (Jun 1957).
Brief statement written for the I.S.C.M. festival in Zürich, June, 1957.

See no. 257 (Stuckenschmidt, Hans Heinz. "Il mondo delle sonorità ignote," Jul 1957).

231 Pfrogner, Hermann. "Elektronik—Lust am Untergang?" NZfM 118:484-489 (Sept 1957). Illus.
Busoni's and Schoenberg's thoughts on new means of musical production; Klangfarbenmelodie. Attacks electronic music.

See no. 260 (Prieberg, Fred K. "Musik: Töne aus der Elektronröhre," Nov 1957).

See no. 261 (Becerra, Gustavo. "¿Que es la música electrónica?" Dec 1957).

See no. 275 (Stuckenschmidt, Hans Heinz. "The third stage" in Electronic music, 1958, p. 11-13).

232 Babbitt, Milton. "Who cares if you listen?" High fidelity 8:38-40, 126-127 (Feb 1958).
A plea for research in experimental electronic music. The author feels that "advanced music" should be intended primarily for specialists.

233 Boulez, Pierre. "Son, verbe, synthèse," Melos 25:310-313 (Oct 1958). [German tr. by Hilde Strobel, p. 313-317.] Illus.
Fusion of sound and word by electronic means, and resulting expansion of sound possibilities.

See no. 70 (Evangelisti, Franco. "Verso una composizione elettronica"/ "Towards electronic composition" in Ordini, Jul 1959).

DESCRIPTION AND HISTORY

See no. 611 (Scriabine, Marina. "Pierre Boulez et la musique concrète," 1952).

234 Eimert, Herbert. "Was ist elektronische Musik?" Melos 20:1-5 (Jan 1953). Illus.
A brief history and description. (For English translation see no. 275.)

235 Beyer, Robert. "Zur Geschichte der elektronischen Musik," Melos 20:278-280 (Oct 1953).
Brief history of electronic music; includes bibliographical notes.

236 Eimert, Herbert. "Möglichkeiten und Grenzen der Elektronischen Musik," Schw MZ 93:445-447 (Nov 1953).

Definition of electronic music; differences from musique concrète. Brief history and summary of objectives.

237   Eimert, Herbert. "Elektronische Musik" in Die Musik in Geschichte und Gegenwart. Kassel, Bärenreiter, 1954, v. 3, col. 1263-1267. Illus.
Includes "nontechnical" bibliography. (For French translation, see no. 253.)

See no. 95 (Wörner, Karl H. "Die Klangwelt der elektronischen Musik" in his Neue Musik in der Entscheidung, 1954, p. 296-302).
History and description of electronic music, especially as developed at the Cologne Studio.

238   Meyer-Eppler, Werner. "Elektronische Musik: Gestaltungsmöglichkeiten, Notation, Technische Einrichtungen," Dt Univ Zt 9:9-10 (Dec 6, 1954). Diagr.
Description of technical considerations.

See no. 98 (Myers, Rollo H. "Music in France in the post-war decade," 1954/55).

239   Gravesano: Musik, Raumgestaltung, Elektroakustik. Hrsg. von Dr. [Werner] Meyer-Eppler. Mainz, Ars Viva [c1955]. 140 p. Diagrs., illus., mus.
A collection of articles, primarily devoted to technical considerations of acoustics and of electronic instruments. Some brief bibliographies.

240   *Klangstruktur der Musik. Neue Erkenntnisse musik-elektronischer Forschung: Vortragsreihe "Musik und Technik" des Ausseninstitutes der Technischen Universität Berlin-Charlottenburg, mit Vorträgen von B[oris] Blacher [et al.] ergänzt durch Beiträge von F. Enkel [et al.]. Im Auftrage des Ausseninstitutes der Technischen Universität zusammengestellt und bearb. von F[ritz] Winckel. Berlin, Verlag für Radio-Foto-Kinotechnik [1955].
Reviewed in Dansk Musiktidsskrift 32:49 (May 1957).

241   "News and comments. Italy. Electronic music," Score, no. 11:67 (Mar 1955).
Very brief résumé of activities at the Milan Studio.

242   Koster, Ernst. "Kinderkrankheiten der elektrogenen Musik," Musica 9:315-317 (Jul 1955). Mus.
Brief description of "experimentelle elektrogene Musik"; explanation of basic terms (sine tone, overtone, timbre, frequency, etc.).

243   Sonner, Rudolf. "Elektronische Musik; ihre drei Arbeitsberichte," ZfM 116:449-452 (Aug/Sept 1955).
Brief history of the development of electronic instruments and of electronic music.

244   Krenek, Ernst. "New development in electronic music," Musical America 75:8 (Sept 1955).
Simple, nontechnical description for the layman.

245   Vlad, Roman. "Die Reihe and electronic music," Score, no. 13:23-24 (Sept 1955).
Current status of electronic music; brief history.

246 Berio, Luciano. "Prospettive nella musica: richerche ed attività dello Studio di Fonologia Musicale di Radio Milano," Elettronica 5:108-115 (1956).
   History of the activities at the Milan Studio.

247 *Prieberg, Fred K. Musik im Technischen Zeitalters. Zürich, Atlantis [1956]. 176 p. Mus.
   Bibliography, p. 173-176.

248 Oesch, Hans. "Einführung in die elektronische Musik," Universitas [Stuttgart] 11:167-175 (Feb 1956).
   The development of electronic music is discussed. Brief bibliography, p. 175.

249 Smith Brindle, Reginald. "The lunatic fringe: I. Electronic music," MT 97:200-201 (Jun 1956).
   A brief historical summary.

250 Pestalozza, Luigi. "L'ultima avanguardia: post-Weberniani, concerti ed elettronici," Ricordiana [nuova serie] 2:333-336 (Jul 1956).
   Brief history and description of the European musical avant-garde (Boulez, Schaeffer, et al.).

251 Forte, Allen. "Composing with electrons in Cologne," High fidelity 6:64-67, 156, 159 (Oct 1956). Illus.
   Nontechnical article, discussing the activities at the Cologne Studios. Describes equipment, discusses composers, defines terminology.

252 Stockhausen, Karlheinz. "A proposito di musica elettronica," Incontri musicali, no. 1:70-78 (Dec 1956).
   Nontechnical; description of electronic music and discussion of its aesthetic problems.

253 Vers une musique expérimentale. Sous la direction de Pierre Schaeffer. Paris, Richard-Masse [1957]. xvi + 141 p. Mus., diagrs. (La revue musicale, no. 236.)
   Partial contents: Schaeffer, Pierre, "Vers une musique expérimentale," p. 11-27; Boulez, Pierre, "Tendances de la musique récente," p. 28-35 (on the music of Varèse, Messiaen, Stockhausen, Cage); Goléa, Antoine, "Tendances de la musique concrète," p. 36-44; Eimert, Herbert, "Musique électronique," tr. by Charles Hebert, p. 45-49 (a translation of his article in M.G.G.; see no. 237); Ussachevsky, Vladimir, "La 'tape music' aux Etats-Unis," p. 50-55; Scherchen, Hermann, "Depassement de l'orchestre," p. 56-59; Tardieu, Jean, "Décade de musique expérimentale," p. 103-104; Poullin, Jacques, "Son et espace," p. 105-114; Moles, André, "Machines à musique," p. 115-127; Arthuys, Philippe, "La pensée et l'instrument," p. 128-134; "Le group de recherches de musique concrète," p. 135-136; "Historique de la musique concrète," p. 137-138; "List des oeuvres de musique concrète," p. 139-141.

254 Tall, Joel. "Music without musicians," Saturday review 40:56-57 (Jan 26, 1957).
   Brief history and description of electronic music, musique concrète, and "music for tape recorder."

255 Maren, Roger. "Electronic music: untouched by human hands."
Reporter 16:40-42 (Apr 18, 1957).
A summary of the activities in Europe and the U.S. in the fields of electronic music and musique concrète.

256 "Das neue Buch: elektronische Musik in Italien," Melos 24:139-140 (May 1957).
On the activities of the Studio di Fonologia Musicale in Milan; review of the periodicals Elettronica and Incontri musicali, and a description of electronic music.

257 Stuckenschmidt, Hans Heinz. "Il mondo delle sonorità ignote: Un contributo all'estetica della musica elettronica," Aut aut, no. 41:399-406 (Jul 1957).
Historical and aesthetical summary.

258 Nettel, Reginald. "Electronic music," Mo mus rec 87:163-168 (Sept/Oct 1957).
Brief summary of the current status of electronic music.

259 Berio, Luciano. "Note sulla musica elettronica," Ricordiana [nuova serie] 3:427-437 (Oct 1957).
Comparatively nontechnical article.

260 Prieberg, Fred K. "Musik: Töne aus der Elektronröhre," Monat 10:62-66 (Nov 1957).
A brief history of mechanical music (from the 1920's) and of electronic music; aesthetic problems are discussed.

261 Becerra, Gustavo. "¿Que es la música electrónica?" Revista musicale chilena 11:27-44 (Dec 1957). Diagrs.
Contents: "Las conjeturas usuales," p. 27-28; "Algunos aspectos fundamentales," p. 28-38; "Actuales compromisos estilísticos de la música electrónica," p. 38-40; "Proyecciones artísticas de la música electrónica," p. 40-42; "Sus efectos económicos y sociales," p. 42-43; "Conclusiones," p. 43-44.

262 Manzoni, Giacomo. "Breve introduzione alla musica elettronica," Rass mus 27:309-315 (Dec 1957).
Explanation of the instruments used; the activities at the studios at Cologne, Paris, and Milan. Mentions some composers and their works. Nontechnical article.

See no. 112 (Prieberg, Fred K. "Elektronische Musik" in his Lexikon der neuen Musik, 1958, p. 116-121).

See no. 116 (Vlad, Roman. "La serialità integrale e la musica elettronica" in his Storia della dodecafonia, 1958).

263 "The progress of science: electronic music," Discovery 19:4-5 (Jan 1958). Illus.
A concise and clear summary of the apparatus and technique used and of the objectives of electronic music. Illustrates the "Darmstadt method of notation for electronic music."

264 Smith Brindle, Reginald. "Reports from abroad: Italy, the R.A.I. Studio di Fonologia Musicale at Milan," MT 99:98 (Feb 1958).

Very brief article commenting on the broadcasts of electronic music given by Luciano Berio. Discusses the use and implications of non-tone sounds derived from "white noise."

265 Prieberg, Fred K. "Italiens elektronische Musik," Melos 6:194-198 (Jun 1958). Illus.
Activity of the Studio di Fonologia Musicale in Milan.

266 Badings, Henk. "Electronic music: its development in the Netherlands," Delta: a review of arts, life and thought in the Netherlands, 1:85-93 (Winter 1958/59). Illus., mus.
A nontechnical history of Dutch electronic music.

See no. 770 (Luening, Otto. "Karlheinz Stockhausen," Winter 1958/59).

267 Experiences musicales: musiques concrète, electronique, exotique, par le Groupe de recherches musicales de la Radiodiffusion Télévision française. Paris, Richard-Masse [c1959]. 72 p. Mus., diagrs. (La revue musicale, no. 244.)
Contents: Messiaen, Olivier, "Préface"; Ferrari, Luc, "Les étapes de la vision"; Schaeffer, Pierre, "Situation actuelle de la musique expérimentale"; Mâche, François-Bernard, "Connaissance des structures sonores"; Xénakis, Yannis, "Notes sur un 'Geste électronique'"; Boucourechliev, André, "La fin et les moyens"; Philippot, Michel, "Espace vital"; Vandella, Romuald, "Musique exotique et musique expérimentale"; Poullin, Jacques, "L'orielle et le malentendu"; Moles, Abraham A., "Instrumentation électronique et musiques expérimentales"; Schaeffer, Pierre, "Le Groupe de recherches musicales . . ."; Chambure, Alaine de, "Infrastructure technique"; Ferrari, Luc, "Les étapes de la production"; "Historiques des recherches de musique concrète"; "Bibliographie sommaire"; "Discographie"; "Notices biographiques" (on Berio, Boucourechliev, Pousseur, Maderna, and other electronic and concrète composers).

268 Hiller, Lejaren Arthur. "Experimental music" in Experimental music: composition with an electronic computer, by Lejaren A. Hiller, Jr., and Leonard M. Isaacson. New York, McGraw-Hill, 1959, p. 36-57, 124-131.
Definition of various types of experimental music: electronic music, musique concrète, tape-recorder music, computational and computer music. Numerous bibliographical footnotes.

268a Rondi, Brunello. Il cammino della musica d'oggi e l'esperienza elettronica. Padova, Rebellato, 1959. 113 p.
Not seen; bibliographical information from the Bibliografia Nazionale Italiana, 1959:V.

269 Stockhausen, Karlheinz. "Elektronische und instrumentale Musik" in Berichte/Analysen. Wien, Universal Edition [c1959], p. 50-58. (Die Reihe: Information über serielle Musik, 5.)
"Dieser Text diente als Vorlage zu einer Reihe von Vorlesungen an amerikanischen Universitäten im November 1958."
A history of electronic music, general estimate of its possibilities, and description of its techniques.

270 Randolph, David. "A new music made with a machine." Horizon [New York] 1:50-55, 124-127 (Jan 1959). Illus., mus.
A brief description of electronic music, musique concrète, and tape music; aesthetic considerations.

271 Winckel, Fritz. "Die Komposition mit elektroakustischen Mitteln." NZfM 120:124-127 (Mar 1959). Illus.
Brief description and history.

272 Walter, Arnold. "Music and electronics." Canadian music journal 3:33-37 (Summer 1959).
General description of the process of creating electronic music. Problem of totally predetermined music. The Cologne group.

COMPOSITIONAL TECHNIQUES

273 Meyer-Eppler, Werner. "Elektronische Kompositionstechnik." Melos 20:5-9 (Jan 1953). Illus.
Describes various electronic instruments and their use.

See no. 95 (Wörner, Karl H. "Neue Musik in der Entscheidung," 1954, p. 296-302).

274 Lindlar, Heinrich. "Elektronische Musik im Kölner Funkhaus." Melos 21:326-327 (Nov 1954).
A review of a concert of electronic music given in Cologne; includes a brief description of the technique used in composing electronic music.

275 Elektronische Musik. Wien, Universal Edition [c1955]. Hrsg. von Herbert Eimert unter Mitarbeit von Karlheinz Stockhausen. 63 p. Illus. (Die Reihe: Information über serielle Musik, 1.)

Electronic music. Bryn Mawr, Pennsylvania, Theodore Presser [c1958]. vi + 62 p. Illus. (Die Reihe: a periodical devoted to developments in contemporary music, ed. by Herbert Eimert and Karlheinz Stockhausen, 1.)
Contents of American edition: Translator's preface, vi; Eimert, Herbert, "What is electronic music?" p. 1-10; Stuckenschmidt, Hans Heinz, "The third stage: some observations on the aesthetics of electronic music," p. 11-13; Krenek, Ernst, "A glance over the shoulders of the young," p. 14-16 (see no. 50); Klebe, Giselher, "First practical work," p. 17-18; Boulez, Pierre, "'At the ends of the fruitful land . . .'" p. 19-29; Pousseur, Henri, "Formal elements in a new compositional material," p. 30-34; Goeyvaerts, Karol, "The sound material of electronic music," p. 35-37; Gredinger, Paul, "Serial technique," p. 38-44; Stockhausen, Karlheinz, "Actualia," p. 45-51; Koenig, Gottfried Michael, "Studio techniques," p. 52-54; Meyer-Eppler, Werner, "Statistic and psychologic problems of sound," p. 55-61 (includes a bibliography). (See no. 245.)

See no. 46 (Kelterborn, Rudolf. "Stilistisch gegensätzliche Entwicklungen auf der Basis der Zwölftontechnik," Apr 1956).

276 Le Caine, Hugh. "Electronic music," Proceedings of the Institute of Radio Engineers 44:457-478 (Apr 1956). Diagrs., illus.
"New musical horizons through electronics," p. 475-478 (the musique concrète and Cologne groups). Technical and important article. Helpful bibliographical footnotes.

277 Enkel, Fritz. "Die Grundlagen der neuen Musik: das neue Klangmaterial (die Technik der elektronischen Klanggestaltung)," Gravesaner Blätter, Heft 6:20-27 (Dec 1956). Diagrs.
Bibliography, p. 27; general article on the technique of electronic music.

278 Xénakis, Janis. "Wahrscheinlichkeitstheorie und Musik," Gravesaner Blätter, Heft 6:28-34 (Dec 1956). Diagrs.
Highly technical article on the mathematical bases of electronic music.

279 Prieberg, Fred K. "Erste elektronische Partitur," NZfM 118:241 (Apr 1957).
Stockhausen's Studie 2.

280 Van San, Hermann. "Einheitswissenschaft und Musik," Gravesaner Blätter, Heft 7/8:39-48 (Apr/May 1957). Diagrs.
Highly technical article on "mathematical-electronic serial composition"; includes a short bibliography.

See no. 261 (Becerra, Gustavo. "¿Que es la música electrónica?" Dec 1957).

281 Badings, Henk, and de Bruyn, J. W. "Electronic music," Philips technical review [English ed.] 19:191-201 (Dec 23, 1957). Diagrs., illus., mus.
A 45 rpm phonorecord is included; it contains illustrations for the text and also an abridged version of Badings' ballet, Cain and Abel.
Primarily an explanation of the method of procedure in composing Bading's Cain and Abel ballet; various electronic techniques are described.

282 Wilkinson, Marc "Two months in the 'Studio di Fonologia,'" Score, no. 22:41-48 (Feb 1958).
Brief, nontechnical account of techniques and equipment used in the Milan Studio. Definition of terms.

283 Koenig, Gottfried Michael. "Studium in Studio" in Berichte/Analysen. Wien, Universal Edition [c1959], p. 74-83. (Die Reihe: Information über serielle Musik, 5.)
The teaching of electronic composition techniques.

See no. 272 (Walter, Arnold. "Music and electronics," Summer 1959).

*283a Prieberg, Fred K. Musica ex machina: über das Verhältnis von Musik und Technik. Berlin, Ullstein [1960]. 299 p.

III
THE VIENNESE SCHOOL

ARNOLD SCHOENBERG (1874-1951)

GENERAL
(Including Collections, Festschriften, etc.)

284   Arnold Schönberg. Mit Beiträgen von Alben Berg [et al.]. München, R. Piper, 1912. 90 p. Illus., mus.
   Partial contents: Webern, Anton, "Schönbergs Musik," p. 22-48 (brief discussion of early works with musical examples); also articles on Schoenberg as a painter and a teacher.

285   Rosenfeld, Paul. "Schoenberg" in his Musical portraits: interpretations of twenty modern composers. New York, Harcourt, Brace [c1920], p. 233-243.
   General; discusses works.

286   Wellesz, Egon. Arnold Schönberg. Leipzig, Tal & Co., 1921.

   _____. Arnold Schönberg. Tr. by W. H. Kerridge. London and New York, Dutton [1925]. vii + 159 p. Mus., port.
   Partial contents: "The new path," p. 10-39; "His teaching," p. 40-58; "His works," p. 59-154; "Chronological table," p. 155-156.
   Biography and discussion of his works, through the first twelve-tone works.

287   Gray, Cecil. "Arnold Schönberg, a critical study," M & L 3:73-89 (Jan 1922). Mus.
   Discussion of works (to 1921) and critical estimate.

288   Arnold Schönberg zum fünfzigsten Geburtstag, 13 September 1924. Wien [1924]. Mus., port. [Sonderheft der Musikblätter des Anbruch, Wien, 6:269-342 (Aug/Sept 1924).]
   Partial contents: Bekker, Paul, "Schönberg: 'Erwartung,'" p. 275-282; Stein, Erwin, "Neue Formenprinzipien," p. 286-303; Berg, Alban, "Warum ist Schönbergs Musik so schwer verständlich?" p. 329-341.
   Stein's article appears in English translation in his book, Orpheus in new guises (see no. 303); Berg's essay has been reprinted several times: in German (see no. 492); in English (see no. 470); in French (see no. 509).

289   *Stefan-Gruenfeldt, Paul. Arnold Schönberg, Wandlung-Legende-Erscheinung-Bedeutung. Wien, Zeitkunst Verlag [c1924]. 101 p.

"Arnold Schönbergs Werke," p. 102-103; "Literatur über Schönberg," p. 103.

290 Wellesz, Egon. "Arnold Schönberg: la voie nouvelle," Rev mus v. 7, no. 6:12-25 (Apr 1926) and v. 7, no. 9:11-23 (Jul 1926). tr. by Stefan Freund.

———. "Arnold Schönberg: la doctrine," Rev mus v. 7, no. 10:126-132 (Aug 1926) and v. 8, no. 1:38-46 (Jan 1927), tr. by Stefan Freund.
Schoenberg's life, works, and philosophy, to 1926.

291 Gray, Cecil. "Arnold Schönberg" in his A survey of contemporary music. 2d ed. London, Oxford University Press, 1927, p. 162-183.
General discussion of works and style.

292 Mersmann, Hans. Die moderne Musik seit der Romantik. Wildpark-Potsdam, Akademische Verlagsgesellschaft Athenaion [c1927]. Mus., illus.
Schoenberg, p. 132-143; Berg (especially Wozzeck), p. 144-147. Brief analyses of works.

293 Arnold Schönberg zum 60. Geburtstag, 13 September 1934. [Wien, Universal Edition, 1934?]. 75 p. Mus., port.
Partial contents: Webern, Anton, "Aus Schönbergs Schriften," p. 11-14; Hába, Alois, "Schönberg und die weiteren Möglichkeiten der Musikentwicklung," p. 15-17; Polnauer, Josef, "Schönbergs 'Verbundenheit,'" p. 44-49 (on the last of the six 'Stücken für Männerchor,' op. 35); Broch, Hermann, "Irrationale Erkenntnis in der Musik," p. 49-60; Berg, Alban, "Glauben, Hoffnung un Liebe," p. 61 (acrostic poem); "Verzeichnis der Werke von Arnold Schönberg," p. 71-75.

294 *Sollertinskii, Ivan Ivanovich. Арнольд Шенберг. [Leningrad, Leningradskaiia Filarmonija, 1934]. 55 p.

See no. 78 (Wind, Hans E. Die Endkrise der bürgerlichen Musik und die Rolle Arnold Schönberg, 1935).

295 Armitage, Merle, ed. Schoenberg. New York, G. Schirmer, 1937. 319 p. Illus.
Partial contents: Sessions, Roger, "Music in crisis," p. 9-39 (reprinted from Modern music; see no. 7); Weiss, Adolph, "The twelve-tone series," p. 75-77 (written 1932); Krenek, Ernst, "Arnold Schoenberg," p. 79-88; Saerchinger, César, "The truth about Schoenberg," p. 89-107 (written 1930; discusses Schoenberg's works); Steuermann, Eduard, "The piano music of Schoenberg," p. 125-133; Viertel, Berthold, "Schoenberg's Jakobsleiter," p. 165-181; Pisk, Paul Amadeus, "Schoenberg's twelve-tone opera," p. 187-194 (reprinted from Modern music; see no. 488); Stefan, Paul, "Schönberg's operas," p. 195-204 (reprinted from Modern music; see no. 428); Slonimsky, Nicholas, "A Schoenberg chronology [1874-1937]," p. 215-245; Schoenberg, Arnold, "Tonality and form," p. 259-264 (reprinted from Pacific coast musician; see no. 185); Schoenberg, Arnold, "Problems of harmony," p. 265-305 (reprinted from Modern music; see no. 184); list of works, p. 307-315.

See no. 81 (Hijman, Julius. Nieuwe oostenrijkse musiek, 1938).

296   Stefan, Paul. "Arnold Schoenberg" in Thompson, Oscar, ed. Great modern composers. New York, Dodd, Mead, 1941, p. 267-277.
      Biographical sketch and discussion of works; catalogue of Schoenberg's works, p. 274-277.

297   Bauer, Marion. "Schoenberg and his innovation: atonality and twelve-tone technique" in her Twentieth century music. New ed. New York, Putnam [c1947], p. 207-230.
      Somewhat superficial but unbiased discussion of Schoenberg's life and works; also some mention of Berg, Webern, and Hauer.

298   Newlin, Dika. Bruckner, Mahler, Schoenberg. New York, King's Crown Press, 1947. 293 p. Mus.

    ————. Bruckner, Mahler, Schönberg. Übers. von C. Nameth und H. Zelzer. Wien, Bergland-Verlag, 1954. 303 p.
      A discussion of his life and works, to 1944.

See no. 84 (Leibowitz, René. "Arnold Schoenberg: the origin and foundations of contemporary music" in his Schoenberg and his school, 1949, p. 43-134).

299   Wörner, Karl H. Musik der Gegenwart. Mainz, Schott [c1949]. 262 p. Illus., mus.
      Chapter 8: "Die jüngere Generations Gruppe des 'Tristan': Arnold Schönberg. Das Zwölftonmusik. Vom Wesen atonaler Musik," p. 70-78; chapter 9: "Die Wiener atonale Schule: Alban Berg und Anton von Webern," p. 84-92.

300   The canon: Australian journal of music [Arnold Schoenberg jubilee issue]. v. 3, no. 2 (Sept 1949).
      Partial contents: Newlin, Dika, "Schoenberg's new 'Fantasy,'" p. 83-84; Leibowitz, René, "Arnold Schoenberg's recent tonal works and the synthesis of tonality," p. 86-90; Pisk, Paul, "Arnold Schoenberg—the influence of my musical youth," p. 94-96.

301   Stuckenschmidt, Hans Heinz. Arnold Schoenberg. Zürich, Atlantis [1951]. 126 p. Mus.

    ————. Arnold Schoenberg. Tr. de l'allemand par Alexandre von Spitzmüller et Claude Rostand. Monaco, Editions du Rocher [1956]. 182 p. Mus. (Domaine musical.)
      Contents of the French edition include: "Note sommaire sur le système dodécaphonique et la méthode sérielle, par Claude Rostand," p. 139-143; "Chronologie," p. 145-167; "Table des oeuvres d'Arnold Schönberg," p. 169-177; "Discographie," p. 179-182.

    ————. Arnold Schoenberg. Tr. by E. T. Roberts and Humphrey Searle. London, Calder [c1959]. 168 p. Illus, mus.
      Contents of the English edition include a letter to the author from Thomas Mann, and a list of Schoenberg's compositions (p. 161-163).

See no. 89 (Reich, Willi. "Versuch einer Geschichte der Zwölftonmusik" in Alte und neue Musik, 1952).

302 Searle, Humphrey. "Schoenberg and the future," Hinrichsen's musical yearbook 7:134-140 (1952). Mus., ports.
List of Schoenberg's works, p. 139-140. A brief summation of Schoenberg's achievements and a discussion of some of his works.

303 Stein, Erwin. Orpheus in new guises. London, Rockliff [c1953]. vii + 167 p. Mus., ports.
Partial contents: "Mahler, Reger, Strauss and Schoenberg: some observations on the technique of composition," p. 36-46 (reprinted from the Jahrbuch 1926 der Universal Edition; see no. 381); "Schoenberg," p. 47-54; "The Gurrelieder," p. 55-56 (from the Christian Science Monitor, Oct 3, 1931); "New formal principles," p. 57-77 (reprinted from Arnold Schönberg zum fünfzigsten Geburtstag; see no. 288); "Some observations on Schoenberg's twelve-note rows," p. 78-81 (reprinted from Anbruch; see no. 382); "Performing Schoenberg's music," p. 83-85 (first published as "Über der Vortrag von Schönbergs Musik," Pult und Tagstock, Sept 1924); "The treatment of the speaking voice in 'Pierrot Lunaire,'" p. 86-89 (published as "Die Behandlung der Sprechstimme in 'Pierrot Lunaire,'" in Pult und Tagstock, Mar/Apr 1927); "Musical thought: Beethoven and Schoenberg," p. 90-95 (reprinted from Anbruch; see no. 383); "Anton Webern—Obituary," p. 99-102 (from MT; see no. 565); "Wozzeck," p. 103-107 (reprinted from Opera; see no. 553); "Berg's opera Lulu in Zürich," p. 108-109 (from the Christian Science Monthly, July 13, 1937).
A useful collection of many of his articles which have appeared in various publications; several of these writings are here translated into English for the first time.

See no. 94 (Rognoni, Luigi. Espressionismo e dodecafonia, 1954).

304 Searle, Humphrey. "Schoenberg, Arnold" in Grove's Dictionary of music and musicians. 5th ed. London, Macmillan, 1954, v. 7:513-523.
Extensive bibliography. Includes a list of his works. Article is arranged into three parts: life, compositions, summary.

See no. 100 (Collaer, Paul. La musique moderne, 1905-1955. 1955, p. 35-77).

See no. 569 (Metzger, Heinz Klaus. "Webern and Schönberg" in Anton Webern, 1955, p. 42-45 [Die Reihe, 2]).

See no. 105 (Goehr, Walter. "Arnold Schönberg's development towards the twelve-note system" in Hartog, Howard, ed. European music, 1957).

305 Magnani, Luigi. Le frontiere della musica, da Monteverdi a Schoenberg. Milano, Ricciardi, 1957, 328 p. Mus.
Partial contents: "Insegnamento di Schoenberg," p. 191-217 (written in 1947; discusses early influences on Schoenberg and expressionism); "Schoenberg e la sua scuola," p. 218-226 (written in 1947; discusses Leibowitz's book of that name; see no. 84).

See no. 112 (Prieberg, Fred K. "Arnold Schoenberg" in his Lexikon der neuen Musik, 1958, p. 381-392).

See no. 116 (Vlad, Roman. Storia della dodecafonia, 1958).

306   Stuckenschmidt, Hans Heinz. "Stil und Ästhetik Schönbergs," Schw MZ 98:97-104 (Mar 1958).
Lecture, given in Basel on Dec 14, 1957; reprinted in his Schöpfer der neuen Musik (see no. 115).
Schoenberg's musical philosophy; his harmonic language; biographical-aesthetic sketch and discussion of works. An important article.

306a Adorno, Theodor Wiesengrund. "Zur Vorgeschichte der Reihenkomposition" in his Klangfiguren. Berlin, Suhrkamp Verlag, c1959, p. 95-120. (His Musikalische Schriften, I.)
"Vortrag für den Nordeutschen Rundfunk 1958, unter Benutzung eines Aufsatzes über die Orchesterstücke op. 16 aus dem Schönbergheft von 'Pult und Taktstock," März/April 1927. Ungedruckt."

See no. 118a (Zillig, Winfried. "Schönberg und sein Weg von der Tonalität zum Zwölftonsystem" in his Variationen über neue Musik, 1959).
Contents: "Letzte Steigerung der Romantik und erste Anzeichen der Zeitenwende," p. 61-69; "An die Grenzen der Tonalität," p. 69-75; "Der absolute Umsturz," p. 75-83; "Die neue Gesetzmässigkeit des Zwölftonsystems," p. 83-94; "Rückkehr zur Tonalität?" p. 94-100; "Schönberg als politischer und religiöser Komponist," p. 100-107.

PHILOSOPHY AND CRITICISM

307   Newman, Ernest. "A propos of Schönberg's Five orchestral pieces," MT 55:87-89 (Feb 1, 1914).
A critical estimate of Schoenberg as a composer. Appended are excerpts from program notes on the Orchestral pieces, written by a Mrs. Newmarch.

308   Calvocoressi, M. D. "The classicism of Arnold Schönberg," MT 55:234-236 (Apr 1, 1914). Mus.
Schoenberg's musical philosophy and classical background.

309   Bekker, Paul. Kritische Zeitbilder. Berlin, Schuster & Loeffler, 1921. 336 p.
Essays on composers and aspects of music. "Schönberg," p. 161-173, is a general discussion of Schoenberg's style.

310   Bücken, Ernst. Führer und Probleme der neuen Musik. Köln, Tonger, 1924. 172 p. Mus.
"Impressionismus und Expressionismus," p. 126-163. (Schoenberg, p. 149-163.) Examples from his op. 11 and 15, and Pierrot.

311   Stein, Erwin. "Schoenberg and the German line," Modern music 3:22-27 (May 1926).
Schoenberg seen as a continuation of the tradition of German music.

312   Cort Van den Linden, R. "Arnold Schoenberg," M & L 7:322-331 (Oct 1926) and 8:38-45 (Jan 1927), tr. by Scott Goddard. Mus.
A discussion of Schoenberg's personality and early works.

313 Stein, Erwin. "Idées d'Arnold Schönberg sur la musique," Rev mus 10:1-6 (Nov 1928), tr. by J. Peyraube.
   In the form of a dialogue between Schoenberg and Stein.

See no. 3 (Adorno, Theodor Wiesengrund. "Zur Zwölftontechnik," Sept/Oct 1929).

314 Collaer, Paul. "Le cas Schoenberg," Revue international de la musique [Brussels] 1:432-440 (July/Sept 1938).
   An attack on Schoenberg as a "cerebral" composer.

315 Feldman, Harry Allen. "Futurism—Arnold Schoenberg" in his Music and the listener. New York, Dutton, 1939, p. 169-182.
   A rather general, anti-Schoenberg article.

316 Stein, Erwin. "Schoenberg's position today," Christian Science Monitor, v. 32, no. 1:9 (Nov 25, 1939).
   An evaluation of Schoenberg's music and of the twelve-tone technique.

317 Taylor, Noel Heath. "Arnold Schoenberg: music in motion," Etc.: a review of general semantics 2:1-9 (Autumn 1944).
   A general semanticist's view of criticisms of Schoenberg's music and of atonality in general.

318 Graf, Max. "Modern music in Vienna: Richard Strauss, Gustav Mahler, Arnold Schönberg" in his Legend of a musical city. New York, Philosophical library, 1945, p. 193-220.
   General Zeitgeist.

319 Graf, Max. "The path of Arnold Schoenberg" in his Modern music: music and composers of our time. Tr. by Beatrice R. Maier. New York, Philosophical Library [c1946], p. 168-196.
   Contains a great many sweeping generalities.

320 Leibowitz, René. "Innovation and tradition in contemporary music: I: The traditional significance of the music of Arnold Schoenberg," Horizon [London] 15:55-63 (Jan 1947).
   Schoenberg seen as a traditional composer. This article, written from an historical viewpoint, attempts to summarize the "principles which determine the character and evolution of Schoenberg's music."

See no. 13 (Adorno, Theodor Wiesengrund. "Schönberg und der Fortschnitt" in his Philosophie der neuen Musik, 1949, p. 19-88).

321 Mitchell, Donald. "Schoenberg the traditionalist," Chesterian 24:1-6 (Jul 1949).
   Schoenberg as a romanticist; discussion of his works.

322 Eimert, Herbert. "Arnold Schönberg, der Fünfundsiebzig-Jährige," Melos 16:226-230 (Sept 1949). Port.
   Essay in honor of Schoenberg's 75th birthday; general evaluation of his works and importance.

323 Wörner, Karl H. "Arnold Schönberg: zu seinem 75. Geburtstag am 13. September," Musica 3:310-312 (Sept 1949).
   Schoenberg's work, accomplishments, and influence.

324 Marcel, Luc-André. "Arnold Schoenberg," Cahiers du Sud [Paris],
v. 34, no. 308:130-136 (1951).
Obituary; estimation of his achievements.

325 Salazar, Adolfo. "Arnold Schoenberg post-mortem: ad usum Delphini," Nuestra musica, v. 6, no. 2:202-221 (1951).
Topics discussed: "Schoenberg y el atonalismo"; "Naturaleza y convencion en la tonalidad"; "Los principios milenarios de la tonalidad"; "Los griegos"; "El superrealismo, las concordancias vizcaínas y otros 'scherzi'"; "Los expresionistas"; "La escuela de las dos sonidos."
A general and nontechnical article.

326 "Notes of the day," Mo mus rec 81:169-170 (Sept 1951) and 81:198-199 (Oct 1951).
Obituary and quite biased attack on Schoenberg as a composer "more intellectual than musical." A reply to this by Humphrey Searle is included in:

_____. Mo mus rec 82:3 (Jan 1952).

327 Reich, Willi. "Arnold Schönberg (1874-1951)," Schw MZ 91:354-355 (Sept 1951).
Obituary; summary of his life, works, and philosophy.

328 Reich, Willi. "Freiwillige für Schoenberg," Melos 18:246-248 (Sept 1951).
Obituary; Schoenberg's influence on the musical world; the importance of the twelve-tone technique.

329 "Arnold Schoenberg, 1874-1951," M & L 32:305-323 (Oct 1951).
A collection of brief and largely unfavorable statements about Schoenberg's music, by various people. (See no. 330.)

330 Neighbour, Oliver W. "In defense of Schönberg," M & L 33:10-27 (Jan 1952). Mus.
A reply to the Schoenberg symposium in M & L (see no. 320). Schoenberg's relation to musical tradition; tonality in his music; his harmonic vocabulary; a discussion of his works.

331 Duhamel, Antoine. "Arnold Schoenberg, la critique, et le monde musical contemporain" in L'oeuvre du XXe siècle. Paris, Richard-Masse, April 1952, p. 77-85. (La revue musicale, no. 212.)
Schoenberg and musical criticism.

332 Boulez, Pierre. "Schoenberg is dead," Score, no. 6:18-22 (May 1952).
Weaknesses in Schoenberg's development of the twelve-tone technique, as seen from the "post-Webern" point of view. Has been an influential article.

333 Glock, William. "Comment," Score, no. 6:3-6 (May 1952).
An appraisal of Schoenberg and the twelve-note technique.

334 Goldbeck, Fred. "The strange case of Schönberg, revolutionary composer and tradition-abiding musician," Score, no. 6:36-39 (May 1952).
Schoenberg and the romantic tradition.

335 Keller, Hans. "The B.B.C.'s victory over Schoenberg," Mus rev 13:130-132 (May 1952).
    Comment on the M & L symposium (see no. 329) and on the B.B.C.'s Third Programme series on Schoenberg.

336 Martin, Frank. "Schoenberg and ourselves," Score, no. 6:15-17 (May 1952). Ports.
    French translation in Le systeme dodécaphonique (see no. 141). Twelve-tone technique seen as an enrichment of composers' musical means.

337 Sessions, Roger. "Some notes on Schönberg and the 'method of composing with twelve tones,'" Score, no. 6:7-10 (May 1952).
    Significance of the twelve-tone technique.

338 Wörner, Karl H. "Der unbekannte Schönberg," Melos 19:342-344 (Dec 1952).
    Schoenberg a relatively unknown composer in Europe at the time of his death, because of few performances.

See no. 27 (Pfrogner, Hermann. Die Zwölfordnung der Töne, 1953).

339 Adorno, Theodor Wiesengrund. "Arnold Schönberg, 1874-1951," Die neue Rundschau 64:80-104 (1953).
    Characteristics of his music and aesthetics; some problems inherent in the twelve-tone technique.

340 Pincherle, Marc. "Aspects de Schoenberg," Schw MZ 93:158-160 (Apr 1953).
    Some aspects of Schoenberg's character.

341 Mitchell, Donald. "Bartók, Stravinsky, and Schoenberg: periods early, middle and late," Chesterian 28:9-16 (Jul 1953).
    Schoenberg, p. 14-16; concerns the implications of Schoenberg's "reversion" to tonality in some of his later works.

342 Pannain, Guido. "Schönberg e la 'Filosofia della musica nuova,'" Rass mus 23:193-209 (Jul 1953).
    Refers to Adorno's book (see no. 13).

See no. 29 (Goléa, Antoine. Esthétique de la musique contemporaine, 1954, p. 48-52, 56-63).

343 Citkowitz, Israel. "Stravinsky and Schoenberg: a note on syntax and sensibility," Juilliard review 1:17-20 (Fall 1954).
    A comparison of the philosophies of Schoenberg and Stravinsky; their reasons for using serial techniques.

See no. 35 (Vlad, Roman. "Elementi metafisici nella poetica schönberghiana" in his Modernità e tradizione nella musica contemporanea, 1955, p. 185-196).

344 Eisler, Hanns. "Arnold Schönberg," Sinn und Form [Berlin] 7:5-15 (1955).
    General essay; discussion of stylistic elements of Schoenberg's "Three periods"; problems of the twelve-tone technique (see nos. 345 and 346).

See no. 37 (Adorno, Theodor Wiesengrund. "Zum Verständnis Schönbergs," Jun 1955).

345 Laux, Karl. "'Die moderne Musik ist tot'—in Amerika und anderswo —in der D.D.R. feiert sie frölich Urständ," Musik und Gesellschaft [E. Berlin] 5:212-217 (Jul 1955).
Claims "decadent bourgeois contemporary music" is dead; attacks Eisler's pro-Schoenberg article (no. 344) on Marxist grounds.

346 Rubin, Marcel. "Was bedeutet uns Schönberg? Eine Antwort an Hanns Eisler," Musik und Gesellschaft [E. Berlin] 5:274-275 (Sept 1955).
Another attack on Eisler's article (see nos. 344 and 345). Compares Schoenberg (unfavorably) with Beethoven, Schubert, Mahler, and Janáček. Finds Schoenberg's music meaningless.

347 Bentzon, Niels Viggo. "Omkring Arnold Schønberg," Dansk Musiktidsskrift 31:9-13 (Feb 1956). Port.
Serial technique; Schoenberg's works and philosophy.

348 Burt, Francis. "An antithesis: the technical aspect," Score, no. 18:7-17 (Dec 1956).

———. "An antithesis: the aesthetic aspect," Score, no. 19:60-74 (Mar 1957).
Reconciliation of the Stravinsky-Schoenberg antithesis.

349 Mellers, Wilfred Howard. "Schoenberg and Hindemith" in his Romanticism and the twentieth century. Fair Lawn, N.J., Essential books, 1957, p. 182-193. Mus.
A general essay on Schoenberg's and Berg's "style" and the twelve-tone technique.

350 Keller, Hans. "The new in review: Schönberg—I: the problem of performance," Mus rev 18:150-153 (May 1957).
Critical comments, especially about critics.

351 Skrebkow, S. "Gegen die Atonalität Schönbergs, für Prokofjew. Einige Forderungen an die Musikästhetik," Sowjetwissenschaft; Kunst und Literatur [E. Berlin] 5:486-495 (May 1957). Mus.
A "socialist realist" interpretation of melody in Prokofief, Schoenberg, and other composers. (None of the musical examples is from Schoenberg.)

See no. 56 (Melichar, Alois. Musik in der Zwangsjacke, 1958).

352 Wolff, Helmut Christian. "Palestrina und Schönberg—zwei Extreme der europäischen Musik" in Bericht über den Internationalen Musikwissenschaftlichen Kongress, Wien; Mozartjahr 1956; hrsg. von Erich Schenk. Graz, Hermann Böhlaus, 1958, p. 749-753.
An aesthetically oriented comparison of Palestrina and Schoenberg.

353 Keller, Hans. "Moses, Freud, and Schönberg," Mo mus rec 88:12-16 (Jan/Feb 1958) and 88:63-67 (Mar/Apr 1958).
The relationship (or lack of relationship) between Freud and Schoenberg; their attitudes toward religion; their interpretation of Moses.

See no. 306 (Stuckenschmidt, Hans Heinz. "Stil und Asthetik Schönbergs," Mar 1958).

354 Blanks, Fred. "Arnold Schoenberg," Canon 11:273-276 (Mar/Apr 1958). Port.
Brief biographical sketch. Discusses the Jewish element in Schoenberg's musik.

See no. 378 (Schoenberg, Arnold. "Aus Briefen Arnold Schönbergs," Dec 1958).

BIOGRAPHY

See no. 284 (Arnold Schönberg. Mit Beiträgen von Alban Berg [et al.], 1912).

355 Maclean, Charles. "London notes," Zeitschrift der Internationalen Musikgesellschaft 15:129-132 (Feb 1914).
An interesting contemporary account of Schoenberg's difficulties in getting performances, and some (biased) comments on Schoenberg's music.

356 Maclean, Charles. "Schönberg: a short sketch of his life," MT 55:302-304 (May 1, 1914).
An account of the dates of Schoenberg's compositions and their performances; some bibliographical data (on reviews) included. "From the Journal of the International Music Society, with additions." (See no. 355.)

357 Schoenberg, Arnold. "Mein Publikum," Der Querschnitt 10:222-224 (Apr 1930).
Reaction of the public to Schoenberg's works.

358 Bach, David Joseph. "A note on Arnold Schoenberg," MQ 22:8-13 (Jan 1936).
Biographical sketch: influences on Schoenberg.

359 Milhaud, Darius. "To Arnold Schoenberg on his 70th birthday: personal reflections," MQ 30:379-385 (Oct 1944). Port.
Reminiscences by Milhaud relating to Schoenberg's music.

360 Leibowitz, René. "Music chronicle; two composers: a letter from Hollywood," Partisan review 15:361-365 (Mar 1948).
On Schoenberg and Stravinsky; Schoenberg's life in California, to 1947.

361 Newlin, Dika. "Schönberg in America, 1933-1948; retrospect and prospect," Mus sur, v. 1, no. 5:128-131 (1949) and v. 1, no. 6:185-189 (1949). Mus.
Biographical; description of his "American" works; discussion of his ideas.

362 Schoenberg, Arnold. "Further to the Schoenberg-Mann controversy," Mus sur 2:77-80 (Autumn, 1949), tr. by Hans Keller.
One of several articles dealing with the controversy between Schoenberg and Thomas Mann over Mann's book Doktor Faustus.

363 Leibowitz, René. "Besuch bei Arnold Schönberg," Schw MZ 89:324-328 (Sept 1949).
"Zum 75. Geburtstag des Komponisten."
Various remarks on the author's experiences with Schoenberg.

364 Schoenberg, Arnold. "Mia evolución," Nuestra musica 4:239-249 (Oct 1949).

———. "My evolution," MQ 38:517-527 (Oct 1952).
Autobiographical essay; his discovery of the "method of composing with twelve tones."

365 Foss, Hubert. "Schoenberg, 1874-1951," MT 92:401-403 (Sept 1951).
Obituary. Contains useful biographical data, including dates of some performances. Some of the information is inaccurate, however, and should be used with caution.

366 Rubsamen, Walter H. "Schoenberg in America," MQ 37:469-489 (Oct 1951). Illus.

———. "Schoenberg in Amerika," Melos 20:132-137 (May 1953) and 20:168-173 (Jun 1953).
Biographical and anecdotal account of Schoenberg's years in America, 1933-1951.

367 Robbins, Michela. "A Schoenberg seminar," Counterpoint 17:9-12 (Feb 1952). Port.
An informal discussion, by some of his pupils, of Schoenberg as composer and teacher.

368 Newlin, Dika. "Arnold Schönberg in Amerika," ÖMZ 7:160-163 (May/Jun 1952).
Biographical sketch and list of works, 1935-1951; brief discussion of the row technique of his Piano concerto. (Not the same article as her "Schönberg in America, 1933-1948"; see no. 361.)

369 Schoenberg, Arnold. "A self-analysis," Musical America 73:14, 172 (Feb 1953). Port.
A brief self-justification. Posthumous MS.

370 Milhaud, Darius. "Begegnungen mit Schönberg," Melos 22:100-103 (Apr 1955).
Dialogue between Claude Rostand and Darius Milhaud, on Schoenberg and the twelve-tone technique.

371 Milhaud, Darius. "Erinnerungen am Arnold Schönberg," ÖMZ 10:406-410 (Dec 1955).
Further reminiscences. (See also no. 359.)

See no. 508 (Reich, Willi. "Alban Berg als Apologet Arnold Schönbergs," Dec 1955).

See no. 376 (Schoenberg, Arnold. Briefe, 1958, p. 13-14, 59-60, 121-122, 193-194, 241-242).

372 Ketting, Otto. "Arnold Schönberg in Amerika," Mens en melodie 13:79-81 (Mar 1958). Port.
Very brief; discusses works written during Schoenberg's American period.

CORRESPONDENCE

See no. 390 (Schoenberg, Arnold [Letter to Nicolas Slonimsky], in Norman, Gertrude, ed., Letters of composers, 1946).

373   Keller, Hans, ed. and tr., "Unpublished Schoenberg letters, early, middle and late," Mus sur 4:449-471 (Jun 1952).
      Letters to Marietta Werndorff, Erwin Stein, Oscar Adler, and Humphrey Searle.

374   Hill, Richard S. "Annual reports on acquisitions: music," Library of Congress quarterly journal of current acquisitions 10:43-44 (Nov 1952).
      A report of the acquisition of the correspondence of Berg, Schoenberg, and Webern.

See no. 192 (Yasser, Joseph, "A letter from Arnold Schoenberg," Spring 1953).

See no. 514 (Rufer, Josef, "Dokumente einer Freundschaft," Feb 1955).

See no. 444 (Reich, Willi, "Ein Briefwechsel über 'Moses und Aron,'" Jun 1957).

375   Birke, Joachim. "Richard Dehmel und Arnold Schönberg; ein Briefwechsel," Die Musikforschung 11:279-285 (1958).

376   Schoenberg, Arnold. Briefe. Ausgewählt und hrsg. von Erwin Stein. Mainz, Schott, 1958. 309 p.
      Letters written from 1910-1951.
      Biographical data, p. 13-14, 59-60, 121-122, 193-194, 241-242.
      Index of works, p. 15, 60, 122, 195, 242. Has a name and subject index.

See no. 581 (Gerhard, Roberto, ed. "Letters of Webern and Schoenberg," Nov 1958).

377   Schoenberg, Arnold. "Briefe aus vier Jahrzehnten," Melos 25:352-356 (Nov 1958).
      These letters also appear in no. 376.

378   [Schoenberg, Arnold]. "Aus Briefen Arnold Schönbergs," NZfM 119:700-705 (Dec 1958). Illus.
      "Die nachfolgen Auszüge beschränken sich auf Grundsätzliches über ästhetische Fragen, Werke, und Aufführungen."
      These letters also appear in no. 376.

379   [Schoenberg, Arnold]. "Ein unbekannter Brief von Arnold Schönberg an Alban Berg," ÖMZ 14:10 (Jan 1959).

COMPOSITIONAL TECHNIQUES

380   Somigli, Carlo. "Il modus operandi di Arnold Schoenberg," <u>Riv mus ital</u> 20:583-606 ([Jul/Sept] 1913). Mus.
      Discussion of Alaleona's theories of atonality (see nos. 176-177); discussion of Schoenberg's techniques in op. 6, 10, 11, and other works.

381   Stein, Erwin. "Mahler, Reger, Strauss und Schönberg; Kompositionstechnische Betrachtungen" <u>in</u> 25. Jahre neue Musik: Jahrbuch 1926 der Universal Edition. Wien, Universal Edition, 1926, p. 63-78.
      English translation <u>in his</u> Orpheus in new guises (see no. 303). Schoenberg, p. 74-78; résumé of his composition technique.

382   Stein, Erwin. "Einige Bemerkungen zu Schönbergs Zwölftonreihen," <u>Anbruch</u> 8:251-253 (Jun/Jul 1926).
      On the development of the twelve-tone technique by Schoenberg. English translation in his Orpheus in new guises (see no. 303).

383   Stein, Erwin. "Das gedankliche Prinzip in Beethovens Musik und seine Auswirkung bei Schönberg," <u>Anbruch</u> 9:117-121 (Mar 1927). Mus.
      The influence of Beethoven's style on Schoenberg. English translation in his Orpheus in new guises (see no. 303).

384   Westphal, Kurt. "Arnold Schönbergs Weg zur Zwölftonmusik: zugleich ein Beitrag zur Entwicklungsgeschichte der modernen Musik," <u>Die Musik</u> 21:491-499 (Apr 1929). Mus.
      The development of Schoenberg's serial technique; some analytical examples from his op. 25 and 26.

385   Weiss, Adolf. "The lyceum of Schönberg," <u>Modern music</u> 9:99-107 (Mar/Apr 1932).
      A codification of the compositional practices of Schoenberg, in general terms.

386   Hill, Richard S. "Schoenberg's tone-rows and the tonal system of the future," <u>MQ</u> 22:14-37 (Jan 1936). Mus., port.
      An important article. Traces the development of the twelve-tone technique; illustrates types of row structure used in various works of Schoenberg. Includes some bibliographical citations.

See no. 186 (Taylor, Noel Heath. "The Schoenberg concept," Apr 1939).

387   Krenek, Ernst. "Homage to Schönberg: the idiom and the technique," <u>Modern music</u> 21:131-134 (Mar/Apr 1944). Port.
      Dodecaphony compared with "atonality"; implications of the twelve-tone technique.

388   Jalowetz, Heinrich. "On the spontaneity of Schoenberg's music," <u>MQ</u> 30:385-408 (Oct 1944). Mus.
      The importance of melodic invention in Schoenberg's music; his Piano concerto is discussed in particular.

See no. 137 (Eschman, Karl. Changing forms in modern music, 1945, p. 104-110).

389 Katz, Adele T. Challenge to musical tradition: a new concept of tonality. New York, Knopf, 1945. Mus.
"Schoenberg," p. 350-397.
An attempt to extend Heinrich Schenker's system of analysis to non-tonal music. Discusses Schoenberg's Verklärte Nacht, D minor quartet, Kammersymphonie op. 9, F minor quartet, Three piano pieces, op. 11, and Suite for piano, op. 25. Also takes up problems of "tonality vs. atonality" and "dissonance."

390 Schoenberg, Arnold. [Letter to Nicolas Slonimsky] in Norman, Gertrude, ed. Letters of composers. New York, Knopf, 1946, p. 341-342.
Describes briefly Schoenberg's development of the twelve-note technique.

391 Wood, Ralph W. "Concerning 'Sprechgesang,'" Tempo, no. 17 [no. 2 of new series]:3-6 (Dec 1946). Mus.
Sprechstimme in Schoenberg's and Berg's vocal works.

See no. 143 (Schoenberg, Arnold. "Composition with twelve tones" in his Style and idea, 1950).

392 Perle, George. "Schönberg's late style," Mus rev 13:274-282 (Nov 1952).
Row structure in Schoenberg's last works; an important article. A reply to this by Hans Keller is included in no. 28.

See no. 154 (Erickson, Robert. The structure of music, 1955).

See no. 43 (Rochberg, George. "Tradition and twelve-tone music," Dec 1955?).

See no. 103 (Gottschalk, Nathan. Twelve-note music as developed by Arnold Schoenberg, 1956).

See no. 160 (Perle, George. Serial composition and atonality, 1956).

See no. 348 (Burt, Francis. "An antithesis: the technical aspect," Dec 1956).

See no. 586 (Pousseur, Henri. "Da Schoenberg a Webern," Dec 1956).

393 Wellesz, Egon. The origins of Schönberg's twelve-tone system. Washington, D.C., 1958. 14 p. Mus.
"A lecture delivered in the Whittall Pavilion of the Library of Congress, January 10, 1957."
The musical influences upon Schoenberg; his development of the twelve-tone technique.

394 Walker, Alan. "Schönberg's classical background," Mus rev 19:283-289 (Nov 1958). Mus.
Schoenbergian techniques derived from Mozart and Beethoven.

GENERAL DESCRIPTIONS OF WORKS

See no. 467 (Wellesz, Egon. "Arnold Schönberg," Sept 1911).

See no. 380 (Somigli, Carlo. "Il modus operandi di Arnold Schoenberg," [Jul-Sept] 1913).

395 Wellesz, Egon. "Schönberg and beyond," MQ 2:76-95 (Jan 1916), tr. by Otto Kinkeldey. Mus.
>Brief biographical sketch. Primarily a discussion of his works, especially the Songs, op. 1-3, Gurrelieder, second String quartet, and George songs.

396 Wellesz, Egon. "Arnold Schönberg et son oeuvre," Rev mus 4:1-18 (May 1923). Mus.
>Early works, through op. 22.

See no. 312 (Cort Van den Linden, R. "Arnold Schoenberg," Oct 1926).

See no. 181 (Erpf, Hermann Robert. Studien zur Harmonie- und Klangtechnik, 1927).

397 Wellesz, Egon. "Schoenberg, Arnold" in Cobbett, Walter W. Cobbett's cyclopedic survey of chamber music. London, Oxford University Press, 1929-30, v. 2:343-352. Mus.
>Brief discussion of the sextet Verklärte Nacht; the first, second, and third String quartets; the first Chamber symphony; Pierrot Lunaire; the Serenade, op. 24; the Wind quintet; and the Suite, op. 29.

398 Harrison, Lou. "Homage to Schonberg: the late works," Modern music 21:135-138 (Mar/Apr 1944).
>The Piano concerto, the Violin concerto, and the fourth String quartet; row structures of the middle and late periods compared.

See no. 141 (Leibowitz, René. "Aspects récents de la technique de douze sons" in Le système dodécaphonique, 1949, p. 32-53).
>On three works of Schoenberg: the Prélude, op. 44; the String trio, op. 45; the Survivor from Warsaw, op. 46.

See no. 361 (Newlin, Dika. "Schönberg in America," 1949).

See no. 300 (Leibowitz, René. "Arnold Schoenberg's recent tonal works" in The canon: Arnold Schoenberg jubilee issue, Sept 1949).

399 Vlad, Roman. "L'ultimo Schönberg," Rass mus 21:106-116 (Apr 1951). Mus.
>A discussion of the works through the String trio, op. 45, and the Survivor from Warsaw. Reprinted in Vlad's Modernità e tradizione nella musica contemporanea, p. 158-173 (see no. 35).

400 Keller, Hans. "Schönberg," Mus sur 3:277-285 (June 1951).
>Discusses the Survivor from Warsaw, the Fantasy for violin, and Schoenberg's book, Style and idea (see no. 143).

401 Stephan, Rudolph. "Unorthodoxe Musik: dem Künstler und Menschen Arnold Schönberg zum Gedachtnis," Dt Univ Zt 6, no. 15/16:16-18 (July 1951). Mus.
   Obituary and discussion of his last works.

402 Redlich, Hans F. "Arnold Schönberg," Mus rev 12:304-306 (Nov 1951). Mus.
   Obituary and discussion of works.

403 Demuth, Norman. Musical trends in the twentieth century. London, Rockliff [c1952]. Illus., mus.
   Biographical sketches and discussion of works. Some row analysis.
   Partial contents: "Arnold Schoenberg," p. 209-232; "Anton von Webern," p. 233-238; "Alban Berg," p. 239-245.

404 Rankle, Karl. "Arnold Schönberg," Score, no. 6:40-43 (May 1952). Mus.
   A very brief discussion of Schoenberg's works, especially the Jakobsleiter, by a former Schoenberg pupil.

405 Keller, Hans. "Concerts and opera: Schoenberg memorial concert," Mus rev 13:216-218 (Aug 1952). Mus.
   A lively review of Schoenberg's three Songs, op. 48, the Suite, and the fourth Quartet.

406 "Catalogue des oeuvres d'Arnold Schoenberg (1874-1951)," Music information record, no. 11:12-15 (winter 1953/54).
   Includes his transcriptions and theoretical writings.

See no. 95 (Wörner, Karl H. Neue Musik in der Entscheidung, 1954, p. 56-67).
   Musical examples from Schoenberg's Survivor from Warsaw, String trio, and Erwartung. Description of works and style.

See no. 155 (Ogden, Wilbur Lee. Series and structure, 1955).

407 Stuckenschmidt, Hans Heinz. "Schönbergs religiöse Werke," Schw MZ 97:256-258 (June 1957).
   Survey of Gurrelieder, Jakobsleiter, Moses und Aron, Moderne Psalmen, Kol Nidre, Survivor from Warsaw, and other religious works by Schoenberg.

408 "Notas del extranjero; Alemania: el legado de Schoenberg," Revista musicale chilena 12:80-81 (Jan/Feb 1958).
   A brief description of a concert which presented several unpublished and previously unperformed works of Schoenberg.

409 Koegler, Horst. "The international scene: Germany," Musical courier 157:29 (Feb 1958).
   Another brief account of the performance of Schoenberg's unpublished works.

410 Rufer, Josef. "A talk on Arnold Schoenberg," Score, no. 22:7-11 (Feb 1958), tr. by Paul Hamburger.
   A discussion of Schoenberg's unpublished works. Originally presented as a talk at the Berlin Akademie der Künste.

411   Rufer, Josef. "Arnold Schönbergs Nachlass," ÖMZ 13:96-106 (Mar 1958). Illus., port.
      A description of Schoenberg's unpublished works: documents, notebooks, compositions.

412   Rufer, Josef. Das Werk Arnold Schönbergs. Kassel, Bärenreiter, 1959. xii + 207 p. Illus., facsim.
      A complete and handsomely printed catalogue of Schoenberg's works. Contents: 1. Music (published and unpublished, including sketchbooks); 2. Writings (theoretical, poetical, articles, etc.); 3. Paintings (includes 10 plates); 4. Chronological list of works and first performances.

413   Gradenwitz, Peter. "Schönbergs religiöse Werke," Melos 11:330-333 (Nov 1959).
      English translation: "The religious works of Arnold Schönberg," Mus rev 21:19-29 (Feb 1960). Mus.
      A brief discussion of Schoenberg's religious philosophy as expressed in Moses und Aron, Jakobsleiter, Moderne Psalmen, Kol Nidre, and other works.

INDIVIDUAL WORKS

Das Buch der hängenden Gärten, op. 15
   See his Songs—op. 15

Chamber symphony, op. 9
   See his Kammersymphonie, op. 9

Choral works
   —op. 13 (Friede auf Erden)

414   Guenther, Siegfried. "Das trochäische Prinzip in Arnold Schoenbergs op. 13: Versuch einer Grundlage zur stilkritischen Erfassung seines gesamten Schaffens," Zeitschrift für Musikwissenschaft 6:158-176 (Dec 1923). Mus.
      A somewhat statistical analysis.

   —op. 27 (Four pieces for mixed chorus)

415   Stein, Erwin. "Neue Chöre von Schönberg," Anbruch 8:421-423 (Dec 1926).
      Review (not an analysis) of op. 27 and 28.

416   Adorno, Theodor Wiesengrund. "Arnold Schönberg: Chöre op. 27 und op. 28," Anbruch 10:411-412 (Nov/Dec 1928).
      Brief descriptive review.

   —op. 28 (Three satires for mixed chorus)

See no. 415 (Stein, Erwin, "Neue Chöre von Schönberg," Dec 1926).

See no. 416 (Adorno, Theodor Wiesengrund. "Arnold Schönberg: Chöre," Nov/Dec 1928).

—op. 35 (Six pieces for male chorus)

417   Reich, Willi. "Schönberg's new Männerchor," Modern music 9:62-66 (Jan/Feb 1932). Mus.
        A discussion of the structure of each chorus. According to Richard Hill (see no. 386), it "should be used with care, since some of the analyses are incorrect."

—op. 35:6

See no. 293 (Polnauer, Josef. "Schönbergs 'Verbundenheit'" in Arnold Schönberg zum 60. Geburtstag, 1934, p. 44-49).

—op. 50a (Dreimal tausend Jahre)

418   Keller, Hans. "The half-year's new music," Mus rev 15:218-219 (Aug 1954).
        Capsule outline of op. 50a and 50b; gives the row of the latter.

—op. 50b (De Profundis)

419   Hill, Richard S. "Music reviews; Arnold Schoenberg: De Profundis," Notes 10:682-683 (Sept 1953).
        Row structure.

See no. 418 (Keller, Hans. "The half-year's new music," Aug 1954).

See no. 204a (Rochberg, George. "The harmonic tendency of the hexachord," Nov 1959).

—op. 50c (Moderne Psalmen)

420   Stuckenschmidt, Hans Heinz. "Moderne Psalmen von Arnold Schönberg," ÖMZ 12:47-50 (Feb 1957). Port.
        Brief discussion of the text and music.

421   Wörner, Karl H. "'Und trotzdem bete ich': Arnold Schönbergs letztes Werk: 'Moderne Psalmen,'" NZfM 118:147-151 (Mar 1957). Mus., port.
        Discussion of the text, with a very brief characterization of the music.

422   Keller, Hans. "The new in review; Schönberg II: the last work," Mus rev 18:221-224 (Aug 1957).
        On the origin of the text, and some general comments about the structure.

423   Vlad, Roman. "Moderne Psalmen von Arnold Schönberg," Melos 24:252-255 (Sept 1957). Illus. [facsim. from the autograph MS.].
        Discussion of Schoenberg's religious compositions; background

of Moderne Psalmen. Not an analysis, but rather a philosophical critique.

Concerto for piano and orchestra

See no. 388 (Jalowetz, Heinrich. "On the spontaneity of Schoenberg's music," Oct 1944).

424 Leibowitz, René. "Schönbergs Klavierkonzert," Melos 16:44-48 (Feb 1949). Mus.
    Principally a row and thematic analysis.

See no. 368 (Newlin, Dika. "Arnold Schönberg in Amerika," May/June 1952).

Concerto for violin and orchestra

425 Rubin, Louis. The idiom of the violin in twentieth century music. 71 l. Mus. (Thesis, M.A., University of California, Berkeley, 1952).
    On performance technique. Many examples from the Schoenberg Concerto; the Berg Violin concerto and Webern's Four pieces for violin and piano are also discussed.

426 Keller, Hans. "First performances," Mus rev 13:307-309 (Nov 1952).
    Witty review of Schoenberg's Violin concerto and Variations on a recitative for organ.

427 Walters, Willard Gibson. Technical problems in modern violin music as found in selected concertos, with related original exercises and études. [Ann Arbor, Mich., University Microfilms], 1958. 261 l. (Thesis, Ph.D., State University of Iowa.)
    Not seen; abstract in Dissertation Abstracts, v. 18, no. 6, p. 2163. Discusses seven concertos, including Berg's and Schoenberg's.

De Profundis
See his Choral works—op. 50b

Drei Klavierstücke, op. 11
See his Piano works—op. 11

Dreimal tausend Jahre
See his Choral works—op. 50a

Erwartung
See also his Operas

See no. 288 (Bekker, Paul. "Schönberg: 'Erwartung'" in Arnold Schönberg zum fünfzigsten Geburtstag, 1924, p. 275-282.

428 Stefan, Paul. "Schönberg's operas," Modern music 7:24-28 (Dec 1929/Jan 1930).
    On Erwartung and Die glückliche Hand. Reprinted in no. 295 (Armitage), p. 195-204.

429 Craft, Robert. "Schoenberg's Erwartung," Counterpoint 17:13-15 (Sept 1952).
    Brief discussion of Schoenberg's operas, particularly Erwartung.

430 Dace, Wallace. "The dramatic structure of Schönberg's Erwartung," Educational theater journal [Austin, Texas] 5:322-327 (Dec 1953).
    Erwartung as a psychological melodrama; the dramatic and musical techniques used.

Fantasy for violin

See no. 300 (Newlin, Dika. "Schoenberg's new Fantasy" in The canon: Arnold Schoenberg jubilee issue, Sept 1949).

See no. 400 (Keller, Hans. "Schoenberg," June 1951).

431 Hill, Richard S. "Music reviews; Arnold Schoenberg: Phantasy for violin, with piano accompaniment, op. 47," Notes 9:647-648 (Sept 1952).
    Discusses the hexachordal treatment of the row.

432 Forte, Allen. Contemporary tone structures. New York, Teachers' College, Columbia University, 1955. 194 p. Mus.
    An attempt to interpret contemporary musical structure in the the light of Heinrich Schenker's analytical theories. Detailed row analysis of Schoenberg's Fantasy, p. 110-127, 175-186.

See no. 103 (Gottschalk, Nathan. Twelve note music as developed by Arnold Schoenberg, 1956).

Five orchestral pieces, op. 16
See his Orchestral pieces, op. 16

Friede auf Erden
See his Choral works—op. 13

Fünf Orchesterstücke, op. 16
See his Orchestral pieces, op. 16

Glückliche Hand
See also his Operas

See no. 428 (Stefan, Paul. "Schönberg's operas," Dec 1929/Jan 1930).

433 Keller, Hans. "New music: two Schönberg problems," Mus rev 17:268-269 (Aug 1956).
    The problems are the meaning of the text and the use of Sprechstimme.

434 Keller, Hans. "The 'lucky' hand and other errors," Listener 58:961 (Dec 5, 1957).
    Corrections of some errors that have been perpetuated in writ-

ings about Schoenberg's opera: the translation of the title, the date of the opera's composition, etc.

Herzgewächse

See no. 74 (Der blaue Reiter, 1914).

Jakobsleiter

See no. 295 (Viertel, Berthold. "Schoenberg's Jakobsleiter" in Armitage, Merle, ed. Schoenberg, 1937, p. 165-181).

See no. 404 (Rankle, Karl. "Arnold Schönberg," May 1952).

435   Zillig, Winfried. "Notes on Arnold Schoenberg's unfinished oratorio, 'Die Jakobsleiter,'" Score, no. 25:7-16 (June 1959). Mus.
   Based on "the entire material connected with the composition of Die Jakobsleiter."

Kammersymphonie, op. 9

436   Berg, Alban. Arnold Schönberg: Kammersymphonie, op. 9. Thematische Analyse. Wien, Universal Edition [192-?] 14 p.
   Thematic form outline; gives measure numbers. No musical examples.

See no. 143 (Schoenberg, Arnold. "Composition with twelve tones" in his Style and idea, 1950).

Kol Nidre

437   Werner, Eric. "Current chronicle: France," MQ 44:242-244 (Apr 1958).
   A description, not an analysis; primarily of the text.

Moderne Psalmen

See his Choral works—op. 50c

Moses und Aron

See also his Operas

438   Bachmann, Claus-Henning. "Ein Wechsel auf die Zukunft," ZfM 115:244-246 (Apr 1954).
   A review of the first performance, with some mention of the row technique and the meaning of the text.

439   Hamel, Fred. "Arnold Schönbergs Bekenntniswerk: zur Uraufführung von Moses und Aron," Musica 8:145-148 (Apr 1954). Illus.
   Background of the opera; its central idea; the first performance.

440   Wörner, Karl H. "Current chronicle: Germany," MQ 40:403-412 (July 1954). Mus.
   Outline of the plot; general description of the music.

441 Rufer, Josef. "Intorno alla genesi del Moses und Aaron di Schoenberg," Aut aut, no. 27:187-195 (May 1955).
History of the composition of Moses und Aron.

442 Babbitt, Milton. "An introduction to the music" in Moses und Aron [a booklet issued with Columbia recording K3L-241]. [New York, Columbia Records, c1957], p. [4-6]. Diagrs.
A technical analysis of the row structure.

443 Zillig, Winfried. "Schoenbergs Moses und Aron," Melos 24:69-71 (Mar 1957). Illus.
General article; discussion of the text and the opera as a whole. Includes a reproduction of a page of the autograph MS.

444 Reich, Willi. "Ein Briefwechsel über 'Moses und Aron,'" Schw MZ 97:259-260 (June 1957).
Letters dating from 1930, between Schoenberg and Berg, concerning Schoenberg's opera.

445 Reich, Willi. "Arnold Schönbergs Oper 'Moses und Aron'; szenische Uraufführung im Stadttheater Zürich," Schw MZ 97:296-298 (July 1957).
Sketch of the plot and general description of the music.

446 Rebling, Eberhard. "Arnold Schönbergs Lebensbekenntnis: Gedanken zu seiner Oper 'Moses und Aron,'" Musik und Gesellschaft [E. Berlin] 7:462-467 (Aug 1957). Illus., port.
Discussion of the work on philosophical grounds; Moses und Aron seen as a sociological commentary.

447 Wörner, Karl H. "Die 39 Schlusstakte von Schönbergs 'Moses und Aron': Polyphonie der Symbole," Melos 24:350-352 (Dec 1957). Mus.
"Abschnitt aus einer grösseren Studie des Verfassers." (See no. 448a.) Analysis of the closing 39 measures of the opera.

See no. 353 (Keller, Hans. "Moses, Freud, and Schönberg," Jan-Apr 1958).

448 Keller, Hans. "The new in review. Schönberg—III: Moses and Aron," Mus rev 19:52-54 (Feb 1958).
A philosophical discussion of the reasons for the opera's being unfinished.

448a Wörner, Karl H. Gotteswort und Magie: die Oper 'Moses und Aron' von Arnold Schönberg. Heidelberg, Lambert Schneider, 1959. 93 p. Mus., port.
Contents: "Das Religiöse in Schönbergs Schaffen," p. 12-18; "'Moses und Aron'—die geistige Welt," p. 20-28; "Zur Dialektik der Idee," p. 29-32; "Die musikalischen Grossformen," p. 33-44; "Gott als Gedanke," p. 45-55; "Gott als Unendlichkeit," p. 56-58; "Gottes Verheissung," p. 59-69; "Aron—der ewige Wandel," p. 70-71; "Musik, Sprache und Symbole," p. 72-76; "Der dritte Akt," p. 77-78; "Der Zwölftoncharacter der Musik," p. 79-87; "Der Aufführungen," p. 88-91.

—Dance around the golden calf

See no. 811 ([Keller, Hans]. "First performances: Schoenbergians and Stravinskyians," Nov 1954).

Ode to Napoleon

449   List, Kurt. "[Homage to Schönberg]: Ode to Napoleon," Modern music 21:139-145 (Mar/Apr 1944). Mus.
      Discusses many aspects of the work: phrase structure, tonality, motivic treatment, etc.

Operas

See also his Erwartung, Glückliche Hand, Moses und Aron, Von Heute auf Morgen.

450   Felber, Erwin. "Arnold Schönberg und die Oper," Musikblätter des Anbruch 9:67-70 (Jan/Feb 1927).
      Wagner's influence on Schoenberg; discussion of Erwartung, Jakobsleiter, Glückliche Hand.

451   Berg, Alban. "Die Stimme in der Oper," Musikblätter des Anbruch 10:349-350 (Nov/Dec 1928).
      Brief description of the voice treatment in Schoenberg's operas and in Berg's Wozzeck.

452   Leibowitz, René. "Les oeuvres d'Arnold Schoenberg ou la conscience du drame futur dans la musique contemporaine" in Le théâtre musical. Paris, Richard-Masse [1947/48], p. 84-104. Mus. (Polyphonie, 1er cahier).
      Erwartung (one of the few articles discussing its construction), Glückliche Hand, Von Heute auf Morgen, and (briefly) Moses und Aron.

453   Mayer, Harry. "Twee toneelwerken van Arnold Schoenberg," Mens en melodie 13:135-139 (May 1958). Mus.
      Erwartung and Von Heute auf Morgen; a brief account of the music and the drama.

454   Mitchell, Donald. "Summer festivals: Von Heute auf Morgen and Erwartung," Opera [London] 9:567-571 (Sept 1958). Illus.
      Brief review and general description.

Orchestral pieces, op. 16

See no. 307 (Newman, Ernest. "A propos of Schönberg's five orchestral pieces," Feb 1, 1914).

455   Deutsch, Max. "Les cinq Pièces pour Orchestre d'Arnold Schönberg," Schw MZ 88:462-464 (Dec 1948).
      "Conférence donnée à Radio-Genève."
      A somewhat philosophical discussion; not an analysis.

456 Cowell, Henry. "Current chronicle: New York," MQ 35:106-111 (Jan 1949). Mus.
   A review and description of Schoenberg's Five orchestral pieces and Webern's Passacaglia.

See no. 306a (Adorno, Theodor Wiesengrund. "Zur Vorgeschichte der Reihenkomposition" in his Klangfiguren, 1959).

Orchestral variations, op. 31
See his Variations for orchestra, op. 31

Phantasy for violin
See his Fantasy for violin

Piano works

457 Deutsch, Leonhard. "Zur Einführung in die Harmonik der zeitgenössischen Klavierliteratur," Musikblätter des Anbruch 9:324-34. (Oct/Nov 1927). Mus.
   "Zwölftontechnik (Schönberg)," p. 339-342.
   Discusses briefly the Three pieces, op. 11; Six little pieces, op. 19; Five pieces, op. 23.

See no. 295 (Steuermann, Eduard. "The piano music of Schoenberg" in Armitage, Merle, ed. Schoenberg, 1937, p. 125-133).

458 Tuttle, T. Temple. "Schönberg's compositions for piano solo," Mus rev 18:300-318 (Nov 1957). Mus.
   Analyses of op. 11, 19, 23, 33a, 33b. Seems to rely on previous analyses by Leibowitz and Dika Newlin.

—op. 11 (Three piano pieces)

See no. 380 (Somigli, Carlo. "Il modus operandi di Arnold Schoenberg," [Jul/Sept] 1913).

See no. 389 (Katz, Adele T. Challenge to musical tradition, 1945).

459 Leichtentritt, Hugo. "Arnold Schönberg: opus 11 and opus 19" in his Musical form. Cambridge, Harvard University Press, 1951, p. 425-450. Mus.
   "The present attempt at analysis . . . is concerned with whether it is possible to discover a rational constructive idea in these pieces . . ."
   The analysis of op. 19 appeared originally in Modern music, May/June 1928.

—op. 11:1

460 Koperberg-Van Wermeskerken, A. "Bij een pianostuk van Schoenberg," Mens en melodie 7:382-384 (Dec 1952). Mus.
   Brief analysis of the variation technique.

—op. 19 (Six little piano pieces)

See no. 459 (Leichtentritt, Hugo. "Arnold Schönberg: opus 11 and opus 19" in his Musical form, 1951).

See no. 586 (Pousseur, Henri. "Da Schoenberg a Webern," Dec 1956).

—op. 19:2

See no. 159 (Ballif, Claude. Introduction à la métatonalité, 1956, p. 111).

—op. 25 (Suite for piano)

See no. 384 (Westphal, Kurt. Arnold Schönbergs Weg zur Zwölftonmusik," Apr 1929).

See no. 389 (Katz, Adele T. Challenge to musical tradition, 1945).

See no. 143 (Schoenberg, Arnold. "Composition with twelve tones" in his Style and idea, 1950).

—op. 33a

See no. 28 ([Keller, Hans]. "First performances and their reviews," Feb 1953).

See no. 155 (Ogdon, Wilbur Lee. Series and structure, 1955, p. 28-92).

461 Mayer, Harry. "Een blik achter de werkwijze van Arnold Schoenberg," Mens en melodie 12:130-133 (May 1957). Mus., port.
Analysis of the row treatment.

Pieces for orchestra, five
See his Orchestral pieces, op. 16

Pierrot Lunaire, op. 21

462 Godet, Robert. "Après une audition de 'Pierrot Lunaire,'" Rev mus 7:19-30 (May 1923).
Impressions of the work; not an analysis.

463 Engel, Carl. "Schönberg Lunaire" in his Dischords mingled. New York, Knopf, 1931, p. 84-97.
A nontechnical essay.

464 Boulez, Pierre. "Trajectories: Ravel, Stravinsky, Schoenberg," Contrepoints 6:122-142 (1949).
Discusses one work each by Ravel, Stravinsky, and Schoenberg (see no. 465).

465 Schaeffner, André. "Chroniques et commentaires; variations Schoenberg," Contrepoints 7:110-129 (1951).
A commentary on Boulez's article (see no. 464).

See no. 303 (Stein, Erwin. "The treatment of the speaking voice in Pierrot Lunaire" in his Orpheus in new guises, 1953, p. 86-89).

See no. 69 (Perle, George. "Theory and practice in twelve-tone music," Jun 1959).

Quartets, Strings

466   Gradenwitz, Peter. "The idiom and development in Schoenberg's quartets," M & L 26:123-142 (Jul 1945). Mus.
      Brief analyses. Includes a list of Schoenberg's works, p. 141-142.

—no. 1, in D minor, op. 7

467   Wellesz, Egon. "Arnold Schönberg," Zeitschrift der Internationalen Musikgesellschaft 12:342-348 (Sept 1911). Mus.
      Discussion of Schoenberg's early works, with outlines of the form of the first and second quartets.

468   Schindler, Kurt. Arnold Schönberg's Quartet in D minor, op. 7: an introductory note . . . delivered . . . at the private performance by the Flonzaley Quartet . . . New York, December 28th, 1913. Followed by an index of musical themes. New York, G. Schirmer [c1914]. 10 p. + 5 p. of "index of themes."

469   "A Schönberg quartet," Musical courier 68:27 (Feb 4, 1914). Port.
      A sympathetic contemporary criticism; discusses the "style" of the work.

470   Berg, Alban. "Why is Schoenberg's music so hard to understand?" Mus rev 13:187-196 (Aug 1952), tr. by Anton Swarowsky and Joseph Lederer.
      Originally appeared as "Warum ist Schönbergs Musik so schwer verständlich?" in Arnold Schönberg zum fünfzigsten Geburtstag (see no. 288); reprinted in Reich's Alban Berg (see no. 492, p. 142-155). French translation—"Pourquoi la musique de Schoenberg est-elle si difficile a comprendre?"—in Berg's Ecrits (see no. 509, p. 65-92).

—no. 2, in F-sharp minor, op. 10

See no. 467 (Wellesz, Egon. "Arnold Schönberg," Sept 1911).

See no. 380 (Somigli, Carlo. "Il modus operandi di Arnold Schoenberg," Jul/Sept 1913).

—no. 3, op. 30

471   Stein, Erwin. "Schönberg's new structural form," Modern music 7:3-10 (Jun/Jul 1930). Mus., port.
      Primarily a row analysis.

See no. 586 (Pousseur, Henri. "Da Schoenberg a Webern," Dec 1956).

—no. 4, op. 37

472 Mangeot, André. "Schoenberg's fourth Quartet," Mus rev 3:33-37 (Feb 1942). Mus.
     A brief thematic analysis.

See no. 206 (Johnson, Martha. A study of linear design in Gregorian chant and music written in the twelve-tone technique, 1954).

See no. 166a (Rufer, Josef. "Was ist Zwölftonmusik?" Jan 1958).

—first movement

473 Neighbor, Oliver. "A talk on Schoenberg for Composers' Concourse," Score, no. 16:19-28 (Jun 1956). Mus.
     An analysis of the first movement.

Quintet, Winds, op. 26

474 Greissle, Felix. "Die formalen Grundlagen des Bläserquintetts von Arnold Schönberg," Musikblätter des Anbruch 7:63-68 (Feb 1925). Mus.
     A brief structural analysis.

475 Pannain, Guido. "L'Internationale Musikgesellschaft für neue Musik e il Festivale musicale di Zurigo; 2° Concerto Schoenberg," Riv mus ital 33:417-421 ([Jul/Sept] 1926).
     Brief description of the twelve-tone technique; characteristics of the Quintet.

See no. 384 (Westphal, Kurt. "Arnold Schönbergs Weg zur Zwölftonmusik," Apr 1929).

See no. 143 (Schoenberg, Arnold. "Composition with twelve tones" in his Style and idea, 1950, p. 102-143).

Satires for mixed chorus
    See his Choral works—op. 28
    (Three satires for mixed chorus)

Sechs kleine Klavierstücke, op. 19
    See his Piano works—op. 19

Septet, op. 29
    See his Suite (Septet), op. 29

Six little piano pieces, op. 19
    See his Piano works—op. 19

Songs

476 Zeiger, Jean Wilson. Early expressionistic songs. (Thesis, M.A., University of California, 1959). 188 l. Mus.
  Bibliography, p. 179-188. Covers songs of Schoenberg, Berg, and Webern "written in a non-tonal idiom prior to Schoenberg's development of the twelve-tone method." Detailed analyses of Schoenberg's op. 15, nos. 4 and 9, Webern's op. 4, no. 2, and Webern's op. 15, no. 4.

—op. 6 (Eight songs)

See no. 380 (Somigli, Carlo. "Il modus operandi di Arnold Schoenberg," Jul/Sept 1913).

—op. 15 (Das Buch der hängenden Gärten)

See no. 476 (Zeiger, Jean Wilson. Early expressionistic songs, 1959).

String quartets
  See his Quartets, Strings

String trio
  See his Trio, Strings

Suite, Piano, op. 25
  See his Piano works—op. 25

Suite (Septet), op. 29

477 Stein, Erwin. "Zu Schönbergs neuer Suite, op. 29," Musikblätter des Anbruch 9:280-281 (Aug/Sept 1927).
  A brief description.

Survivor from Warsaw

478 Leibowitz, René. "Arnold Schoenberg's 'Survivor from Warsaw' or the possibility of 'committed' art," Horizon [London] 20:122-131 (Aug 1949).
  A philosophical discussion of the political questions involved; brief summary of the "plot" and some general statements about the music. [Summarized by Paul Hamburger in Mus sur 2:183 (Winter 1950).]

479 Hill, Richard S. "Music reviews; Arnold Schoenberg: A survivor from Warsaw," Notes 7:133-135 (Dec 1949).
  Discusses the row treatment.

See no. 400 (Keller, Hans. "Schoenberg," Jun 1951).

Theme and variations in G minor for orchestra, op. 43b

480 Goehr, Walter. "Musica-Umschau: Schönbergs Aussöhnung mit der Tonalität," Musica 1:219-220 (May/Aug 1947).
Surveys Schoenberg's various "periods" of composition and briefly describes these tonal variations.

Trio, Strings, op. 45

481 Hymanson, William. "Schoenberg's String trio (1946)," Mus rev 11:184-194 (Aug 1950). Mus., tables.
The work as a whole; its row treatment.

482 Hill, Richard S. "Music reviews: Arnold Schoenberg: String trio, op. 45," Notes 8:127-129 (Dec 1950).
Hexachordal row treatment discussed at some length.

483 Neighbor, Oliver W. "Dodecaphony in Schoenberg's String trio," Mus sur 4:489-490 (Jun 1952). Mus.
Very brief account of the row treatment.

See no. 204a (Rochberg, George. "The harmonic tendency of the hexachord," Nov 1959).

Variations for orchestra, op. 31

484 Leibowitz, René. Introduction à la musique de douze sons. Les Variations pour orchestre, op. 31, d'Arnold Schoenberg. Paris, L'Arche [1949]. 351 p. Mus.
Partial contents: Première partie: "Nécessités et genèse de la technique de douze sons," p. 25-52; "La 'Reihenkomposition' antérieure à la technique de douze sons," p. 53-80; "La technique de douze sons," p. 81-108. Deuxième partie: "Les Variations pour orchestre," p. 113-220. Troisième partie: "Les dernières oeuvres de Schoenberg, de Webern et de Berg," p. 223-249; "Les nouvelles générations de compositeurs 'dodécaphonistes' et leurs caractéristiques générales," p. 250-276; "Les survivances de l'ordre tonal à l'intérieur de la technique de douze sons et les possibilités de leur dépassement," p. 279-302; "Les aspects les plus récents de la technique de douze sons," p. 303-335; "Oeuvres d'Arnold Schoenberg," p. 339-342; "Oeuvres d'Alban Berg," p. 342-343; "Oeuvres d'Anton Webern," p. 343-345.

See no. 143 (Schoenberg, Arnold. "Composition with twelve tones" in his Style and idea, 1950, p. 102-143).

485 Kloppenburg, W. C. M. "Het thema van Schoenbergs Variationen Für Orchester," Mens en melodie 12:362-365 (Dec 1957). Mus.
An analysis of the theme.

See no. 170 (Nono, Luigi. "Die Entwicklung der Reihentechnik" in Steinecke, Wolfgang, ed. Darmstädter Beiträge zur neuen Musik, 1958, p. 25-37).

485a Schoenberg, Arnold. "The orchestral variations, op. 31: a radio talk," Score, no. 27:27-40 (Jul 1960). Mus.
An analysis; originally given over the Frankfurt radio in 1931.

Variations on a recitative for organ, op. 40

See no. 426 (Keller, Hans. "First performances," Nov 1952).

486 Keller, Hans. "First performances: their pre- and reviews," Mus rev 16:145-147 (May 1955).
Discusses "tonality and harmony," "counterpoint," "melody and rhythmic structure" very briefly.

Von Heute auf Morgen
See also his Operas

487 Adorno, Theodor Wiesengrund. "Arnold Schönberg: Von Heute auf Morgen," Anbruch 13:72-74 (Feb 1930).
A brief description.

488 Pisk, Paul. "Schoenberg's twelve-tone opera," Modern music 7:18-21 (Apr/May 1930).
Discusses the plot and musical structure. Reprinted in no. 295 (Armitage).

489 Reich, Willi. "Berichte aus dem Ausland: Schönberg-Premier nach 22 Jahren," Melos 20:27-28 (Jan 1953). Illus.
General description of the work and of its first performance since 1930.

490 Keller, Hans. "Schoenberg's comic opera," Score, no. 23:27-36 (Jul 1958).
A discussion of its history, bibliography, libretto, and music.

Wind quintet, op. 26
See his Quintet, Winds, op. 26

ALBAN BERG (1885-1935)

GENERAL
(Including Collections, Festschriften, etc.)

491 Mantelli, Alberto. "Note su Alban Berg," Rass mus 9:117-132 (Apr 1936). Mus.
Berg's works, especially Wozzeck, and his significance.

492 Reich, Willi, ed. Alban Berg: mit Bergs eigenem Schriften und Beiträgen von Theodor Wiesengrund Adorno und Ernst Krenek.

Wien, Herbert Reichner [c1937]. 208 p. Mus., ports.
Contents: Biography, p. 7-18; analyses of Berg's works, by Reich, Adorno, and Krenek, p. 19-133; essays by Berg, p. 135-203.

See no. 81 (Hijman, Julius. Nieuwe oostenrijkse musiek, 1938).

493 Reich, Willi. "Alban Berg" in Thompson, Oscar, ed. Great modern composers. New York, Dodd Mead, 1941, p. 10-14.
Includes a short catalog of Berg's works, p. 14.

See no. 82 (Salazar, Adolfo. Music in our time, 1946).

494 Hübner, Herbert. "Berg, Alban" in Die Musik in Geschichte und Gegenwart. Kassel, Bärenreiter, 1949-1951, v. 1, col. 1680-1684. Illus.
Bibliography and list of works included.

See no. 84 (Leibowitz, René. "Alban Berg: the awareness of the past in contemporary music" in his Schoenberg and his school, 1949, p. 137-186).

See no. 299 (Wörner, Karl H. Music der Gegenwart, 1949).

495 Reich, Willi. "Berg, Alban" in Grove's Dictionary of music and musicians. 5th ed., London, Macmillan, 1954, v. 1, p. 635-639.
Includes a list of works and a bibliography.

See no. 94 (Rognoni, Luigi. Espressionismo e dodecafonia, 1954).

See no. 100 (Collaer, Paul. La musique moderne, 1905-1955, 1955).

See no. 105 (Hamilton, Iain. "Alban Berg and Anton Webern" in Hartog, Howard, ed. European music in the twentieth century, 1957, p. 94-117).

496 Redlich, Hans Ferdinand. Alban Berg, the man and his music. New York, Abelard-Schuman [c1957]. 316 p. Mus., ports.

_____. Alban Berg: Versuch einer Würdigung. Wien, Universal Edition, 1957.
Contents: Part 1: "The second Viennese school," p. 13-18; "The problem of tonality," p. 19-31. Part 2: "The music of Alban Berg," p. 35-202. Part 3: "The life of Alban Berg," p. 217-242. Part 4: appendices: "Arnold Schoenberg on Alban Berg" (1949), p. 245-246; "Facsimile of Berg's Variations for piano on a theme of his own" (1908), p. 247-259; "Berg's lecture on Wozzeck" (1929), p. 261-285; "Catalogue of works," p. 287-298; "Discography," p. 299-304; "Bibliography," p. 305-312.
Review by Ernst Krenek in MQ 43:403-406 (July 1957).

See no. 112 (Prieberg, Fred K. Lexikon der neuen Musik, 1958, p. 36-41).

See no. 115 (Stuckenschmidt, Hans Heinz. "Alban Berg" in his Schöpfer der neuen Musik, 1958, p. 180-191).

See no. 116 (Vlad, Roman. "Berg e la libera articolazione della dodecafonia" in his Storia della dodecafonia, 1958, p. 115-124).

497   Adorno, Theodor Wiesengrund. "Alban Berg" in his Klangfiguren. Berlin, Suhrkamp Verlag, c1959, p. 121-137. (His Musikalischen Schriften, I.)
"Ursprünglich ein Vortrag für den Norddeutschen Rundfunk, veröffentlich in 'Merkur,' 10. Jahrgang, Heft 7, Juli 1956, S. 643 ff."

498   Vogelsang, Konrad. Alban Berg, Leben und Werk. Berlin-Halensee, Max Hesses Verlag [c1959]. 88 p. Ports. (Hesses kleine Bücherei, Band 5.)
Contents: Part 1: "Leben," p. 9-54. Part 2: "Werkanalysen," p. 55-77; "Werkverzeichnis," p. 79-81; "Discographie," p. 81-85; "Bibliographie," p. 86-88.

See no. 118a (Zillig, Winifried. "Alban Berg und die Wiener Schule" in his Variationen über neue Musik, 1959, p. 140-148).

498a   Boulez, Pierre. "Alban Berg heute gesehen," Melos 27:33-36 (Feb 1960).
Exerpted from his article in Fasquelle's Encyclopèdie de la musique [c1958]; tr. by Pierre Stoll.

PHILOSOPHY AND CRITICISM

499   Pijper, Willem. "Alban Berg," MT 77:414-415 (May 1936), tr. by Herbert Antcliffe.
Obituary; general evaluation of Berg's work. The author feels that, with Berg's death, the "period of atonal composition is for the time being already concluded."

500   Holländer, Hans. "Alban Berg," MQ 22:375-382 (Oct 1936), tr. by "G. R." Port.
General essay on the importance of Berg.

501   Menasce, Jacques. "Berg and Bartók," Modern music 21:76-81 (Jan/Feb 1944).
Affinities between the two composers.

502   Leibowitz, René. "Innovation and tradition in contemporary music: III. Alban Berg, or the seduction to truth," Horizon [London] 16: 140-152 (Aug 1947).
Conclusion of his series of articles on Schoenberg, Webern, and Berg (see nos. 320 and 575).

503   Boulez, Pierre. "Incidences actuelles de Berg; à propos de la Quinzaine de Musique autrichienne à Paris" in Le rythme musical. Paris, Richard-Masse [1948], p. 104-108. Mus. (Polyphonie, 2e cahier.)
Berg's relation to musical tradition.

See no. 29 (Goléa, Antoine. "Alban Berg" in his Esthétique de la musique contemporaine, 1954, p. 52-56, 66-71).

504 Lindlar, Heinrich. "'Mir fehlt die grosse Freude'; zum 20. Todestag Alban Bergs," Musica 9:594-596 (Dec 1955). Illus.
An evaluation of Berg's works twenty years after his death.

505 Rubin, Marcel. "Alban Berg und die Zukunft der Schönberg-Schule," Musik und Gesellschaft [E. Berlin] 5:384-386 (Dec 1955). Mus.
Feels that Berg's works, having tonal implications, could more practically have been written within a tonal idiom. Finds Berg the only twelve-tone composer who appeals to the masses, and therefore the one by which the trend of dodecaphony should be judged. Discusses folk elements in Wozzeck.

BIOGRAPHY

506 Reich, Willi. "Erinnerungen an Alban Berg," Schw MZ 91:1-3 (Jan 1951).
"Gesprochen im Südwestfunk in Baden-Baden im Dezember 1950."

507 Schmidt-Garre, Helmut. "Berg als Lehrer," Melos 22:40-41 (Feb 1955). Illus.
A brief comment by a former Berg pupil.

508 Reich, Willi. "Alban Berg als Apologet Arnold Schönbergs: mit einem unbekannten Aufsatz Bergs," Schw MZ 95:475-477 (Dec 1955).
Gives the first part of an article by Berg. (The second part of Berg's article was previously published as "Zwei Feuilletons: Ein Beitrag zum Kapitel, 'Schönberg und die Kritik'" in the Neuer Wiener Journal, July 17, 1920).

509 Berg, Alban. Ecrits: choisis, traduits, et commentés par Henri Pousseur. Monaco, Editions du Rocher [1957]. 182 p. Mus. (Domaine musical.)
Partial contents: "La société viennoise d'exécutions privées" (1919), p. 29-37; "Pourquoi la musique de Schoenberg est-elle si difficile à comprendre?" (1924), p. 65-92; "Lettre ouverte à Schoenberg" (1925), p. 93-108; "A propos des formes employées dans Wozzeck" (1924), p. 109-117; "Indications pratiques pour l'étude de Wozzeck" (1930), p. 141-155; "Credo" (1930), p. 157-166; "Chronologie," p. 167-178.

*509a Reich, Willi, ed. Alban Berg, Bildnis im Wort: Selbstzeugnisse und Aussagen der Freunde. Zürich, Die Arche [c1959]. 89 p. Illus., mus., ports.

510 Schoenberg, Arnold. "Über Alban Berg," Schw MZ 99:221-225 (Jun 1959).
Originally written for Reich's book on Berg (see no. 492).

CORRESPONDENCE

See no. 374 (Hill, Richard S. "Annual reports on acquisitions: music," Nov 1952).

511 Reich, Willi. "Aus unbekannten Briefen von Alban Berg an Anton Webern: Alban Berg als Opernkomponist und Musikschriftsteller," Schw MZ 93:49-52 (Feb 1953).
Brief note concerning the friendship between Berg and Webern; texts of five letters.

See no. 555 (Blaukopf, Kurt. "New light on Wozzeck," Sept 26, 1953).

512 Redlich, Hans Ferdinand. "Alle guten Dinge," Melos 22:39-40 (Feb 1955).
Excerpts from letters of Berg to Schoenberg and Webern concerning Berg's Chamber concerto. Reprinted in Redlich's Alban Berg (see no. 496).

513 Reich, Willi. "Aus Alban Bergs Jugendzeit," Melos 22:33-38 (Feb 1955). Port.
The young Berg; selections from early letters.

514 Rufer, Josef. "Dokumente einer Freundschaft," Melos 22:42-46 (Feb 1955). Illus., port.
Letters from Berg to Schoenberg.

See no. 444 (Reich, Willi. "Ein Briefwechsel über 'Moses und Aron,'" Jun 1957).

See no. 379 ([Schoenberg, Arnold]. "Ein unbekannter Brief von Arnold Schönberg an Alban Berg," Jan 1959).

COMPOSITIONAL TECHNIQUES

See no. 391 (Wood, Ralph W. "Concerning 'Sprechgesang,'" Dec 1946).

See no. 154 (Erickson, Robert. The structure of music, 1955).

See no. 160 (Perle, George. Serial composition and atonality, 1956 [c1959].)

GENERAL DESCRIPTIONS OF WORKS

See no. 292 (Mersmann, Hans. Die moderne Musik seit der Romantik, 1927).

515 Reich, Willi. "Alban Berg," Die Musik 22:347-353 (Feb 1930). Mus., port.
A discussion of Berg's works and "style." Includes the complete music of Berg's two settings of "Schliesse mir die Augen beide," made in 1900 and 1925.

516 Adorno, Theodor Wiesengrund. "Berg and Webern—Schoenberg's heirs," Modern music 8:29-38 (Jan 1931).
    Discussion and comparison of Berg's and Webern's works and "styles."

517 Reich, Willi. "Les dernières oeuvres d'Alban Berg," Rev mus 12:148-154 (Feb 1931).
    A brief discussion.

518 Mantelli, Alberto. "Elenco delle opere di Berg," Rass mus 9:163-164 (May 1936).
    A list of Berg's works.

See no. 492 (Reich, Willi, ed. Alban Berg, 1937, p. 19-133).

See no. 484 (Leibowitz, René. "Les dernières oeuvres de Schoenberg, de Webern et de Berg" in his Introduction à la musique de douze sons, 1949, p. 223-249).

See no. 403 (Demuth, Norman. "Alban Berg" in his Musical trends in the twentieth century, 1952, p. 239-245).

519 "Oeuvres d'Alban Berg (1885-1935)," Music information record, no. 11:15, 17 (Winter 1953/1954).
    List of works with dates of publication.

See no. 95 (Wörner, Karl H. Neue Musik in der Entscheidung, 1954).

INDIVIDUAL WORKS

Altenberger Lieder
See his Songs—op. 4

Chamber concerto for violin, piano, and 13 winds

520 Deutsch, Max. "Le Concerto de chambre d'Alban Berg," Schw MZ 89:328-333 (Sept 1949).
    The background of the work, its symbolism, its general characteristics.

See no. 94 (Berg, Alban. "Lettera aperta ad Arnold Schoenberg" in Rognoni, Luigi. Espressionismo e dodecafonia, 1954, p. 277-282).
    Originally published in Pult und Taktstock, 1925.

See no. 512 (Redlich, Hans Ferdinand. "Alle guten Dinge," Feb 1955).

Concerto, Violin and orchestra

521 Smith, Moses. "Alban Berg—finale: a requiem," Modern music 13:29-34 (Mar 1936). Port.
    Some comments on Lulu, but primarily an essay on the Violin concerto: its genesis and character.

522   Carner, Mosco. "Alban Berg (1885-1935)" in Hill, Ralph. The concerto. London, Penguin Books, 1952, p. 362-379. Mus.
      An extended but nontechnical analysis.

See no. 425 (Rubin, Louis. The idiom of the violin in twentieth century music, 1952).

See no. 649 (Gavazzeni, Gianandrea. "La critica soggettivistica e il Concerto per violino di Berg" in his Musicisti d'Europa, 1954, p. 124-129).

523   Rostal, Max, and Hans Keller. "Berg's Violin concerto: a revision," MT 95:87-88 (Feb 1954). Mus.
      Problems of alternate versions of the cadenza in the second movement.

524   Redlich, Hans Ferdinand. "Alban Bergs Violinkonzert," Melos 24: 316-321 (Nov 1957) and 24:352-357 (Dec 1957). Mus.
      An analysis. Reprinted from Redlich's Alban Berg (see no. 496).

See no. 427 (Walters, Willard Gibson. Technical problems in modern violin music, 1958).

Five songs to postcard texts
See his Songs—op. 4

Kammerkonzert
See his Chamber concerto

Lulu
See also his Operas

525   Collaer, Paul. "Une nouvelle oeuvre d'Alban Berg: Loulou," Rev mus 16:169-174 (Mar 1934). Mus.
      The structure of the drama and the music; a survey-analysis.

526   Bach, David Joseph. "New music by Berg, Webern, Krenek," Modern music 12:31-38 (Nov/Dec 1934).
      A review of the music (Berg's Lulu, Webern's Songs, op. 23, and Krenek's Cantata, op. 72) and a summary of the trends of twelve-tone music in the mid-1930's.

527   Reich, Willi. "Lulu, the text and music," Modern music 12:103-111 (Mar/Apr 1935). Port.
      A summary of the drama and a brief general discussion of the music.

528   Reich, Willi. "Alban Berg's Lulu," MQ 22:383-401 (Oct 1936), tr. by M. D. Herter Norton. Mus.
      The dramatic and musical structure of the opera.

529   List, Kurt. "Lulu, after the première," Modern music 15:8-12 (Nov/Dec 1937).

A general summation of Berg's achievements; a review of Lulu—the performance and the music.

530 Thoresby, Christina. "Lulu d'Alban Berg au théâtre," Contrepoints 6:156-159 (1949). Mus.
Brief summary of the plot and the musical technique.

531 Reich, Willi. "Deutsche Première nach 15 Jahren: Alban Bergs Oper 'Lulu,'" Melos 19:337-342 (Dec 1952). Illus., port.
Background of the opera; outline of the plot.

532 Hill, Richard S. "Reviews of records; Berg: Lulu," MQ 39:134-138 (Jan 1953).
Comparison of Lulu with Wozzeck and Schoenberg's Erwartung; the origin of the text of Lulu; the character of the music.

533 Werker, Gerard. "Alban Berg en zijn opera Lulu," Mens en melodie 8:167-172 (Jun 1953). Mus., port.
Some row analysis; a sketch of the drama.

534 Mitchell, Donald. "The character of Lulu: Wedekind's and Berg's conceptions compared," Mus rev 15:268-274 (Nov 1954). Mus.
Berg and Wedekind as librettists; Berg's musical treatment of the drama.

535 Krenek, Ernst. "Alban Bergs 'Lulu'" in his Zur Sprache Gebracht: Essays über Musik. München, Albert Langen [c1958], p. 241-250.
Reprinted from the Wiener Zeitung, June 6, 1937.

See no. 69 (Perle, George. "Theory and practice in twelve-tone music," Jun 1959).

Lulu Symphonie

535a Adorno, Theodor Wiesengrund. "Bergs Lulu-Symphonie," Melos 27:43-46 (Feb 1960).
Reprinted from the fall 1935 issue of 23, eine Wiener Musikzeitschrift.

535b Reich, Willi. "An der Seite von Alban Berg," Melos 27:36-42 (Feb 1960). Mus.
Includes facsimiles of three sketches for Lulu.

Lyric suite for string quartet

536 Bouquet, Fritz. "Alban Bergs 'Lyrische Suite'; eine Studie über Gestalt, Klang und Ausdruck," Melos 15:227-231 (Aug/Sept 1948). Mus.
Analysis, especially of the row treatment and the form.

See no. 144 (Brainard, Paul. "Lyric suite" in his A study of the twelve-tone technique, 1951, p. 34-58).

537 Smith Brindle, Reginald. "The symbolism in Berg's 'Lyric suite,'" Score, no. 21:60-63 (Oct 1957). Mus.
A deciphering of Berg's musical symbolism.

See no. 69 (Perle, George. "Theory and practice in twelve-tone music," Jun 1959).

Operas
See also his Lulu, Wozzeck

538 Leibowitz, René. "Alban Berg et l'essence de l'opéra," L'arche [pt. 1] "Réflexions sur la musique dramatique sub una specie," no. 13:130-134 (Feb 1946); [pt. 2] "Problèmes et architecture des opéras de Berg," no. 14:158-166 (Mar 1946).
Berg and the problems of opera.

539 Grout, Donald Jay. "Opera between two wars" in his A short history of opera. One-volume ed. New York, Columbia University Press [c1947], p. 532-535. Mus.
Brief outline of the dramatic and musical structure of Wozzeck and Lulu. Bibliographical notes.

Schliesse mir die Augen beide
See his Songs—Schliesse mir die Augen beide

Songs

540 Adorno, Theodor Wiesengrund. "Die Instrumentation von Bergs frühen Liedern" in his Klangfiguren. Berlin, Suhrkamp Verlag, c1959, p. 138-156. (His Musikalischen Schriften, I.)
Originally published in Schweizerische Musikzeitschrift und Sängerblatt, 5/6:158 ff., 198 ff. (Mar 1932). Revised.

See no. 476 (Zeiger, Jean Wilson. Early expressionistic songs, 1959).

—op. 2, no. 4
See no. 74 (Der blaue Reiter, 1914).

—op. 4
(Five songs to postcard texts by Peter Altenberg)

541 Leibowitz, René. "Alban Berg's Five orchestral songs, after postcard texts by Peter Altenberg, op. 4," MQ 34:487-511 (Oct 1948). Mus., port.
"A brief survey of the essential elements of the first four songs and a complete analysis of the last song" (the music of which is reproduced in a piano reduction).

542 Ringger, Rolf Urs. "Zur formbildenden Kraft des vertonten Wortes: analytische Untersuchen an Liedern von Hugo Wolf und Alban Berg," Schw MZ 99:225-229 (Jun 1959). Mus.
A comparison of Wolf's "Das verlassene Mägdlein" (Mörikelieder) and Berg's op. 4 songs. The score of op. 4, no. 2, is given complete.

—Schliesse mir die Augen beide
See no. 515 (Reich, Willi. "Alban Berg," Feb 1930).

—Der Wein
See his Der Wein

Variations for piano
See no. 496 (Redlich, Hans Ferdinand. Alban Berg, 1957, p. 247-259).

Violin concerto
See his Concerto, Violin and orchestra

Der Wein

543 Reich, Willi. "Berg's new work, 'Der Wein,'" Modern music 7:41-43 (Apr/May 1930).
A description; the row is quoted.

Wozzeck
See also his Operas

544 Viebig, Ernst. "Bergs 'Wozzeck': ein Beitrag zum Opernproblem," Die Musik 15:506-510 (Apr 1923).
The background of the opera; the text, the musical forms used; its place in operatic tradition.

545 Alban Bergs 'Wozzeck' und die Musikkritik. Herausgeber: Musikblätter des Anbruch. Wien [1925?]. 31 p. Mus. (Musik der Gegenwart; eine Flugblätterfolge, nr. 9.)
Contemporary reviews of Berg's opera; some analyses.

546 Winkler, Hans. Georg Büchners "Woyzeck." Greifswald, E. Hartmann, 1925. 238 p.
An analysis of Büchner's drama (not of Berg's opera); bibliography, p. 235-236.

547 Adorno, Theodor Wiesengrund. "Alban Berg: zur Uraufführung des 'Wozzeck,'" Musikblätter des Anbruch 7:531-537 (Dec 1925).
General comments on the first performance.

548 Reich, Willi. Alban Berg's Wozzeck; a guide to the text and music of the opera. New York, G. Schirmer [c1927]. 22 p. Mus., port.
"Reprinted from the monograph originally published by the League of Composers' Quarterly Review, Modern Music."
Contents: "Synopsis of the opera," p. 1-2; "Berg's organization of the text," p. 2-4; "The musical structure as a whole," p. 4-6; "Scheme of the dramatic and musical forms," p. 7; "Analysis of the individual scenes," p. 8-21; "Postscript by Alban Berg," p. 21-22.

See no. 451 (Berg, Alban. "Die Stimme in der Oper," Nov/Dec 1928).

549   Sabin, Robert. "Alban Berg's Wozzeck," Musical America 71:6-7, 34 (Apr 1, 1951). Illus.
Fritz Mahler's analytical charts are explained. (Fritz Mahler was a pupil of Berg.) (See no. 561.)

550   Keller, Hans. "First performances: the eclecticism of Wozzeck," Mus rev 12:309-315 (Nov 1951) and 13:133-137 (May 1952). Mus.

551   Gerhard, Roberto. "Wozzeck," Foyer [London], no. 2:16-20 (Winter, 1951/52). Mus., port.
A brief outline of the plot and the musical structure.

552   Berg, Alban. "The musical form in Wozzeck," Opera [London] 3:23-24 (Jan 1952), tr by Erwin Stein. Illus.
Originally published as "Das Opernproblem" in the Neue Musikzeitung [Stuttgart] 49:285 ff. (Nov 1928).
A brief article stating that Berg's various "closed forms" are used in Wozzeck for compactness but are not to be perceived by the audience as such.

553   Stein, Erwin. "Wozzeck," Opera [London] 3:17-22 (Jan 1952). Illus.
History of Wozzeck; its performances and general characteristics; the drama and a few comments on the music. Reprinted in Stein's Orpheus in new guises, p. 103-107 (see no. 303).

554   Jouve, Pierre Jean. Wozzeck ou le nouvel opéra, [par] Pierre-Jean Jouve [et] Michel Fano. Paris, Plon [1953]. 242 p. Mus., port.
Contents: "Argument d'après le drame de Georg Büchner," p. 9-30; "Introduction," p. 31-40; "Structure," p. 41-211; "Forme et invention," p. 215-242.
Musical and dramatic analysis of the work, scene by scene.

555   Blaukopf, Kurt. "New light on Wozzeck," Saturday review 36:62, 76 (Sept 26, 1953). Port.
A description of "some recently discovered correspondence written by Alban Berg during his army career in World War I [which] gives strong evidence of Berg's personal identification with . . . Wozzeck."

556   Reich, Willi. "Alban Berg: 'Wozzeck'" in Oper im XX. Jahrhundert. Bonn, Boosey & Hawkes [c1954], p. 27-34. (Musik der Zeit: eine Schriftenreihe zur zeitgenössischen Musik, 6.)
"Formgesinnung; Textgestaltung; Musikalischer Aufbau; Analytische Bemerkungen zu den einzelnen Szenen."

557   Kerman, Joseph. "Terror and self-pity: Alban Berg's Wozzeck; an analysis of a modern operatic masterpiece," Perspectives USA, no. 10:43-57 (Winter 1955).
The style and mood of Wozzeck; a discussion of the opera as drama, not a musical analysis.

558   Kerman, Joseph. "Wozzeck and the Rake's progress" in his Opera as drama. New York, Knopf, c1956, p. 219-249. Mus.

Drawn from his earlier article (see no. 557). Comparison of Wozzeck with Stravinsky's opera. Reprinted by Vintage Books, 1959.

559 Newman, Ernest. "Wozzeck" in his From the world of music; essays from the Sunday Times. London, John Calder [1956], p. 148-159.
Five brief essays, on the music, the drama, the first performance in England, and Berg's use of Sprechgesang.

560 Redlich, Hans Ferdinand. "Wozzeck; Dramaturgie und musikalische Form," Musica 10:120-125 (Feb 1956).
The layout of Büchner's text compared to Berg's; a table of the musical forms used in each scene.

See no. 509 (Berg, Alban. "A propos des formes employées dans Wozzeck" in his Ecrits, 1957, p. 109-117).

561 *Mahler, Fritz. Zu Alban Bergs Oper Wozzeck; szenische und musikalische Ubersicht. Wien, Universal Edition, c1957. 9 p. (See no. 549.)

562 Opera news v. 23, no. 19 (Mar 9, 1959), 33 p. Illus., mus.
The entire issue is devoted to the Metropolitan Opera's first production of Wozzeck. Includes articles on the drama, the music, the singers, staging problems, Berg, and Büchner.

—act 3, scene 4

563 Jouve, Pierre Jean. "Wozzeck d'Alban Berg (Acte III, Scène IV)" in L'Oeuvre du XXe siècle. Paris, Richard-Masse, 1952, p. 87-98. Mus. (La revue musicale, no. 212.)
An extract from his book (see no. 554).

ANTON WEBERN (1883-1945)

GENERAL

(Including Collections, Festschriften, etc.)

564 Anton Webern zum 50. Geburtstag. 23, eine Wiener musikzeitschrift no. 14 (Feb 1934), 25 p. Ports.
Contents: "Zur Einleitung," p. 3; Webern, Anton, "Der Schönbergschüler," p. 4-5; Reich, Willi, "Weberns Musik," p. 5-8; "Meister und Jünger," p. 8-9; Krenek, Ernst, "Freiheit und Verantwortung," p. 10-11; Humplik, Josef, "Dem Freunde," p. 12-13; Zenk, Ludwig, "Mein Lehrer," p. 13; Reich, Willi, "Weberns Vorträge," p. 17-22; "Die Presse," p. 22-23; Reich, Willi, "Lieber Freund Doktor Ploderer!" p. 24; "An die Leser," p.[25].

See no. 81 (Hijman, Julius. Nieuwe oostenrijkse musiek, 1938).

565   Leibowitz, René. "La musique: Anton Webern," L'arche, no. 11:130-134 (Nov 1945).
Obituary; brief summary of life and works.

See no. 82 (Salazar, Adolfo. Music in our time, 1946).

566   Stein, Erwin. "Anton Webern," MT 87:14-15 (Jan 1946). Mus.
An obituary. Brief discussion of Webern's works and style. Reprinted in Stein's Orpheus in new guises (see no. 303, p. 99-102).

See no. 297 (Bauer, Marion. Twentieth century music, 1947).

567   Dallapiccola, Luigi. "In memoria di Anton Webern," Emporium 105:18-20 (Jan 1947). Port.
Obituary; biographical and critical article.

See no. 84 (Leibowitz, René. "Anton Webern: the awareness of the future in contemporary music" in his Schoenberg and his school, 1949, p. 187-255).

See no. 299 (Wörner, Karl H. Musik der Gegenwart, 1949).

568   Baruch, Gerth-Wolfgang. "Anton von Webern," Melos 20:337-342 (Dec 1953). Port.
Biographical sketch; discussion of Webern's contributions. Includes a list of Webern's works, p. 342.

See no. 94 (Rognoni, Luigi. Espressionismo e dodecafonia, 1954).

569   Searle, Humphrey. "Webern, Anton (von)" in Grove's Dictionary of music and musicians. 5th ed., London, Macmillan, 1954, v. 9:225-228.
Includes a bibliography and list of Webern's works.

570   Anton Webern. Tr. from the German by Leo Black, Eric Smith, and others. Bryn Mawr, Pa., Theodore Presser [c1955, 1958].
vii + 100 p. Diagrs., illus., mus. (Die Reihe, a periodical devoted to developments in contemporary music, ed. by Herbert Eimert and Karlheinz Stockhausen, no. 2.)
Contents: Stravinsky, Igor, "Foreword," p. vii; Wildgans, Friedrich, "Biographical table: index of works," p. 1-6; Jone, Hildegard, "A cantata," p. 7-8; Schoenberg, Arnold, "Foreword to Webern's Six Bagatelles, op. 6," p. 8; Webern, Anton, "Homage to Arnold Schoenberg," p. 9-10; "Anton Webern as a conductor," p. 11; Krenek, Ernst, "The same stone . . ." p. 12; "From the the correspondence [of Webern]," p. 13-21; Webern, Anton, "Choralis Constantinus," p. 23-25; Eimert, Herbert, "A change of focus," p. 29-36; Stockhausen, Karlheinz, "For the 15th of September, 1955," p. 37-39; Boulez, Pierre, "The threshold," p. 40-41; Metzger, Heinz-Klaus, "Webern and Schönberg," p. 42-45; Spinner, Leopold, "Analysis of a period: Concerto for 9 instruments, op. 24, second movement," p. 46-50; Pousseur, Henri, "Webern's organic chromaticism," p. 51-60; Wolff, Christian, "Movement," p. 61-63; Stockhausen, Karlheinz, "Structure and experimental time," p. 64-74; Metzger, Heinz-Klaus, "Analysis of the Sacred song, op. 15, no. 4," p. 75-80; Klammer, Armin,

"Webern's Piano variations, op. 27, 3rd movement," p. 81-92; Eimert, Herbert. "Interval proportions: String quartet, 1st movement," p. 93-99; "The published works of Anton Webern," p. 100. A lengthy review of this symposium, by Peter Stadlen, is found in Score, no. 25:65-68 (Jun 1959).

See no. 100 (Collaer, Paul. La musique moderne, 1905-1955. 1955).

See no. 105 (Hamilton, Iain. "Alban Berg and Anton Webern" in Hartog, Howard, ed. European music in the twentieth century, 1957, p. 94-117).

571 Stuckenschmidt, Hans Heinz. "Anton Webern," Ricordiana [nuova serie] 3:274-277 (Jun 1957).
Brief résumé of his life and works.

See no. 112 (Prieberg, Fred K. Lexikon der neuen Musik, 1958, p. 446-449).

See no. 115 (Stuckenschmidt, Hans Heinz. "Anton von Webern" in his Schöpfer der neuen Musik, 1958, p. 192-203).

See no. 116 (Vlad, Roman. "I traguardi del radicalismo di Webern" in his Storia della dodecafonia, 1958, p. 125-130).

572 Adorno, Theodor Wiesengrund. "Anton von Webern" in his Klangfiguren. Berlin, Suhrkamp, c1959, p. 157-181. (His Musikalische Schriften, I.)
"Ursprünglich ein Vortrag für den Norddeutschen Rundfunk, veröffentlicht in 'Merkur,' 13. Jahrg., Heft 3, März 1959, S. 201 ff."

See no. 118a (Zillig, Winfried. "Anton Webern, Aussenseiter und Vorbild" in his Variationen über neue Musik, 1959, p. 181-190).

PHILOSOPHY AND CRITICISM

573 Adorno, Theodor Wiesengrund. "Anton Webern: zur Aufführung der fünf Orchesterstücke in Zürich," Musikblätter des Anbruch 8:280-282 (May 1926).
Very general essay on Webern's music; not an analysis.

574 List, Kurt. "Anton von Webern," Modern music 21:27-30 (Nov/Dec 1943).
An essay in honor of Webern's 60th birthday; the character of his music.

575 Leibowitz, René. "Innovation and tradition in contemporary music: II. The tragic art of Anton Webern," Horizon [London] 15:282-293 (May 1947).
Similar to his article on Schoenberg in this series (see no. 320), but somewhat more technical regarding row technique.

576 Craft, Robert. "Discoveries and convictions," Counterpoint 18:16-18 (Feb 1953).
   Review of an all-Webern concert and discussion of the essential points of Webern's music.

See no. 29 (Goléa, Antoine. Esthétique de la musique contemporaine, 1954, p. 63-66).

577 Maren, Roger. "The music of Anton Webern: prisms in twelve tones," Reporter 16:38-41 (May 30, 1957).
   A review of the recording of Webern's complete works; also some general comments about Webern's style and about the twelve-tone technique.

See no. 170 (Pousseur, Henri. "Webern und die Theorie" in Steinecke, Wolfgang, ed. Darmstädter Beiträge zur neuen Musik, 1958, p. 38-43).

578 Wildgans, Friedrich. "Anton von Webern; zu seinem 75. Geburtstag am 3. Dezember 1958," ÖMZ 13:456-460 (Nov 1958). Illus. (autograph of a Webern MS), port.
   Webern's posthumous influence and importance.

579 Hampton, Christopher. "Anton Webern and the consciousness of time," Mus rev 20:45-51 (Feb 1959).
   An interpretation of the importance of Webern.

BIOGRAPHY

580 Searle, Humphrey. "Conversations with Webern," MT 81:405-406 (Oct 1940).
   Searle's experiences as a student of Webern. Includes a list of Webern's works through op. 29.

See no. 83 (Schlee, Alfred. "Vienna since the Anschluss," Spring 1946).

See no. 569 (Anton Webern. 1955, 1958 [Die Reihe, 2]).

580a Dorian, Frederick Deutsch. "Webern als Lehrer," Melos 27:101-106 (Apr 1960). Port.
   Webern as a teacher.

CORRESPONDENCE

See no. 374 (Hill, Richard S. "Annual reports on acquisitions: music," Nov 1952).

See no. 511 (Reich, Willi. "Aus unbekannten Briefen von Alban Berg an Anton Webern," Feb 1953).

See no. 569 ("From the correspondence" in Anton Webern, 1955, 1958, p. 13-21 [Die Reihe, 2]).

581 Gerhard, Roberto, ed. "Letters of Webern and Schoenberg" [to Roberto Gerhard], Score, no. 24:36-41 (Nov 1958).
These letters date from 1931-1934.

582 Webern, Anton von. Briefe an Hildegard Jone und Josef Humplik. Hrsg. von Josef Polnauer. Wien, Universal Edition, 1959, 106 p. Port., mus.
Extensive explanatory notes included.

COMPOSITIONAL TECHNIQUES

583 Stein, Erwin. "Anton Webern," Anbruch 13:107-109 (Jun/Jul 1931). Mus.
A brief and general discussion of his compositional techniques.

See no. 569 (Anton Webern. 1955, 1958 [Die Reihe, 2]).

See no. 154 (Erickson, Robert. The structure of music, 1955).

584 Vlad, Roman. "Anton von Webern e la composizione atematica," Rass mus 25:98-102 (Apr/Jun 1955). Mus.
The replacement of thematic content in Webern's works by structural design. Deals especially with the Concerto for 9 instruments, op. 24; the Variations for piano, op. 27; and the Variations for orchestra, op. 30.
An extract from chapter 7 of Vlad's Storia della dodecafonia (see no. 116).

See no. 43 (Rochberg, George. "Tradition and twelve-tone music," Dec 1955).

See no. 160 (Perle, George. Serial composition and atonality, 1956).

585 Stephan, Rudolph. "Anton von Webern," Dt Univ Zt 13/14:26-29 (Jul 19, 1956). Mus.
General discussion of Webern's works and compositional technique, including use of the row.

586 Pousseur, Henri. "Da Schoenberg a Webern: una mutazione," Incontri musicali 1:3-39 (Dec 1956), tr. by Vittorio Armanni. Mus.
A continuation of his study of Webern begun in Die Reihe, 2 (see no. 569, p. 51-60), and a comparison of Webern's and Schoenberg's compositional techniques. Examples from Schoenberg's op. 19 and 30 and from Webern's op. 5, 16, 26, 27 and other works.

GENERAL DESCRIPTIONS OF WORKS

587 Evans, Edwin. "Webern, Anton von" in Cobbett, Walter W. Cobbett's cyclopedic survey of chamber music. London, Oxford University Press, 1929/30, p. 571-574. Mus.

Discusses, very briefly, the Five movements for string quartet, the Four pieces for violin and piano, the Six bagatelles for string quartet, and the Three little pieces for cello and piano.

588 Reich, Willi. "Anton von Webern," Die Musik 22:812-816 (Aug 1930).
Description of works through 1929.

See no. 516 (Adorno, Theodor Wiesengrund. "Berg and Webern—Schoenberg's heirs," Jan 1931).

See no. 484 (Leibowitz, René. "Les dernières oeuvres de Schoenberg, de Webern, et de Berg" in his Introduction à la musique de douze sons, 1949, p. 232-244).

See no. 403 (Demuth, Norman. Musical trends in the twentieth century, 1952, p. 233-238).

589 "Oeuvres d'Anton Webern (1883-1945)," Music information record 11:17-18 (Winter 1953/54).
Lists of works with dates of publication.

See no. 95 (Wörner, Karl H. Neue Musik in der Entscheidung, 1954, p. 94-98).

590 Stephan, Rudolf. "Über einige geistliche Kompositionen Anton von Weberns," Musik und Kirche 24:152-160 (Jul/Aug 1954). Mus.
Discussion and analysis of op. 15, 16, 17, 18, 23, 26, 29, 31.

See no. 155 (Ogdon, Wilbur Lee. Series and structure, 1955).

591 Craft, Robert. "Anton Webern," Score, no. 13:9-22 (Sept 1955).
Biographical sketch; brief discussion of each group of works, and a list of Webern's compositions, with timings.

See no. 586 (Pousseur, Henri. "Da Schoenberg a Webern," Dec 1956).

592 Mason, Colin. "Webern's later chamber music," M & L 38:232-237 (Jul 1957).
A discussion of the chamber works from op. 15 on.

INDIVIDUAL WORKS

Bagatelles for string quartet, op. 9

See no. 569 (Schoenberg, Arnold. "Foreword to Webern's Six bagatelles, op. 6" in Anton Webern, 1955, 1958, p. 8 [Die Reihe, 2]).

Cantatas
—no. 2, op. 31

593 Mason, Colin. "New music," Chesterian 26:25-27 (Oct 1951).
Review of the score; some analytical comments, especially concerning the row structure.

594 Castiglioni, Niccolò. "Sul rapporto tra parola e musica nella seconda Cantata di Webern," Incontri musicali, no. 3:112-127 (Aug 1959).
Includes a translation of the text of the cantata into Italian.

Concerto for 9 instruments, op. 24

595 Leibowitz, René. Qu'est-ce que la musique de douze sons? Le concerto pour neuf instruments, op. 24, d'Anton Webern. Liège, Editions Dynamo, 1948. 63 p. + 8 p. "exemples musicaux."
Contents: "Le sens des problèmes soulevés par Schoenberg," p. 8-15; "L'évolution d'Anton Webern," p. 16-18; "Le concerto pour neuf instruments, op. 24, d'Anton Webern," p. 19-53; "Conclusion: les possibilités de reconnaissance d'une oeuvre," p. 55-61.
Includes a theme-by-theme analysis of the concerto.

See no. 584 (Vlad, Roman. "Anton von Webern e la composizione atematica," Apr/Jun 1955).

—First movement

596 Stockhausen, Karlheinz. "Weberns Konzert für 9 Instrumente, op. 24; Analyse der ersten Satzes," Melos 20:343-348 (Dec 1953). Mus. Interesting not only as a detailed analysis of the Webern, but also as an example of Stockhausen's analytical technique.

—Second movement

See no. 569 (Spinner, Leopold. "Analysis of a period: Concerto for 9 instruments, op. 24, second movement" in Anton Webern, 1955, 1958, p. 46-50 [Die Reihe, 2]).

Five movements for string quartet, op. 5
See his Movements for string quartet, op. 5

Five orchestral pieces, op. 10
See his Orchestral pieces, op. 10

Five sacred songs, op. 15
See his Songs—op. 15

Geistliche Lieder, op. 15
See his Songs—op. 15

Klavier Variationen, op. 27
See his Variations for piano, op. 27

Movements for string quartet, op. 5

597 Asuar, José Vicente. "Una incursion por el Op. 5 di Anton Webern," Revista musicale chilena 12:19-41 (Mar/Apr 1958). Mus.
A detailed analysis.

Orchestral pieces, op. 10

See no. 573 (Adorno, Theodor Wiesengrund. "Anton Webern: zur Aufführung der fünf Orchesterstücke in Zürich," May 1926).

Orchestral variations, op. 30
See his Variations for orchestra, op. 30

Passacaglia for orchestra, op. 1
See no. 456 (Cowell, Henry. "Current chronicle: New York," Jan 1949).

Piano quintet (1907)
See his Quintet, piano and strings

Piano variations, op. 27
See his Variations for piano, op. 27

Quartet, strings, op. 28

598 Wellesz, Egon. "Reviews of music: Webern, Anton, String Quartet, op. 28," Mus rev 1:177-178 (May 1940).
An interesting contemporary review; brief discussion of "atonality" and the twelve-tone technique; mention of the main musical ideas of the quartet.

See no. 206 (Johnson, Martha. A study of linear design, 1954).

599 Elston, Arnold. "Some rhythmic practices in contemporary music," MQ 42:318-329 (Jul 1956). Mus.
Webern, p. 325-329.

—First movement

See no. 569 (Eimert, Herbert. "Interval proportions: string quartet, first movement" in Anton Webern, 1955, 1958, p. 93-99 [Die Reihe, 2]).

—Second movement

See no. 569 (Stockhausen, Karlheinz. "Structure and experimental time" in Anton Webern, 1955, 1958, p. 64-74 [Die Reihe, 2]).

Quintet, piano and strings (1907)

600 Newlin, Dika. "Music reviews; Anton von Webern: Quintet for string quartet and piano," <u>Notes</u> 10:674-675 (Sept 1953).
General comments about the structure and "style."

Sacred songs, op. 15
See his <u>Songs—op. 15</u>

Sätze für Streichquartet, op. 5
See his <u>Movements for string quartet, op. 5</u>

Songs

<u>See no. 590</u> (Stephan, Rudolf. "Über einige geistliche Kompositionen Anton von Weberns," Jul/Aug 1954).

<u>See no. 476</u> (Zeiger, Jean Wilson. Early expressionistic songs, 1959).

601 Mayer, Harry. "De liedkunst van Anton Webern," <u>Mens en melodie</u> 14:114-117 (Apr 1959). Mus., port.
A brief discussion of his songs.

—op. 4 (Five songs)
—op. 4:2

<u>See no. 476</u> (Zeiger, Jean Wilson. Early expressionistic songs, 1959).

—op. 15 (Five sacred songs)
—op. 15:4

<u>See no. 569</u> (Metzger, Heinz-Klaus. "Analysis of the sacred song, op. 15, no. 4" <u>in</u> Anton Webern, 1955, 1958, p. 75-80 [Die Reihe, 2]).

<u>See no. 476</u> (Zeiger, Jean Wilson. Early expressionistic songs, 1959).

—op. 23 (Three songs)

<u>See no. 526</u> (Bach, David Joseph. "New music by Berg, Webern, Krenek," Nov/Dec 1934).

String quartet, op. 28
See his <u>Quartet, strings, op. 28</u>

String quartet, Six bagatelles for
See his <u>Bagatelles for string quartet, op. 9</u>

Stücke für Orchester, op. 10
See his <u>Orchestral pieces, op. 10</u>

Three songs with piano accompaniment, op. 23
See his Songs—op. 23

Variations for orchestra, op. 30

See no. 584 (Vlad, Roman. "Anton von Webern e la composizione atematica," Apr/Jun 1955).

See no. 170 (Nono, Luigi. "Die Entwicklung der Reihentechnik" in Steinecke, Wolfgang, ed. Darmstädter Beiträge zur neuen Musik, 1958, p. 25-37).

Variations for piano, op. 27

See no. 155 (Ogdon, Wilbur Lee. Series and structure, 1955).

See no. 584 (Vlad, Roman. "Anton von Webern e la composizione atematica," Apr/Jun 1955).

See no. 57 (Stadlen, Peter. "Serialism reconsidered," Feb 1958).

See no. 59 (Gerhard, Roberto. "Apropos Mr. Stadlen," Jul 1958).

See no. 66 (Stadlen, Peter. "No real casualties?" Nov 1958).

—third movement

See no. 569 (Klammer, Armin. "Webern's Piano variations, op. 27, 3rd movement" in Anton Webern, 1955, 1958, p. 81-92 [Die Reihe, 2]).

IV
OTHER COMPOSERS

MILTON BABBITT

602   Bruno, Anthony. "Two American twelve-tone composers: Milton Babbitt and Ben Weber represent opposing views," <u>Musical America</u> 71:22, 170 (Feb 1951).
        Row technique as used by the two composers.

<u>See no. 99a</u> (Chase, Gilbert. "Twelve tone composers" <u>in his</u> America's music, 1955).

<u>See no. 204a</u> (Rochberg, George. "The harmonic tendency of the hexachord," Nov 1959).

All set

603   Gottlieb, Louis. "Brandeis festival album," <u>Jazz: a quarterly of American music</u>, no. 2:151-160 (Spring 1959). Mus.
        Brief serial analysis of <u>All set</u>, p. 152-156.

Quartet, woodwinds

604   Rochberg, George. "Music reviews; Milton Babbitt: Woodwind quartet in one movement," <u>Notes</u> 13:695-696 (Sept 1956).
        Capsule description of Babbitt's structural procedures.

LUCIANO BERIO

<u>See no. 106</u> (Pestalozza, Luigi. "I compositori milanesi del dopoguerra," Mar 1957).

605   "Luciano Berio," <u>Schw MZ</u> 97:233 (Jun 1957).
        Very brief list of works, with dates.

<u>See no. 112</u> (Prieberg, Fred K. Lexikon der neuen Musik, 1958, p. 42).

<u>See no. 116</u> (Vlad, Roman. Storia della dodecafonia, 1958, p. 262-263, 268).

<u>See no. 118a</u> (Zillig, Winfried. "Die Jungen: Stockhausen, Boulez, Nono, Berio" <u>in his</u> Variationen über neuen Musik, 1959, p. 190-199).

See no. 637 (Metzger, Heinz-Klaus. "John Cage o della liberazione," Aug 1959).

Alleluia

606 Berio, Luciano. "Aspetti di artigianato formale," Incontri musicali 1:55-69 (Dec 1956). Mus.
    A detailed explanation of the organizing principles of this work.

607 Thomas, Ernst. "Ein 'Allelujah' aus dem Jahre 1956," NZfM 118: 433-434 (Jul/Aug 1957).
    A very brief review, giving some background on Berio.

Nones

See no. 168 (Santi, Piero. "Luciano Berio" in Junge Komponisten, 1958, p. 98-102 [Die Reihe, 4]).

608 Smith Brindle, Reginald. "Current chronicle: Italy," MQ 44:95-101 (Jan 1958). Mus.
    An explanation of the principle of "total control," with examples drawn from the beginning of the work.

Quartet, string

See no. 168 (Santi, Piero. "Luciano Berio" in Junge Komponisten, 1958, p. 98-102 [Die Reihe, 4]).

Sequenza per flauto solo

See no. 71 (Eco, Umberto. "L'opera in movimento e la coscienza dell'epoca," Aug 1959).

Thema: Omaggio a Joyce

609 Berio, Luciano. "Poesie e musica—un'esperienza," Incontri musicali, no. 3:98-111 (Aug 1959). Diagrs.
    Experiments in new means of combining text and music; Berio's setting of the begginning of the 11th chapter of Joyce's Ulysses (see no. 174).

PIERRE BOULEZ

GENERAL

610 Goldbeck, Frederick. "Current chronicle: France," MQ 36:291-295 (Apr 1950). Mus.
    One of the first articles on "totally controlled" serial music.

611 Scriabine, Marina. "Pierre Boulez et la musique concrète" in Les carnets critiques. Paris, Richard-Masse [1952], p. 14-15. (La revue musicale, no. 215.)
   Boulez as organizer of electronic experiments in the Paris Studio.

612 Goldbeck, Fred E. "Boulez, Pierre" in Grove's Dictionary of music and musicians. 5th ed. London, Macmillan, 1954, v. 1: 844.
   Includes a very brief list of selected works.

See no. 29 (Goléa, Antoine. Esthétique de la musique contemporaine, 1954, p. 176-189, 193).

See no. 30 (La musique et ses problèmes contemporains, 1954, p. 3-24).

See no. 98 (Myers, Rollo H. "Music in France in the post-war decade," 1954/55).

613 Myers, Rollo H. "Some personalities and trends in contemporary French music," Chesterian 30:14-18 (Jul 1955).
   Boulez, p. 16-17.

614 Hodeir, Andre. "The young French music," Saturday review 40:41-42, 53 (May 25, 1957), tr. by David Noakes. Port.
   Brief summary of Boulez's musical philosophy, p. 42, 53.

615 Goléa, Antoine. Rencontres avec Pierre Boulez, avec trois hors-texte. Paris, R. Julliard [1958]. 259 p. Port., facsims., mus.
   A lengthy discussion of Boulez's life, works, compositional techniques, and aesthetics. Difficult to use: no table of contents, chapter headings, or index.

See no. 112 (Prieberg, Fred K. Lexicon der neuen Musik, 1958, p. 53-55).

See no. 116 (Vlad, Roman. Storia della dodecafonia, 1958, p. 257-261).

616 Lesure, François. "Profili di musicisti contemporanei," Musica d'oggi 1:19-21 (Jan 1958).
   Principally a discussion of his musical philosophy; includes a list of works.

See no. 118a (Zillig, Winfried. "Die Jungen: Stockhausen, Boulez, Nono, Berio" in his Variationen über neuen Musik, 1959, p. 190-199).

See no. 637 (Metzger, Heinz-Klaus. "John Cage o della liberazione," Aug 1959).

COMPOSITIONAL TECHNIQUES

See no. 208 (Boulez, Pierre. "Propositions" in Le rythme musical, 1948, p. 65-72 [Polyphonie, 2^e cahier]).

617 Cowell, Henry. "Current chronicle: New York," MQ 38:132-134 (Jan 1952). Illus., mus.
   Boulez's serial technique and its relation to the experiments of John Cage.

See no. 150 (Krenek, Ernst. "Is the twelve-tone technique on the decline?" Oct 1953).
    Discusses Boulez's Piano sonata no. 2 and his Polyphonie X.

618 Barraqué, Jean. "Rythme et développement" in Inventaire des techniques rédactionnelles. Paris, Richard-Masse [1954], p. 47-73. (Polyphonie, 9e/10e cahier.)
    Boulez, p. 63-73. Examples from his Piano sonata no. 2, String quartet, and Polyphonie pour 18 instruments.

INDIVIDUAL WORKS

Le marteau sans maître

619 Saathen, Friedrich. "'Le Marteau sans maître' von Pierre Boulez," Schw MZ 97:289-290 (Jul 1957).
    Not an analysis. Discusses Boulez's musical philosophy. Includes a German translation of the text of 'Le marteau.'

See no. 170 (Stockhausen, Karlheinz. "Sprache und Musik" in Steinecke, Wolfgang, ed. Darmstädter Beiträge zur neuen Musik, 1958, p. 57-81).

620 Mason, Colin. "Reviews of music," M & L 39:198-199 (Apr 1958). Mus.
    Brief review, indicating the rhythmic complexity of the work.

621 Craft, Robert. "Boulez and Stockhausen," Score, no. 24:54-62 (Nov 1958).
    "Notes written in the course of preparing a record . . . for American Columbia." Principally discusses influences and structure.

622 Skulsky, Abraham. "After Webern, who?" American record guide 23:316-319 (Jan 1959). Illus.
    Description for the layman of Boulez's and Stockhausen's compositional techniques; review of the recording.

L'Orestie

623 Rostand, Claude, "La musique de scène de Pierre Boulez pour 'L'Orestie' d'Eschyle," Schw MZ 96:11-13 (Jan 1956). Mus.
    Discusses declamation of the text and theatrical effect.

Poésie pour pouvoir

624 Heck, Ludwig. "Klänge in Schmelztiegel," Melos 25:320-329 (Oct 1958). Diagrs., illus.
    Technological problems encountered in setting up Boulez's Poésie pour pouvoir, a piece combining three orchestras and electronically produced sounds.

625 Wörner, Karl H. "Current chronicle: Germany," MQ 45:239-241 (Apr 1959).
    A brief description of the work.

Polyphonie X for 18 solo instruments

626 Morton, Lawrence. "Los Angeles letter," Counterpoint 17:33-34 (Nov 1952).
    A review and general summary.

Sonatas, piano
—no. 2

627 Demuth, Norman. French piano music; a survey with notes on its performance. London, Museum Press [c1959]. 179 p. Mus.
    Boulez, p. 152-156; a brief description of the Sonata.

—no. 3

628 Ligeti, György. "Zur III. Klaviersonate von Boulez" in Berichte/Analysen. Wien, Universal Edition [c1959], p. 38-40. (Die Reihe, 5.)
    Very brief; no musical examples.

Sonatina, flute and piano

629 Pestalozzi, Luigi. "Vita musicale: musiche nuovissime," Rass mus 26:298-299 (Oct 1956).
    Review of the first concert of the Incontri Musicali in Milan.

Structures, for two pianos, four hands

630 Vlad, Roman. "Recensioni: Pierre Boulez, Structures per 2 pianoforti a 4 mani," Rass mus 26:153-155 (Apr 1956).
    General review; not an analysis.

See no. 170 (Nono, Luigi. "Die Entwicklung der Reihentechnik" in Steinecke, Wolfgang, ed. Darmstädter Beiträge zur neuen Musik, 1958, p. 25-37).

—no. 1a

See no. 168 (Ligeti, György. "Pierre Boulez" in Junge Komponisten, 1958, p. 38-63 [Die Reihe, 4]).

631 Wilkinson, Mark. "Pierre Boulez' 'Structure 1a': Bemerkungen zur Zwölfton-technik/Some thoughts on twelve-tone method," Gravesaner Blätter, Heft 10:12-29 (1958). Tables.
    In German (p. 12-18) and English (p. 23-29). An analysis of the serial technique in the Structure 1a.

JOHN CAGE

632   Cowell, Henry. "Current chronicle: New York," MQ 38:123-127 (Jan 1952).
        Cage's rhythmic structural principles. Discusses his Imaginary landscape and Music of changes. Influences on Morton Feldman and Pierre Boulez.

633   Glanville-Hicks, Peggy. "Cage, John" in Grove's Dictionary of music and musicians. 5th ed. London, Macmillan, 1954, v. 2:16-17.
        Includes a list of his works.

See no. 29 (Goléa, Antoine. Esthétique de la musique contemporaine, 1954, p. 183-184).

634   Curjel, Hans. "Cage oder das wohlpräparierte Klavier," Melos 22:97-100 (Apr 1955). Illus., port.
        One of the few articles attempting to evaluate Cage's experiments seriously.

635   Cage, John. "Experimental music," Score, no. 12:65-68 (Jun 1955).
        Rather whimsical article in dialogue form, discussing Cage's style.

See no. 253 (Boulez, Pierre. "Tendances de la musique récente" in Vers une musique expérimentale, 1957, p. 28-35).

See no. 112 (Prieberg, Fred K. Lexikon der neuen Musik, 1958, p. 67-68).

636   Maren, Roger. "The musical numbers game," Reporter 18:37-39 (Mar 6, 1958).
        The compositional philosophies of Cage and of Stockhausen.

See no. 63 (Porena, Boris. "L'avanguardia musicale di Darmstadt," Sept 1958).

637   Metzger, Heinz-Klaus. "John Cage o della liberazione," Incontri musicali, no. 3:16-31 (Aug 1959), tr. by Sylvano Bussotti.
        Cage's aesthetic philosophy; freedom of choice for the performer in Cage's works; similar techniques in Stockhausen, Boulez, Berio, Pousseur.

Music for piano 21-52

See no. 166 (Cage, John. "To describe the process of composition used in 'Music for piano 21-52'" in Musical craftsmanship, 1957, 1959, p. 41-43 [Die Reihe, 3]).

Sonata, piano, no. 4

See no. 87 (Thomson, Virgil. "Atonality today," Nov 1951).

LUIGI DALLAPICCOLA

GENERAL

638 Searle, Humphrey. "Luigi Dallapiccola," Listener 40:780 (Nov 18, 1948).
Brief discussion of some of his works; his background and influences.

639 Skulsky, Abraham. "Dallapiccola felt impelled to introduce a new romantic era," Musical America 69:6, 40-41 (May 1949). Port.
Brief discussion of his life and works.

640 Dallapiccola, Luigi. "Sulla strada della dodecafonia," Aut aut 1:30-45 (Jan 1951).

———. "On the twelve-note road," Mus sur 4:318-332 (Oct 1951).
Dallapiccola's account of his adoption of the twelve-tone technique; the character of dodecaphony (especially compared with literary techniques, e.g., Joyce and Proust).

641 Mila, Massimo. "Dallapiccola, Luigi" in Die Musik in Geschichte und Gegenwart. Kassel, Bärenreiter, 1952. v. 2, col. 1874-1875, tr. by Anna Amalie Abert. Mus.
Includes a bibliography and a list of works.

642 Amico, Fedele d'. "Luigi Dallapiccola," Melos 20:69-74 (Mar 1953). Illus., port.
Biographical sketch; general discussion of his works and style, through 1952.

643 Gatti, Guido M. "Dallapiccola, Luigi" in Grove's Dictionary of music and musicians. 5th ed. London, Macmillan, 1954, v. 2:582-583.
Includes a list of his works; no bibliography.

See no. 29 (Goléa, Antoine. Esthétique de la musique contemporaine, 1954, p. 143-147).

See no. 151 ("Contemporary composers on their experiences of composition with twelve notes: Luigi Dallapiccola" in Rufer, Josef. Composition with twelve notes, 1954, p. 178-181).

See no. 100 (Collaer, Paul. La musique moderne, 1905-1955. 1955, p. 272-274).

See no. 105 (Smith Brindle, Reginald. "Italian contemporary music" in Hartog, Howard, ed. European music in the twentieth century, 1957, p. 176-181).

See no. 112 (Prieberg, Fred K. Lexikon der neuen Musik, 1958, p. 87-90).

See no. 115 (Stuckenschmidt, Hans Heinz. Schöpfer der neuen Musik, 1958, p. 228-240).

See no. 118a (Zillig, Winfried. "Die Erneuerung der italienischen Musik von Malipiero bis Dallapiccola" in his Variationen über neue Musik, 1959, p. 165-173).

GENERAL DESCRIPTIONS OF WORKS

644 Paoli, Domenico de. "Chroniques et notes; Italie: Luigi Dallapiccola," Rev mus 16:65-67 (Jun 1935).
Brief general article on Dallapiccola's early works.

645 "Voci aggiunte a un dizionario dei musicisti italiani contemporanei: Luigi Dallapiccola," Rass mus 9/10:284-285 (Sept/Oct 1936) and 20:40-41 (Jan 1950).
A list of his works.

646 Ballo, Ferdinando. "Le musiche chorali di Dallapiccola," Rass mus 10:136-141 (Apr 1937).
The early choral works; a general essay, not an analysis.

647 "Un musicien d'aujourd'hui: Luigi Dallapiccola" in Le théâtre musical. Paris, Richard-Masse [1947/48]. (Polyphonie, 1er cahier.) Mus., port.
Contents: "Chronologie et portrait," p. 135-138 (gives dates of performances); Dallapiccola, Luigi, "Notes sur mon opéra," p. 139-142 (on Il prigioniero); "Bibliographie," p. 143-146 (list of compositions with dates of first performance, timings, and publishers); "Supplement musical hors-texte: 'La canzona dei Pezzenti,' extraite de 'Il prigioniero,' opéra de L. Dallapiccola."

648 Vlad, Roman. "Luigi Dallapiccola," Horizon [London] 20:379-391 (Dec 1949/Jan 1950), tr. by Toni del Renzio.
A discussion of his works through the Due pezzi.

649 Gavazzeni, Gianandrea. Musicisti d'Europa: studi sui contemporanei. [Milano] Suvini Zerboni [1954]. 275 p.
A collection of critical essays on various composers. Studi su Dallapiccola, p. 191-224: "Cori e laudi" (1937), p. 191-201; "Dai Canti di prigionia a Rencesvals" (1946), p. 202-218; "Il piccolo concerto per Muriel Couvreux" (1943), p. 219-224.

650 Valentin, Erich. "Klassiker aus antikem Geist: Luigi Dallapiccola fünfzig Jahre," ZfM 115:94-95 (Feb 1954).
A brief survey of his works.

See no. 35 (Vlad, Roman. Modernità e tradizione nella musica contemporanea, 1955, p. 197-211).

651 Vlad, Roman. "Dallapiccola, 1948-55," Score, no. 15:39-62 (Mar 1956). Mus.
A continuation of the survey of Dallapiccola's works (begun in his article in Horizon; see no. 648) through the cantata An Mathilde (1955). Includes a complete score of Dallapiccola's Improvisation after Tartini, for violin and piano, p. 56-62.

652 Vlad, Roman. Luigi Dallapiccola. Tr. by Cynthia Jolly. Milano, Suvini Zerboni, 1957. 62 p. Mus.
Biographical sketch, p. 60; list of works, p. 61-62. A translation of the Dallapiccola chapter from his Storia della dodecafonia (see no. 116), p. 275-314.

653 Nathan, Hans. "The twelve-tone compositions of Luigi Dallapiccola," MQ 44:289-310 (Jul 1958). Mus.
   A list of his "completely dodecaphonic" compositions, p. 309-310. A general discussion, with musical illustrations, of Dallapiccola's style and the main influences that have shaped it.

654 Basart, Ann P. The twelve-tone compositions of Luigi Dallapiccola. (Thesis, M.A., University of California, 1960.) iii + 117 l. Mus.
   Contents: "Il prigioniero," p. 7-29; "Quaderno musicale di Annalibera," p. 30-55; "Canti di liberazione," p. 56-78; "Cinque canti per baritono," p. 79-99; "Conclusions," p. 110-113. Primarily an analysis.

INDIVIDUAL WORKS

An Mathilde

655 Mila, Massimo. "L'incontro Heine-Dallapiccola," Rass mus 27:301-308 (Dec 1957). Mus.
   Somewhat extensive analysis, with emphasis on the textual meaning as reflected in the music.

Canti di liberazione

See no. 161 (Smith Brindle, Reginald. "The lunatic fringe, III: computational composition," Jul 1956).

656 Vlad, Roman. "Vita musicale: Roma," Rass mus 27:54-55 (Mar 1957).
   Gives some background of the text; a general review.

657 Smith Brindle, Reginald. "Current chronicle: Italy," MQ 43:240-245 (Apr 1957). Mus.
   Emphasis on the rhythmic structure.

658 Drew, David. "The arts and entertainment: Dallapiccola," New statesman 57:363-365 (Mar 14, 1959).
   Discusses the Canti di liberazione in relation to the other works of his trilogy on prisoners and freedom.

See no. 654 (Basart, Ann P. "Canti di liberazione" in her The twelve-tone compositions of Luigi Dallapiccola, 1960, p. 56-78).

Canti di prigionia

659 Amico, Fedele d'. "'Canti di prigionia,'" Società [Roma] 1:95-100 (Jan/Jun 1945).
   Philosophical background of the work.

See no. 669 (Goldman, Richard Franco. "Current chronicle: New York," Jul 1951).

660 Morton, Lawrence. "Los Angeles letter," Counterpoint 18:35-36 (Feb 1953).
A brief review.

See no. 670 (Dallapiccola, Luigi. "The genesis of the Canti di prigionia and Il prigioniero," Jul 1953).

Cinque canti per baritono

661 Wildberger, Jacques. "Dallapiccolas 'Cinque Canti,'" Melos 26:7-10 (Jan 1959). Mus.
Brief analysis, especially of serial and rhythmic structure.

See no. 654 (Basart, Ann P. "Cinque canti per baritono" in her The twelve-tone compositions of Luigi Dallapiccola, 1960, p. 79-99).

Greek lyrics
See his Liriche greche

Improvisation after Tartini, for violin and piano

See no. 651 (Vlad, Roman. "Dallapiccola, 1948-55," Mar 1956, p. 56-62).

Job, una sacra rappresentazione

662 Wörner, Karl H. "Dallapiccolas Job," Melos 21:208-210 (Jul/Aug 1954). Mus.
An excellent article on the musical structure and on the implications of the drama. Gives, however, an incorrect quotation of the principal twelve-note row.

663 Skulsky, Abraham. "Opera, 1954," Juilliard review 2:34-43 (Winter, 1955). Mus.
Job, p. 37-38. Brief summary of the musical and dramatic structure; one page from the full score is reproduced.

Liriche greche

664 Amico, Fedele d'. "Recensioni: Luigi Dallapiccola," Rass mus 17:165-170 (Apr 1947).
A general review; no musical examples.

Marsia

665 Gatti, Guido M. "Current chronicle: Italy," MQ 35:136-139 (Jan 1949). Mus.
Review of a performance at Venice; background of the work, brief sketch of the central dramatic and musical ideas.

666 Smith Brindle, Reginald. "Current chronicle: Italy," MQ 41:524-526 (Oct 1955).
Gives a capsule idea of the character of this ballet.

Orchestral variations
See his <u>Variations for orchestra</u>

Il prigioniero

<u>See no. 647</u> (Dallapiccola, Luigi. "Notes sur mon opéra" <u>in</u> Le théâtre musical, 1947/48, p. 139-142 [Polyphonie, 1]).

667 Keller, Hans. "XIII Maggio musicale fiorentino," <u>Mus rev</u> 11:211 (Aug 1950).
   A psychological approach to the text.

668 Mila, Massimo. "'Il prigioniero' di Luigi Dallapiccola," <u>Rass mus</u> 20:303-311 (Oct 1950). Mus.
   Background of the libretto; discussion of the music, including row technique.

669 Goldman, Richard F. "Current chronicle, New York," <u>MQ</u> 37:405-410 (Jul 1951). Mus.
   A comparison of the opera with the Canti di prigionia; discussion of the text and the musical materials.

670 Dallapiccola, Luigi. "The genesis of the Canti di prigionia and Il prigioniero: an autobiographical fragment," <u>MQ</u> 39:355-372 (Jul 1953), tr. by Jonathan Schiller. Port.
   The origins of the central ideas of these works from literature and from events in Dallapiccola's life.

671 Rufer, Josef. "Luigi Dallapiccola: Il prigioniero" <u>in</u> Oper im XX. Jahrhundert. Bonn, Boosey & Hawkes [c1954], p. 56-64. Illus., mus. (Musik der Zeit: eine Schriftenreihe zur zeitgenössischen Musik, 6.)
   Brief background on the development of Italian music in the 20th century; sketch of the plot and of the central musical ideas of Il prigioniero.

672 Mason, Colin. "Dallapiccola and the twelve-note method," <u>Listener</u> 51:757 (Apr 29, 1954).
   The use of dodecaphony in Il prigioniero.

<u>See no. 35</u> (Vlad, Roman. "'Il prigioniero'" in his Modernità e tradizione nella musica contemporanea, 1955, p. <u>212-216</u>).

<u>See no. 654</u> (Basart, Ann P. "Il prigioniero" <u>in her</u> The twelve-tone compositions of Luigi Dallapiccola, 1960, p. <u>7-29</u>).

Quaderno musicale di Annalibera
See also his <u>Variations for orchestra</u>

673 Keller, Hans. "The half-year's new music," <u>Mus rev</u> 15:214-215 (Aug 1954).
   An outline sketch of the form and techniques used.

<u>See no. 654</u> (Basart, Ann P. "Quaderno musicale di Annalibera" <u>in her</u> The twelve-tone compositions of Luigi Dallapiccola, 1960, p. 30-55).

Songs of imprisonment
    See his Canti di prigionia

Songs of liberation
    See his Canti di liberazione

Variations for orchestra
    See also his Quaderno musicale di Annalibera

674 Herz, Gerhard. "Current chronicle: Louisville, Kentucky," MQ 41:79-85 (Jan 1955). Mus.
    A brief analysis of each variation.

WOLFGANG FORTNER

675 Stephan, Rudolf. "Gegenwärtiges Komponieren; Ein Überblick: Fortner, Pepping, Orff, Egk, Hartmann," Dt Univ Zt 6:12-15 (Sept 28, 1951).
    A brief characterization of each composer's style.

See no. 703 (Stuckenschmidt, Hans Heinz. "Synthesis and new experiments: four contemporary German composers," Jul 1952).

676 Wörner, Karl H. "Wolfgang Fortner in seinen Werken seit 1945," Schw MZ 93:260-263 (Jun 1953).
    Discussion of Fortner's works and style, 1945-1953.

See no. 151 ("Contemporary composers on their experiences of composition with twelve notes: Wolfgang Fortner" in Rufer, Josef. Composition with twelve notes, 1954, p. 181-183).

See no. 95 (Wörner, Karl H. Neue Musik in der Entscheidung, 1954, p. 101-104).

677 Laaff, Ernst. "Wolfgang Fortner," Melos 21:307-310 (Nov 1954). Port.
    List of works, p. 309-310. Brief summary of life and works.

678 Friedländer, Walther. "Moderner Kompositionsunterricht bei Wolfgang Fortner an der nordwestdeutschen Musikakademie," NZfM 116:113-114 (Nov 1955).
    Fortner as a teacher of composition.

679 Helm, Everett. "Six modern German composers," American-German review 23:12-15 (Dec 1956/Jan 1957).
    Wolfgang Fortner: p. 13-14; Hans Werner Henze: p. 14-15. Very brief summaries of style and works.

680 Driesch, Kurt. "Wolfgang Fortner: Zum fünfzigsten Geburtstag des deutschen Komponisten," Geist und Zeit [Düsseldorf], no. 6:119-124 (1957).
    General discussion of life and works.

See no. 112 (Prieberg, Fred K. Lexikon der neuen Musik, 1958, p. 139-142).

See no. 116 (Vlad, Roman. Storia della dodecafonia, 1958, p. 146-147).

See no. 118a (Zillig, Winfried. "Neue Musik in Deutschland" in his Variationen über neue Musik, 1959, p. 254-263).

Bluthochzeit

681   Fortner, Wolfgang. "Bluthochzeit nach Federico Garcia Lorca," Melos 24:71-73 (Mar 1957). Illus.
     A description of the drama, by the composer.

Concerto, violin

682   Helm, Everett. "Current chronicle: Germany," MQ 38:606-610 (Oct 1952). Mus.
     Brief summary; gives some themes and motives.

Fantasy for two pianos and orchestra on BACH

683   Helm, Everett. "Current chronicle: Germany," MQ 37:267-269 (Apr 1951). Mus.
     Shows how Fortner treats the "BACH" motive throughout.

684   Engelmann, Hans Ulrich. "Fortners Phantasie über B-A-C-H," Melos 21:131-135 (May 1954). Mus.
     Analysis, especially of serial and rhythmic aspects.

Impromptus

684a Dangel, Arthur. "Wolfgang Fortner [Impromptus]," Melos 27:79-84 (Mar 1960) and 27:107-112 (Apr 1960). Mus.
     Serial analyses.

Kammermusik

See no. 213 (Unger, Udo. "Analyse von W. Fortners Fuge aus 'Kammermusik,' komp. 1943" in his Die Klavierfuge im zwanzigsten Jahrhundert, 1956, p. 91-92).

ROBERTO GERHARD

See no. 88 (Mitchell, Donald. "The emancipation of the dissonance," 1952, p. 144).

685   Mason, Colin. "Gerhard, Roberto" in Grove's Dictionary of music and musicians. 5th ed., London, Macmillan, 1954, v. 3:599-601.
     Includes a list of works (no bibliography).

See no. 151 ("Contemporary composers on their experiences of composition with twelve notes: Roberto Gerhard" in Rufer, Josef. Composition with twelve notes, 1954, p. 183-185).

686   Redlich, Hans Ferdinand. "Gerhard, Roberto" in Die Musik in Geschichte und Gegenwart. Kassel, Bärenreiter, 1955, v. 4, col. 1786-1787.
Includes a list of his works and a bibliography.

687   Drew, David. "Roberto Gerhard: the musical character," Score, no. 17:39-49 (Sept 1956). Mus.
Biography and a discussion of his works.

See no. 163 (Gerhard, Roberto. "Developments in twelve-tone technique," Sept 1956).

688   "Roberto Gerhard: catalog of works," Score, no. 17:54-60 (Sept 1956).

689   Vlad, Roman. "My first impressions of Roberto Gerhard's music," Score, no. 17:27-38 (Sept 1956). Mus.
Includes the score of the Capriccio movement of the String quartet. Discusses the general characteristics of Gerhard's music; analyzes his Symphony and String quartet.

See no. 116 (Vlad, Roman. Storia della dodecafonia, 1958, p. 137-144).

690   Mason, Colin. "A Spanish composer in exile," Listener 60:484 (Sept 25, 1958).
Brief survey of his life and works.

Concerto, violin

691   del Mar, Norman. "Gerhard as an orchestral composer," Score, no. 17:13-19 (Sept 1956). Mus.
Analyses of his ballet suite, Don Quixote; Symphony, Homenaje a Pedrell; and Violin concerto.

Don Quixote (ballet suite)

See no. 691 (del Mar, Norman. "Gerhard as an orchestral composer," Sept 1956).

The Duenna

692   Gardner, John. "The Duenna (1945-47)," Score, no. 17:20-26 (Sept 1956). Mus.
Synopsis of the story and a brief analysis of the music.

Homenaje a Pedrell (symphony)

See no. 691 (del Mar, Norman. "Gerhard as an orchestral composer," Sept 1956).

See no. 689 (Vlad, Roman. "My first impressions of Roberto Gerhard's music," Sept 1956).

Quartet, string

See no. 689 (Vlad, Roman. "My first impressions of Roberto Gerhard's music," Sept 1956).

Symphony
See his Homenaje a Pedrell

JOSEF MATTHIAS HAUER

See no. 126 (Hauer, Josef Matthias. Vom Wesen des Musikalischen, 1923).

See no. 127 (Hauer, Josef Matthias. "Atonale Musik," Nov 1923).

See no. 129 (Hauer, Josef Matthias. Von Melos zur Pauke, 1925).

See no. 130 (Hauer, Josef Matthias. Zwölftontechnik, die Lehre von den Tropen, 1926).

693   Stuckenschmidt, Hans Heinz. "Josef Matthias Hauer," Musikblätter des Anbruch 10:245-249 (Aug/Sept 1928).
      Discussion of his music and his theories.

694   Machabey, Armand. "La singulière figure de Jean-Mathias Hauer, musicien autrichien," Rev mus 12:221-233 (Mar 1931). Mus.
      Discussion of his theories and his compositions.

695   Reich, Willi. "Josef Matthias Hauer," Die Musik 23:577-581 (May 1931). Mus., port.
      Discussion of his theories and his compositions; includes a facsimile of a page of his Salambo.

See no. 137 (Eschman, Karl. Changing forms in modern music, 1945).

See no. 82 (Salazar, Adolfo. Music in our time, 1946).

See no. 83 (Schlee, Alfred. "Vienna since the Anschluss," Spring 1946).

See no. 297 (Bauer, Marion. "Schoenberg and his innovation" in her Twentieth century music, 1947, p. 207-230).

696   Schmale, Erich. "Die Zwölftonmusik von Josef Matthias Hauer," Schw MZ 88:305-306 (Jul 1948).
      Brief bibliography, p. 306. An explanation of Hauer's system of tropes.

697   Eisenmann, Will. "Zur Sache Hauer," Schw MZ 88:353-354 (Sept 1948).
      A reply to Schmale's article (see no. 696).

See no. 89 (Reich, Willi. "Versuch einer Geschichte der Zwölftonmusik" in Alte und neue Musik, 1952, p. 106-132).

See no. 27 (Pfrogner, Hermann. Die Zwölfordnung der Töne, 1953, p. 184-232).

698   Redlich, Hans Ferdinand. "Hauer, Josef (Matthias)" in Grove's Dictionary of music and musicians, 5th ed., London, Macmillan, 1954, v. 4:135-137.
   Includes a list of works and a very brief bibliography.

See no. 153 (Searle, Humphrey. "Twelve-note music" in Grove's Dictionary of music and musicians, 5th ed., London, Macmillan, 1954, 8:617-623).

699   Mila, Massimo. "Lettera da Venezia," Rass mus 24:352 (Oct/Dec 1954).
   Capsule résumé of Hauer's system of tropes.

See no. 196 (Perle, George. "The harmonic problem in twelve-tone music," Nov 1954).

700   Eimert, Herbert. "Hauer, Josef Matthias" in Die Musik in Geschichte und Gegenwart. Kassel, Bärenreiter, 1956. v. 5, col. 1823. Mus.
   Bibliography and list of works.

See no. 164 (Simbriger, Heinrich. "Die Situation der Zwölftonmusik," Sept/Oct 1956).

701   Schwieger, Johannes. "Josef Matthias Hauer," ÖMZ 12:108-109 (Mar 1957). Port.
   Brief discussion of the three periods, 1911, 1918, and 1920; his compositions are listed.

See no. 56 (Melichar, Alois. Musik in der Zwangsjacke, 1958).

See no. 112 (Prieberg, Fred K. Lexikon der neuen Musik, 1958, p. 185).

702   Wildgans, Friedrich. "Josef Matthias Hauer zum 75. Geburtstag," ÖMZ 13:108-110 (Mar 1958). Port.
   Hauer's theories and works.

See no. 204a (Rochberg, George. "The harmonic tendency of the hexachord," Nov 1959).

HANS WERNER HENZE

703   Stuckenschmidt, Hans Heinz. "Synthesis and new experiments: four contemporary German composers," MQ 38:353-368 (Jul 1952), tr. by Abram Loft. Mus.
   German version in Schw MZ 93:1-10 (Jan 1953); Italian translation in Rass mus 23:210-224 (Jul 1953).
   On Boris Blacher, Giselher Klebe, Wolfgang Fortner, and Hans Werner Henze (p. 364-368).

704 Bartlett, K. W. "Henze, Hans Werner" in Grove's Dictionary of music and musicians. 5th ed., London, Macmillan, 1954, v. 4:244-245.
   A list of his principal works is included.

See no. 679 (Helm, Everett. "Six modern German composers," Dec 1956/Jan 1957).

705 Stuckenschmidt, Hans Heinz. "Henze, Hans Werner" in Die Musik in Geschichte und Gegenwart. Kassel, Bärenreiter, 1957, v. 6, col. 176-179. Mus.
   List of works; reproduction of part of autograph of König Hirsch.

706 Stuckenschmidt, Hans Heinz. "Hans Werner Henze: Porträt eines Komponisten," NZfM 118:491-492 (Sept 1957). Port.
   Discussion of works and style. Reprinted in the author's Schöpfer der neuen Musik (see no. 115, p. 290-301).

See no. 112 (Prieberg, Fred K. Lexikon der neuen Musik, 1958, p. 187-189).

See no. 168 (Stephan, Rudolf. "Hans Werner Henze" in Junge Komponisten, 1958, p. 32-37 [Die Reihe, 4]).

See no. 116 (Vlad, Roman. Storia della dodecafonia, 1958, p. 148-150).

See no. 118a (Zillig, Winfried. "Neue Musik in Deutschland: Pepping, Genzmer, Fortner, Henze, Klebe" in his Variationen über neue Musik, 1959, p. 254-263).

707 Helm, Everett. "Current chronicle: Germany," MQ 45:241-248 (Apr 1959). Mus.
   Includes biographical information and a discussion of his works and stylistic development.

708 Pauli, Hansjörg. "Hans Werner Henze's Italian music," Score, no. 25:26-37 (Jun 1959). Mus.
   Discussion of his works since 1953.

König Hirsch

709 Rostand, Claude. "König Hirsch de H. Werner Henze," La table ronde [Paris], no. 109:157-158 (Jan 1957).
   A brief description.

710 Stuckenschmidt, Hans Heinz. "'König Hirsch' (Re Cervo) di Hans Werner Henze," Rass mus 27:153-155 (Jun 1957).
   A brief description.

HANNS JELINEK

711 Fiechtner, Helmut A. "Hanns Jelinek," Melos 20:242-245 (Sept 1953). Port.
> List of his works, p. 244-245. A brief biographical sketch and discussion of his works and theories.

712 Krenek, Ernst. "Reviews of books," MQ 40:250-256 (Apr 1954).
> Reviews Jelinek's Anleitung zur Zwölftonkomposition (see no. 190) and briefly discusses his compositional technique and his works.

713 Wildgans, Friedrich. "Jelinek, Hanns" in Die Musik in Geschichte und Gegenwart. Kassel, Bärenreiter, 1957, v. 6, col. 1847-1849.
> Includes a list of his works and a brief bibliography.

See no. 112 (Prieberg, Fred K. Lexikon der neuen Musik, 1958, p. 221-222).

713a Redlich, Hans F. "Hanns Jelinek," Mus rev 21:66-72 (Feb 1960). Mus.
> Brief discussion of his works and of his theory of twelve-tone composition.

Symphonia brevis, op. 16

714 Blaukopf, Kurt. "Current chronicle: Austria," MQ 37:413-416 (Jul 1951). Mus.
> His method of using the twelve-tone technique.

Zwölftonwerk, op. 15

715 Tenschert, Roland. "Hanns Jelinek; zu seinem 'Zwölftonwerk, op. 15,'" Schw MZ 91:452-454 (Nov 1951). Mus.
> Brief biographical sketch; summary of dodecaphonic theories; analysis of op. 15, particularly regarding serial technique. Review of Jelinek's book (see no. 190).

See no. 190 (Jelinek, Hanns. Anleitung zur Zwölftonkomposition nebst allerlei Paralipomena, 1952).

See no. 151 ("Contemporary composers on their experiences of composition with twelve notes: Hanns Jelinek" in Rufer, Josef. Composition with twelve notes, 1954, p. 186-188).

GISELHER KLEBE

See no. 703 (Stuckenschmidt, Hans Heinz. "Synthesis and new experiments: four contemporary German composers," Jul 1952).

See no. 275 (Klebe, Giselher. "First practical work" in Electronic music, 1958, p. 17-18 [Die Reihe, 1]).

See no. 112 (Prieberg, Fred K. Lexikon der neuen Musik, 1958, p. 228-229).

See no. 118a (Zillig, Winfried. "Neue Musik in Deutschland: Pepping, Genzmer, Fortner, Henze, Klebe" in his Variationen über neue Musik, 1959, p. 254-263).

Elegia appassionata (piano trio)

716   Mann, Robert W. "Vita musicale: Stoccolma," Rass mus 26:141-142 (Apr 1956).
  Brief and general.

See no. 168 (Lewinsky, Wolf-Eberhard von. "Giselher Klebe" in Junge Komponisten, 1958, p. 89-97 [Die Reihe, 4]).

Quartet, string, op. 9

See no. 703 (Stuckenschmidt, Hans Heinz. "Synthesis and new experiments: four contemporary German composers," Jul 1952).

See no. 168 (Lewinsky, Wolf-Eberhard von. "Giselher Klebe" in Junge Komponisten, 1958, p. 89-97 [Die Reihe, 4]).

Die Räuber

717   Klebe, Giselher. "Über meine Oper 'Die Räuber,'" Melos 24:73-76 (Mar 1957). Mus.
  "Grundform und dominierende Gestaltungsordnungen; Charakteristik der vier Hauptpersonen."

718   Helm, Everett. "Operas by Egk, Klebe, and Fortner," Mus rev 18:226-228 (Aug 1957).
  Discussion of the libretto and the style of the music.

Die tödlichen Wünsche

719   Wörner, Karl H. "Current chronicle: Germany," MQ 46:80-83 (Jan 1960). Mus.
  A review of Klebe's second opera. A piano reduction of the Prelude (21 ms.) is included.

Trio, piano
See his Elegia appassionata

ERNST KRENEK

GENERAL

See no. 82 (Salazar, Adolfo. Music in our time, 1946).

720 Krenek, Ernst. Selbstdarstellung. Zürich, Atlantis [1948]. 66 p. Port.
List of his compositions, p. 63-66. "Keine Selbstbiographie, sondern der Versuch einer Selbstanalyse." Last chapter reprinted as "Der musikalische Fortschnitt," Melos 16:71-75 (Mar 1949). Port. (See no. 723.)

721 Krenek, Ernst. "Versuch einer Selbstanalyse: Vom 'Jonny' zur Zwölftonmusik," Melos 16:33-38 (Feb 1949).
Krenek discusses the development of his compositional technique in general terms.

See no. 88 (Mitchell, Donald. "The emancipation of the dissonance," 1952, p. 142-143).

722 Reich, Willi. "Ernst Krenek als Musikschriftsteller," Schw MZ [Ernst Krenek Heft] 93:113-114 (Mar 1953).
A summary of Krenek's thought, as expressed in his writings.

723 Krenek, Ernst. "Self-analysis," New Mexico quarterly 23:5-57 (Spring 1953). Mus., port.
List of works, with opus number, year, and publisher, p. 51-56; discography, p. 56-57. "Revised and considerably enlarged version of a work originally published in German under the title, Selbstdarstellung." (See no. 720.)

See no. 151 ("Contemporary composers on their experiences of composition with twelve notes: Ernst Krenek" in Rufer, Josef. Composition with twelve notes, 1954, p. 188-191).

See no. 95 (Wörner, Karl H. Neue Musik in der Entscheidung, 1954, p. 99-100).

724 Redlich, Hans Ferdinand. "Křenek, Ernst" in Grove's Dictionary of music and musicians. 5th ed., London, Macmillan, 1954, v. 4: 844-848.
Includes a bibliography and a list of his works.

725 Colucci, Matthew Joseph. A comparative study of contemporary musical theories in selected writings of Piston, Krenek, and Hindemith. [Ann Arbor, Mich., University Microfilms], 1957. 195 p. (University Microfilms, no. 23, 583.) (Thesis, Ph.D., music, University of Pennsylvania.)
Not seen; abstract in Dissertation Abstracts 17:2628 (1957). "Brief sketch of each composer's life; analysis of the musical theories."

726 Wörner, Karl H. "Krenek (Křenek), Ernst" in Die Musik in Geschichte und Gegenwart. Kassel, Bärenreiter, 1958, v. 7, col. 1759-1763.
Includes a list of his works.

See no. 118a (Zillig, Winfried. "Krenek, der Sucher" in his Variationen über neue Musik, 1959, p. 236-239).

727   Saathen, Friedrich. "Ernst Kŕeneks Botschaft im Wort." Schw MZ 99:45-50 (Feb 1959).
      Discusses Krenek's writings on music

GENERAL DESCRIPTIONS OF WORKS

728   Weissmann, Adolph. "Ernst Krenek," Modern music 6:17-23 (Nov/Dec 1928).
      An evaluation of Krenek's works through the late 1920's.

729   Preussner, Eberhard. "Ernst Krenek," Anbruch 11:154-159 (Apr 1929). Port.
      Discussion of works and style.

730   Redlich, Hans Ferdinand. "Heimat und Freiheit: zur Ideologie der jüngsten Werken Ernst Kreneks," Anbruch 13:54-58 (Feb 1930).
      A discussion of his works.

731   Schneider, J. Marius. "Ernst Krenek," Rev mus 11:126-134 (Aug/Sept 1930).
      A survey of his works and style.

732   Günther, Siegfried. "Der Kurs in Ernst Kreneks jungstem Schaffen," Die Musik 23:587-592 (May 1931).
      Krenek's works, op. 54-64; comparison with earlier works.

733   Erickson, Robert. "Krenek's later music (1930-1947)," Mus rev 9:29-44 (Feb 1948). Mus.
      Emphasis on row technique. A list of Krenek's works, 1930-Jan 1947, p. 43-44.

See no. 721 (Krenek, Ernst. "Versuch einer Selbstanalyse," Feb 1949).

734   Reich, Willi. "Ernst Kŕeneks Arbeit in der Zwölftontechnik," Schw MZ 89:49-53 (Feb 1949). Mus.
      Krenek's serial technique, especially his use of "modes" (six-note rows). Examples from his Sixth string quartet, his Lamentatio Jeremiae Prophetae, and his Sinfonischen Stück für Streichorchester.

735   Krenek, Ernst. "Kurzer Rechenschaftsbericht," Schw MZ 90:299-301 (Jun 1950).
      The use of a modified twelve-tone technique in his works, 1939-1950. Includes a list of his works of that period, p. 301.

736   Fiechtner, Helmut A. "Ernst Krenek," Musica 7:7-10 (Jan 1953). Port.
      Discussion of his works and of his various "periods" of composition. List of works, 1938-1952, p. 10.

737 Erickson, Robert. "Křeneks amerikanische texte," Schw MZ 93:104-108 (Mar 1953).
Krenek's settings of English texts (Five prayers, Cantata for wartime, Santa Fé timetable, Tarquin, Dark waters, etc.).

738 Krenek, Ernst. "Zu meinem Kammermusikwerken 1936-1950," Schw MZ [Ernst Krenek Heft] 93:102-104 (Mar 1953).
Primarily a discussion of row technique, in his Sixth and Seventh Quartets, Variations for piano, Sonatine for flute and clarinet, Sonata for viola solo, Lamentatio Jeremiae Prophetae, Third and Fourth Piano sonatas, and other chamber works.

See no. 155 (Ogdon, Wilbur Lee. Series and structure, 1955).

739 Joachim, Heinz. "Ernst Křenek," Schw MZ 95:1-5 (Jan 1955). Mus.
Includes a list of his works, 1948-1954. Analysis of the first movement of his Sonata for violin and piano, 1944/45.

See no. 116 (Vlad, Roman. Storia della dodecafonia, 1958, p. 133-136, 270-271).

739a Krenek, Ernst. "Extents and limits of serial techniques," MQ [special issue on the Princeton Seminar in Advanced Musical Studies] 46:210-232 (Apr 1960). Diagrs., mus.
The principles of serial rotation, indeterminacy, and other techniques, especially in Krenek's Lamentatio Jeremiae Prophetae; Kette, Kreis und Spiegel; Spiritus intelligentiae, sanctus; Sestina; and Sechs Vermessene.

INDIVIDUAL WORKS

Cantata, op. 72

See no. 526 (Bach, David Joseph. "New music by Berg, Webern, Krenek," Nov/Dec 1934).

Five prayers
See his Prayers, Five

Five short pieces for strings
See his Pieces for strings, Five

Invention for flute and clarinet

740 Schuh, Willi. "Zu Ernst Kreneks Invention," Schw MZ [Ernst Krenek Heft] 93:115 (Mar 1953). Mus.
Includes a facsimile of the entire piece. This brief composition was written especially for the Schw MZ and is "ein einfaches Beispiel für die 'klassische' Reihentechnik." A short row analysis is given.

See no. 31 (Burkhard, Willy. "Versuch einer kritischen Auseinandersetzung mit der Zwölftontechnik," Mar 1954).

Kette, Kreis und Spiegel

741   Reich, Willi. "Musica-Bericht: Krenek und Martinu," Musica 12:161 (Mar 1958).
        Very brief explanation of the row technique used.

See no. 739a (Krenek, Ernst. "Extents and limits of serial techniques," Apr 1960).

Lamentatio Jeremiae Prophetae

See no. 206 (Johnson, Martha. A study of linear design in Gregorian chant and music written in the twelve-tone technique, 1954).

See no. 52 (Rössler, Ernst Karl. "Zeitgenössische Kirchenmusik und christliche Gemeinde," Jan/Feb 1957).

742   Vellekoop, Gerrit. "De 'Lamentatio Jeremiae Prophetae' van Ernst Krsjenek," Mens en melodie 13:326-329 (Nov 1958). Mus.
        Illustrates Krenek's use of hexachords.

See no. 739a (Krenek, Ernst. "Extents and limits of serial techniques," Apr 1960).

Pallas Athene weint

743   Koegler, Horst. "The international scene: Hamburg," Musical courier 152:27-28 (Nov 15, 1955). Illus.
        Capsule description of the plot and the musical structure.

744   Joachim, Heinz. "Current chronicle: Germany," MQ 42:92-98 (Jan 1956). Mus.
        General summation of Krenek's work and importance; the plot of the opera and the character of its music.

Pieces for strings, Five

See no. 46 (Kelterborn, Rudolf. "Stilistisch gegensätzliche Entwicklungen auf der Basis der Zwölftontechnik," Apr 1956).

Prayers, Five

745   Ogdon, Wilbur Lee. "The twelve-tone series and cantus firmus: a discussion of Ernst Krenek's 'Five Prayers,'" BAMS 11/13:86-88 (1948).
        An abstract only.

Quartets, string
—no. 1

746   Evans, Edwin. "Krenek, Ernst" in Cobbett, Walter W. Cobbett's cyclopedic survey of chamber music. London, Oxford University Press, 1929/30, p. 76-79. Mus.
A brief description of the first and third String quartets.

—no. 3

See no. 746 (Evans, Edwin. "Krenek, Ernst," 1929/30).

—no. 6

See no. 484 (Leibowitz, René. "Les nouvelles générations de compositeurs 'dodécaphonistes' et leurs caractéristiques générales" in his Introduction à la musique de douze sons, 1949, p. 255-259).

Sestina

747   Krenek, Ernst. "Sestina," Melos 7/8:235-238 (Jul/Aug 1958). Mus.
A quite technical analysis by the composer. The complete poem is quoted on p. 238.

See no. 739a (Krenek, Ernst. "Extents and limits of serial techniques," Apr 1960).

Sonata for violin and piano
—first movement

See no. 739 (Joachim, Heinz. "Ernst Křenek," Jan 1955).

Symphonic elegy

See no. 155 (Ogdon, Wilbur Lee. Series and structure, 1955, p. 162-231).

RENÉ LEIBOWITZ

See no. 141 ("Un musicien d'aujourd'hui: René Leibowitz" in Le système dodécaphonique, 1949, p. 80-83 [Polyphonie, 4]).

See no. 29 (Goléa, Antoine. Esthétique de la musique contemporaine, 1954, p. 179-180).

748   Searle, Humphrey. "Leibowitz, René" in Grove's Dictionary of music and musicians. 5th ed., London, Macmillan, 1954, v. 5:117.
Includes a list of his compositions and published theoretical writings.

See no. 98 (Myers, Rollo H. "Music in France in the post-war decade," 1954/55).

See no. 155 (Ogdon, Wilbur Lee. Series and structure, 1955).

Chamber symphony, op. 16

See no. 141 (Saby, Bernard. "Un aspect des problèmes de la thématique sérielle; à propos de la Symphonie de chambre, op. 16, de René Leibowitz" in Le système dodécaphonique, 1949, p. 54-63 [Polyphonie, 4]).

Quartets, strings
—no. 3

See no. 155 (Ogdon, Wilbur Lee. Series and structure, 1955).

Tourist death
(Air pour soprano et orchestre, op. 7)

See no. 484 (Leibowitz, René. "Les nouvelles générations de compositeurs 'dodécaphonistes' et leurs caractéristiques générales" in his Introduction à la musique de douze sons, 1949, p. 263-265).

BRUNO MADERNA

See no. 161 (Smith Brindle, Reginald. "The lunatic fringe, III: computational composition," Jul 1956).

See no. 105 (Smith Brindle, Reginald. "Italian contemporary music" in Hartog, Howard, ed. European music in the twentieth century, 1957, p. 184, 185-186).

See no. 106 (Pestalozza, Luigi. "I compositori milanesi del dopoguerra," Mar 1957).

See no. 168 (Manzoni, Giacomo. "Bruno Maderna" in Junge Komponisten, 1958, p. 113-118 [Die Reihe, 4]).

See no. 112 (Prieberg, Fred K. Lexikon der neuen Musik, 1958, p. 263).

See no. 116 (Vlad, Roman. Storia della dodecafonia, 1958, p. 261-262).

749 Smith Brindle, Reginald. "Current chronicle: Italy," MQ 45:388-392 (Jul 1959). Mus.
    Brief description of his String quartet in two movements and his Serenata no. 2 for eleven instruments. Gives some biographical background.

LUIGI NONO

See no. 29 (Goléa, Antoine. Esthétique de la musique contemporaine, 1954).

See no. 30 (Goléa, Antoine. "Deux portraits: Luigi Nono—Karlheinz Stockhausen" in La musique et ses problèmes contemporains, 1954, p. 112-114).

See no. 105 (Smith Brindle, Reginald. "Italian contemporary music" in Hartog, Howard, ed. European music in the twentieth century, 1957, p. 184, 186-187).

See no. 112 (Prieberg, Fred K. Lexikon der neuen Musik, 1958, p. 318-320).

See no. 116 (Vlad, Roman. Storia della dodecafonia, 1958, p. 264-265).

See no. 63 (Porena, Boris. "L'avanguardia musicale di Darmstadt," Sept 1958).

See no. 118a (Zillig, Winfried. "Die Jungen: Stockhausen, Boulez, Nono, Berio" in his Variationen über neue Musik, 1959, p. 190-199).

Il canto sospeso

750 Koegler, Horst. "The international scene: Germany," Musical courier 155:41 (Apr 1957).
    Very brief description.

See no. 170 (Stockhausen, Karlheinz. "Sprache und Musik" in Steinecke, Wolfgang, ed. Darmstädter Beiträge zur neuen Musik, 1958, p. 57-81).

See no. 168 (Unger, Udo. "Luigi Nono" in Junge Komponisten, 1958, p. 9-17 [Die Reihe, 4]).

Coro di Didone

751 Helm, Everett. "Current chronicle: Germany," MQ 45:101-102 (Jan 1959).
    A brief description.

Polifonica-Monodia-Ritmica

See no. 168 (Unger, Udo. "Luigi Nono" in Junge Komponisten, 1958, p. 9-17 [Die Reihe, 4]).

Varianti, for violin and orchestra

752 Kolisch, Rudolf. "Nonos Varianti," Melos 24:292-296 (Oct 1957). Mus.
    A short analysis; shows the use of permutation as a factor in composition.

HENRI POUSSEUR

753 "Henri Pousseur," Schw MZ 97:233 (Jun 1957).
Very brief; gives biographical data and lists some of his works.

See no. 168 (Koenig, Gottfried Michael. "Henri Pousseur" in Junge Komponisten, 1958, p. 18-31 [Die Reihe, 4]).

See no. 112 (Prieberg, Fred K. Lexikon der neuen Musik, 1958, p. 344-345).

See no. 166 (Pousseur, Henri. "Outline of a method" in Musical craftsmanship, 1959, p. 44-88 [Die Reihe, 3]).

See no. 637 (Metzger, Heinz-Klaus. "John Cage o della liberazione," Aug 1959).

Impromptu for piano

See no. 166 (Pousseur, Henri. "Outline of a method" in Musical craftsmanship, 1957, 1959, p. 56-63 [Die Reihe, 3]).
Includes a score of the work.

Quintet in memory of Webern

See no. 166 (Pousseur, Henri. "Outline of a method" in Musical craftsmanship, 1957, 1959, p. 48-55 [Die Reihe, 3]).

Scambi

754 Pousseur, Henri. "Scambi," Gravesaner Blätter, v. 4, no. 13:36-47 (1959). Diagrs.
English translation, p. 48-54. Details of the composition of Pousseur's electronic piece, Scambi.

See no. 71 (Eco, Umberto. "L'opera in movimento e la coscienza dell'epoca," Aug 1959).

Variations for piano

See no. 166 (Pousseur, Henri. "Outline of a method" in Musical craftsmanship, 1957, 1959, p. 64-88).

HUMPHREY SEARLE

755 Gorer, Richard. "An interim report on Humphrey Searle's music," Mus sur 1:137-140 (1949). Mus.
Brief outline of Searle's background and musical training; discussion of his style and works. List of works, p. 140.

See no. 88 (Mitchell, Donald. "The emancipation of the dissonance," 1952, p. 144).

756 Mason, Colin. "Searle, Humphrey" in Grove's Dictionary of music and musicians. 5th ed., London, Macmillan, 1954, v. 7:679-681.
Includes a list of his "principal compositions."

See no. 151 ("Contemporary composers on their experiences of composition with twelve notes: Humphrey Searle" in Rufer, Josef. Composition with twelve notes, 1954, p. 193-195).

757 Lockspeiser, Edward. "Humphrey Searle," MT 96:468-472 (Sept 1955). Mus.
Biographical sketch and discussion of works; list of compositions and writings, p. 472.

See no. 105 (Milner, Anthony. "English contemporary music" in Hartog, Howard, ed. European music in the twentieth century, 1957, p. 146-147).

See no. 112 (Prieberg, Fred K. Lexikon der neuen Musik, 1958, p. 398-399).

See no. 116 (Vlad, Roman. Storia della dodecafonia, 1958, p. 150-151).

Shadow of Cain

See no. 28 (Keller, Hans. "First performances and their reviews," Feb 1953).

Sonata for piano

758 Keller, Hans. "First performances," Mus rev 13:43-44 (Feb 1952).
An outline of the structure.

MÁTYÁS SEIBER

759 Weissmann, John S. "Mátyás Seiber: Style and technique," Listener 55:476 (Mar 22, 1951).
A brief survey of his works and method of using the twelve-tone technique.

See no. 88 (Mitchell, Donald. "The emancipation of the dissonance," 1952, p. 144).

760 Weissmann, John S. "Seiber, Mátyás (György)" in Grove's Dictionary of music and musicians. 5th ed., London, Macmillan, 1954, v. 7:687-689.
Includes a bibliography and catalog of his works.

See no. 151 ("Contemporary composers on their experiences of composition with twelve notes: Mátyás Seiber" in Rufer, Josef. Composition with twelve notes, 1954, p. 196-198).

761 Schweizer, Gottfried. "Komponistenporträt: Mátyás Seiber 50 Jahre," Musica 9:233-234 (May 1955). Port.
Biographical data and brief characterization of Seiber's music.

762 Schweizer, Gottfried. "Zwischen Bartók und Schönberg: das Bild Mátyás Seibers," ZfM 116:269-272 (May 1955). Port.
Influences on Seiber; brief discussion of works and style.

763 Keller, Hans. "Mátyás Seiber," MT 96:580-584 (Nov 1955). Mus.
Biographical sketch; discussion of Seiber's row technique in some detail. List of published compositions, recordings, and writings, p. 583-584.

See no. 112 (Prieberg, Fred K. Lexikon der neuen Musik, 1958, p. 399-401).

See no. 116 (Vlad, Roman. Storia della dodecafonia, 1958, p. 151-153).

Quartets, string

—no. 1

764 Weissmann, John S. "Die Streichquartette von Mátyás Seiber," Melos 22:344-347 (Dec 1955) and 23:38-41 (Feb 1956). Mus.
Tr. from the English by Willi Reich. Analyses of the first three quartets.

—no. 2

See no. 764 (Weissmann, John S. "Die Streichquartette von Mátyás Seiber," Dec 1955 and Feb 1956).

—no. 3

(Quartetto lirico)

765 Helm, Everett. "Current chronicle: Germany," MQ 41:521-524 (Oct 1955). Mus.
A brief analysis of the form with some examples of the contrapuntal technique.

See no. 764 (Weissmann, John S. "Die Streichquartette von Mátyás Seiber," Dec 1955 and Feb 1956).

Ulysses

766 Carner, Mosco. "Mátyás Seiber and his Ulysses," Mus rev 12:105-112 (May 1951). Mus.
A textual and musical analysis.

767 Seiber, Mátyás. "A note on 'Ulysses,'" Mus sur 3:263-270 (Jun 1951). Mus.
The composer's description of the structure of his cantata.

KARLHEINZ STOCKHAUSEN

See no. 253 (Boulez, Pierre. "Tendances de la musique récente" in Vers une musique expérimentale, 1957, p. 28-35).

See no. 105 (Hartog, Howard. "German contemporary music" in his European music in the twentieth century, 1957, p. 201-202).

See no. 168 (Schnebel, Dieter. "Karlheinz Stockhausen" in Junge Komponisten, 1958, p. 119-133 [Die Reihe, 4]).

See no. 170a (Stephan, Rudolf. Neue Musik, 1958).

See no. 116 (Vlad, Roman. Storia della dodecafonia, 1958, p. 265-266).

768   Maegaard, Jan "Karlheinz Stockhausen," Nordisk Musikkultur 7:11-14 (Mar 1958). Port., mus.
Discussion of Stockhausen's philosophy of composition and the characteristics, especially rhythmical, of his music.

See no. 636 (Maren, Roger. "The musical numbers game," Mar 6, 1958).

769   Manzoni, Giacomo. "Profili di musicisti contemporanei: Karlheinz Stockhausen," Musica d'oggi [new series] 1:229-233 (Apr 1958).
A survey of his background and works.

See no. 63, (Porena, Boris. "L'avanguardia musicale di Darmstadt," Sept 1958).

770   Luening, Otto. "Karlheinz Stockhausen," Juilliard review 6:10-11 (Winter 1958/59). Port.
A brief critical appraisal of Stockhausen and a chronological outline of the history of the Cologne group of electronic composers.

See no. 166 (Stockhausen, Karlheinz. ". . . how time passes . . ." in Musical craftsmanship, 1959, p. 10-40 [Die Reihe, 3]).

See no. 118a (Zillig, Winfried. "Die Jungen: Stockhausen, Boulez, Nono, Berio" in his Variationen über neue Musik, 1959, p. 190-199).

See no. 637 (Metzger, Heinz-Klaus. "John Cage o della liberazione," Aug 1959).

Gesang der Jünglinge

See no. 170 (Stockhausen, Karlheinz. "Sprach und Musik" in Steinecke, Wolfgang, ed. Darmstädter Beiträge zur neuen Musik, 1958, p. 57-81).

Gruppen für 3 Orchester

771   Stockhausen, Karlheinz. "Musik im Raum," Melos 25:317-320 (Oct 1958). Illus.
Stockhausen's theories of music in space, particularly as worked out in his Gruppen für 3 Orchester; problems of concert hall design. (See no. 772.)

772   Stockhausen, Karlheinz. "Musik im Raum" in Berichte/Analysen. Wien, Universal Edition [c1959], p. 59-73. Illus. (Die Reihe, 5.)
"Dieser Text diente als Vorlage für eine Vorlesung, die während der Internationalen Ferienkurse für Neue Musik 1958 in Darmstadt gehalten wurde." (An expansion of no. 771; see also no. 174.)

773   Wörner, Karl H. "Current chronicle: Germany," MQ 45:237-239 (Apr 1959).
A brief description of the work.

Klavierstücke

—nr. 2

774   Mason, Colin. "Review of music," M & L 36:307-308 (Jul 1955).
A brief review, including some discussion of rhythmic elements.

See no. 629 (Pestalozzi, Luigi. "Vita musicale: musiche nuovissime," Oct 1956).
Discusses the fifth, sixth, seventh, and eighth pieces.

—nr. 11

See no. 71 (Eco, Umberto. "L'opera in movimento e la coscienza dell'epoca," Aug 1959).

Komposition nr. 2

See no. 30 (Stockhausen, Karlheinz. "Une expérience électronique" in La musique et ses problèmes contemporains, 1954, p. 82-93).

See no. 170 (Nono, Luigi. "Die Entwicklung der Reihentechnik" in Steinecke, Wolfgang, ed. Darmstädter Beiträge zur neuen Musik, 1958, p. 25-37).

Kontrapunkten

775   Scherchen, Hermann. "Stockhausen und die Zeit: zur Geschichte einer Geschichte," Gravesaner Blätter, v. 4, no. 13:29-31 (1959).
English translation, p. 32-34. Implications of changes made by Stockhausen in his Kontrapunkten.

Studie nr. 2

See no. 279 (Prieberg, Fred K. "Erste elektronische Partitur," Apr 1957).

Zeitmasse

See no. 170 (Nono, Luigi. "Die Entwicklung der Reihentechnik" in Steinecke, Wolfgang, ed. Darmstädter Beiträge zur neuen Musik, 1958, p. 25-37).

776   Pade, Else Marie, and Blyme, Anker. "Efter Stockhausen...," Dansk musiktidsskrift 33:48-49 (Apr 1958). Port.
Review of Zeitmasse and discussion of Stockhausen's musical philosophy.

777 Helm, Everett. "Current chronicle: France," MQ 44:520-521 (Oct 1958).
The rhythmic structure is briefly discussed.

See no. 621 (Craft, Robert. "Boulez and Stockhausen," Nov 1958).

See no. 622 (Skulsky, Abraham. "After Webern, who?" Jan 1959).

IGOR STRAVINSKY

GENERAL

See no. 343 (Citkowitz, Israel. "Stravinsky and Schoenberg," Fall, 1954).

See no. 99 (Neighbor, Oliver. "The evolution of twelve-note music," 1954/1955).

778 Strawinsky in Amerika; das kompositorische Werk von 1939 bis 1955. Bonn, Boosey & Hawkes [c1955]. 87 p. Illus., mus. (Musik der Zeit; eine Schriftenreihe zur zeitgenössischen Musik, Heft 12.)
Partial contents: Lindlar, Heinrich, "Cantata" (Jan 1953), p. 30-34; Eimert, Herbert, "Die drei Shakespeare-Lieder (1953)," p. 35-38; Keller, Hans, "In Memoriam Dylan Thomas: Strawinskys Schönbergische Technik," p. 39-42 (from Tempo, Spring 1955; see no. 806); Craft, Robert, "Reihenkompositionen: vom 'Septett' zum 'Agon'" (Sept 1955), p. 43-54; list of works, 1939-55, p. 84-85.

See no. 160 (Perle, George. Serial composition and atonality, 1956).

See no. 348 (Burt, Francis. "An antithesis," Dec 1956 and Mar 1957).

779 Lindlar, Heinrich. Igor Strawinskys sakraler Gesang: Geist und Form der Christ-kultischen Kompositionen. Regensburg, Bosse Verlag, 1957. 93 p. Illus., mus. (Forschungsbeiträge zur Musikwissenschaft, Band 6.)
Partial contents: Cantata, p. 68-72; Shakespeare songs, p. 72-73; In Memoriam Dylan Thomas, p. 73; Canticum Sacrum, p. 74-79. (See nos. 787, 796.)

780 Le musiche religiose di Igor Strawinsky, con il catalogo analitico completo di tutte le sue opera. Venezia, Lombroso [1957]. 79 p. Illus., mus.
Contents: Piovesan, Alessandro, "Promesso," p. 5-9; Vlad, Roman, "Le musiche religiose di Strawinsky," p. 11-21; Craft, Robert, "Il 'Canticum sacrum,'" p. 23-36; Craft, Robert, "Bach-Strawinsky: Choral und Variationen über . . . 'Von Himmel hoch'. . ." p. 37-46; Piovesan, Alessandro, and Borri, Biancamaria, "Catalogo generale delle opere di Igor Strawinsky," p. 47-79.
The Craft articles first appeared under the title, "A concert for St. Mark" in Score, Dec 1956 (see no. 799).

781 Mason, Colin. "Stravinsky's contribution to chamber music," Tempo, no. 43:6-16 (Spring 1957). Mus.

Discussion of the Septet, In memoriam Dylan Thomas, and the Shakespeare songs. A list of Stravinsky's chamber music, p. 15-16. (See no. 787.)

782 Pfaundler, Geertruy von. "De jongste werken van Igor Strawinsky (uit de jaren 1952-1957)," Mens en melodie 12:133-137 (May 1957). Mus., port.
Discusses briefly the Canticum Sacrum, the Shakespeare songs, and the Septet.

783 Gerhard, Roberto. "Twelve-note technique in Stravinsky," Score, no. 20:38-43 (Jun 1957). Mus.
A description of Stravinsky's use of dodecaphonic elements. For a German translation, see no. 787.

784 Stravinsky, Igor. "35 Antworten auf 35 Fragen," Melos 24:161-170 (Jun 1957). Port.
Translation, as "Answers to 34 [sic] questions; an interview with Igor Stravinsky," Encounter, no. 46:3-7 (Jul 1957). Some of the questions concern Stravinsky's serial technique.

785 Milner, Anthony. "Melody in Stravinsky's music," MT 98:370-371 (Jul 1957). Mus.
Very brief general article on the characteristics of Stravinsky's melody; includes an illustration from the Canticum Sacrum.

786 Kirchmeyer, Helmut. Igor Strawinsky; Zeitgeschichte im Persönlichkeitsbild: Grundlagen und Voraussetzungen zur modernen Konstruktionstechnik. Regensburg, Gustav Bosse, 1958. xvi + 792 p. Illus., mus. (Kölner Beiträge zur Musikforschung, Band 10.)
Contents: Erster Teil, "Die musik- und geistegeschichtliche Stellung Igor Strawinskys"; Zweiter Teil, "Kritik und Polemic— Dokumente zur Zeitgeschichte"; Dritter Teil, "Die Umgestaltung des musikalischen Materials"; Vierter Teil, "Die Konstruktion: Prinzipien der Konstruktion; Musiktheoretische Voraussetzungen; Folgen der Konstruktion; Sonderformen der Konstruktion." Bibliography, p. 653-711 (general, not limited to Stravinsky); list of works, p. 715-764 (very complete information, giving description, instrumentation, names of sections, timing, publishers, recordings, history of performances, etc., for each work).
An attempt to establish Stravinsky's place in the history of contemporary music. Much of the book is devoted to background material, including Schoenberg and the development of the twelve-tone technique.

See no. 112 (Prieberg, Fred K. Lexikon der neuen Musik, 1958, p. 405-416).

787 Strawinsky: Wirklichkeit und Wirkung. Bonn, Boosey & Hawkes [c1958]. 88 p. Illus., mus., ports. (Musik der Zeit: eine Schriftenreihe zu Musik und Gegenwart. Neue Folge, Heft 1.)
Partial contents: Gerhard, Roberto, "Die Reihentechnik des Diatonikers," p. 18-22 (tr. by Alfred Becker from Gerhard's article in Score; see nos. 783, 796); Lindlar, Heinrich, "Der Sakralkomponist: Cantata/In memoriam Dylan Thomas, Canticum Sacrum/ Threni," p. 66-68 (from his Igor Strawinskys sakraler Gesang;

see no. 779); Mason, Colin. "Die Kammermusik," p. 72-81 (tr. by Alfred Becker from Mason's article in Tempo, see no. 781).

See no. 115 (Stuckenschmidt, Hans Heinz. "Igor Strawinsky" in his Schöpfer der neuen Musik, 1958, p. 128-161).

See no. 116 (Vlad, Roman. "Strawinsky e la dodecafonia" in his Storia della dodecafonia, 1958, p. 161-174).

788 Füssl, Karl Heinz. "Selbstbesinnung am Beispiel Strawinskys," ÖMZ 13:461-466 (Nov 1958). Port.
Primarily an article about Stravinsky's influence on the author, but with some discussion of the implications of Stravinsky's adaptation of serial techniques.

See no. 118a (Zillig, Winfried. "Strawinsky und das Zwölftonsystem" in his Variationen über neue Musik, 1959, p. 50-59).

SERIAL WORKS

Agon

789 Craft, Robert. "Ein Ballett für zwölf Tänzer," Melos 24:284-288 (Oct 1957). Mus.
A brief formal analysis; the row technique is discussed in some detail.

790 Morton, Lawrence. "Current chronicle: Los Angeles," MQ 43:535-541 (Oct 1957). Mus.
A brief analysis, with some examples of the row technique.

791 Vlad, Roman. "Vita musicale: Roma," Rass mus 27:322-324 (Dec 1957).
A review, not an analysis.

See no. 116 (Vlad, Roman. "'Agon' di Strawinsky" in his Storia della dodecafonia, 1958, p. 329-338).

792 Lewkovitch, Bernhard. "Agon: Ballet for 12 dansere af Igor Strawinsky," Nordisk musikkultur 7:89, 91, 93 (Oct 1958). Mus.
An outline-analysis of the work.

793 Wouters, Jos. "Nieuwe balletmuziek van Strawinsky," Mens en melodie 13:301-306 (Oct 1958). Mus.
The row, contrapuntal treatment, and rhythmic structure are discussed.

Canticum Sacrum ad Honorem Sancti Marci Nominis

794 Stein, Erwin. "Igor Stravinsky: Canticum Sacrum ad Honorem Sancti Marci Nominis," Tempo, no. 40:3-5 (Summer 1956).
A very brief description, dealing with the over-all shape of the work and of its several sections.

795 Mila, Massimo. "Vita musicale: Venezia," Rass mus 26:204-206 (Jul 1956).
    A review, not an analysis.

796 Lindlar, Heinrich. "Strawinskys sakraler Gesang," NZfM 117:548-552 (Oct 1956). Diagrs.
    Parallels between the structure of the Canticum Sacrum and that of the Basilica of St. Mark in Venice. (See also nos. 779, 787.)

797 Swarowsky, Hans. "Canticum Sacrum," ÖMZ 11:399-405 (Nov 1956). Mus.
    A description, with some row analysis.

798 Schuh, Willi. "Uraufführungen neuer Kirchenmusik: Strawinskys 'Canticum Sacrum,'" Musik und Kirche 26:296-298 (Nov/Dec 1956). Reprinted from the Neue Züriche Zeitung (Fernausgabe), nr. 257, Sept 18, 1956. A fairly detailed description of the work's structure.

799 Craft, Robert. "A concert for Saint Mark," Score, no. 18:35-45 (Dec 1956). Mus., port.
    Italian translation in Le musiche religiose di Igor Strawinsky, no. 780. Analyses of the Canticum Sacrum and the Von Himmel Hoch variations.

800 Rostand, Claude. "Canticum Sacrum d'Igor Stravinsky," La table ronde [Paris], no. 109:155-157 (Jan 1957).
    Review and general brief description.

801 Weissmann, John S. "Current chronicle: Italy," MQ 43:104-110 (Jan 1957). Mus.
    Survey of the structure as a whole; aesthetic implications.

802 Winter, Carl. "Canticum Sancti Marci: Strawinskys neues geistliches Chorwerk," Musica sacra 77:8-17 (Jan 1957). Mus., port.
    Gives an outline of the form and a general description of each section.

See no. 782 (Pfaundler, Geertruy von. "De jongste werken van Igor Strawinsky," May 1957).

803 Andriessen, Hendrik. "Het 'Canticum Sacrum' van Strawinsky," Mens en melodie 12:285-289 (Sept 1957). Mus.
    A discussion of the structure.

804 Reck, Albert von. "Gestaltzusammenhänge in 'Canticum Sacrum' von Strawinsky: Tonalität und Form," Schw MZ 98:49-68 (Feb 1958). Diagrs., mus.
    An elaborate structural analysis.

Double canon for string quartet
    See his Movements for piano and orchestra

Epitaphium für das Grabmal des
Prinzen Max Egon zu Fürstenburg
See his Movements for piano and orchestra

In Memoriam Dylan Thomas

805   Turchi, Guido. "Letture critiche: Igor Strawinsky—In memoriam Dylan Thomas," Riv mus ital 57:69-72 (Jan/Mar 1955).
      Philosophical considerations, not an analysis. Rather negative review.

806   Keller, Hans. "In memoriam Dylan Thomas: Stravinsky's Schoenbergian technique," Tempo, no. 35:13-20 (Spring 1955). Mus.
      "The present article is no more than an illustration appended to my analytic music example of the complete central song [p. 16-20]." The analysis is indicated on the score. (German translation in no. 778.) (See also no. 807.)

807   Shawe-Taylor, Desmond. "The arts and entertainment: Stravinsky as serialist," New statesman and nation [ser. 2] 50:12-13 (Jul 2, 1955).
      An answer to Keller's analysis (see no. 806); a reply by Keller in New statesman and nation [ser. 2] 50:72 (Jul 16, 1955).

808   Keller, Hans. "A serial masterpiece," Mus rev 16:342-344 (Nov 1955). Diagr.
      A brief serial and thematic analysis.

809   Goldman, Richard F. "Current chronicle: New York," MQ 42:236-239 (Apr 1956). Mus.
      Illustrates some of the canonic techniques; claims that the piece is "augenmusik."

See no. 781 (Mason, Colin. "Stravinsky's contribution to chamber music," Spring 1957).

Movements for piano and orchestra

809a Mason, Colin. "Stravinsky's newest works," Tempo, no. 53/54:2-10 (Spring/summer 1960), mus.
      Serial analysis of the Movements; also brief analyses of two miniature works, the Double canon for string quartet and the Epitaphium.

809b Goldman, Richard F. "Current chronicle: New York," MQ 46:260-264 (Apr 1960).
      A brief description of the Movements and also of the Double canon for string quartet.

809c Briner, Andreas. "Guillaume de Machaut 1958/59, oder Strawinskys 'Movements for piano and orchestra,'" Melos 27:184-186 (Jun 1960). Mus.
      A brief analysis.

Septet

810 Stein, Erwin. "Stravinsky's Septet (1953) . . . an analysis," <u>Tempo</u>, no. 31:7-10 (Spring 1954). Mus., illus.
A formal analysis.

811 [Keller, Hans]. "First performances: Schönbergians and Stravinskyians," <u>Mus rev</u> 15:307-310 (Nov 1954).
Aesthetic considerations.

812 Redlich, Hans. "New music: a critical interim report," <u>Mus rev</u> 16:167-168 (May 1955). Mus.
Brief example of "thematic integration" in the work.

813 Schilling, Hans Ludwig. "Zur Instrumentation in Igor Strawinskys Spätwerk aufgezeigt an seinem 'Septett 1953,'" <u>Archiv für Musikwissenschaft</u> 13:181-196 (1956). Mus.
A discussion of the instrumentation only.

<u>See no. 781</u> (Mason, Colin. "Stravinsky's contribution to chamber music," Spring 1957).

<u>See no. 782</u> (Pfaundler, Geertruy von. "De jongste werken van Igor Strawinsky," May 1957).

Shakespeare songs

<u>See no. 778</u> (Eimert, Herbert. "Die drei Shakespeare-Lieder (1953)" <u>in</u> Strawinsky in Amerika, 1955, p. 35-38 [Musik der Zeit, 12]).

<u>See no. 781</u> (Mason, Colin. "Stravinsky's contribution to chamber music," Spring 1957).

<u>See no. 782</u> (Pfaundler, Geertruy von. "De jongste werken van Igor Strawinsky," May 1957).

Threni, id est Lamentationes
Jeremiae Prophetae

814 Pauli, Hansjörg. "On Stravinsky's 'Threni,'" <u>Tempo</u>, no. 49:16-33 (Autumn 1958). Mus.

_____. "Zur seriellen Struktur von Igor Strawinskys 'Threni,'" <u>Schw MZ</u> 98:450-456 (Dec 1958). Mus.
Detailed analysis of the textual and musical structure.

815 Mila, Massimo. "Vita musicale: Venezia; I 'Threni' di Strawinsky," <u>Rass mus</u> 28:215-217 (Sept 1958).
General description and aesthetic discussion; not an analysis.

816 Ruppel, K. H. "Berichte aus dem Ausland; Strawinskys neues Werk: 'Threni,'" <u>Melos</u> 25:369-371 (Nov 1958).
Brief account of Stravinsky's road to serial technique; general description of the work.

817 Smith Brindle, Reginald. "Reports from abroad: Venice Contemporary Music Festival," <u>MT</u> 99:619-620 (Nov 1958).
Very brief review.

Igor Stravinsky 127

818 Glock, William. "The arts and entertainment: Stravinsky's Threni," New statesman 56:723-724 (Nov 22, 1958).
A brief description and evaluation.

819 Schuh, Willi. "Strukturanalyse eines Fragments aus Strawinskys 'Threni,'" Schw MZ 98:456-460 (Dec 1958). Mus.
Analysis of the first section (ms. 322-342) of the "Solacium" from the third part of Threni, "De elegia tertia."

820 Weissmann, John S. "Current chronicle: Italy," MQ 45:104-110 (Jan 1959). Mus.
Brief analytical description, including row technique.

821 Vlad, Roman. "Igor Strawinskys 'Threni,'" Melos 26:36-39 (Feb 1959). Mus.
A brief description of the row technique and the general form.

822 Weissmann, John S. "The new in review; Venice 1958: Stravinsky's Threni," Mus rev 20:74-76 (Feb 1959). Mus.
A brief description.

823 Lewkovitch, Bernhard. "Stravinskijs klagensange," Dansk musiktidsskrift 34:37-40 (Mar 1959). Mus.
A brief description.

AUTHOR INDEX

Ackere, Jules van. Muziek van onze eeuw, 1900-1950, 92; Schönberg en de atonale school, 92

Adorno, Theodor Wiesengrund. Alban Berg (1957), 492; ___ (1959), 497; Alban Berg: zur Uraufführung des 'Wozzeck,' 547; Das Altern der neuen Musik, 36; Anton von Webern, 572; Anton Webern: zur Aufführung der fünf Orchesterstücke, 573; Arnold Schoenberg, 1874-1951, 339; Arnold Schönberg: Chöre op. 27 und op. 28, 416; Arnold Schönberg: Von Heute auf Morgen, 487; Berg and Webern—Schoenberg's heirs, 516; Bergs Lulu Symphonie, 535a; Die Funktion des Kontrapunkts in der neuen Musik, 214; Die Instrumentation von Bergs frühen Liedern, 540; Invecchiamento della musica nuova, 36; Klangfiguren, 306a, 497, 540, 572; Kritieren, 170; Musica e tecnica oggi, 70; Philosophie der neuen Musik, 13; Technique, technology, and music today, 70; Zum Verständnis Schönbergs, 37; Zur Vorgeschichte der Reihenkomposition, 306a; Zur Zwölftontechnik, 3

Alaleona, Domenico. L'armonia modernissima, 177; I moderni orizzonti della tecnica musicale, 176

Alban Bergs 'Wozzeck' und die Musikkritik, 545

Almeyda, Renato. Atonalistas brasileños, 85

Alte und neue Musik, 89

Amico, Fedele d'. 'Canti di prigionia,' 659; Luigi Dallapiccola, 642; Recensioni: Luigi Dallapiccola, 664

Andriessen, Hendrik. Het 'Canticum Sacrum' van Strawinsky, 803; Twaalf contra twaalf, 203

Anton Webern (Die Reihe, 2), 570

Anton Webern zum 50. Geburtstag, 564

Armitage, Merle, ed. Schoenberg, 295

Arnold Schönberg (Festschrift, 1912), 284

Arnold Schoenberg, 1874-1951 [special issue of Music and letters], 329

Arnold Schönberg zum fünfzigsten Geburtstag, 288

Arnold Schönberg zum 60. Geburtstag, 293

Arthuys, Philippe. La pensée et l'instrument, 253

Asuar, José Vicente. Una incursion por el op. 5 de Anton Webern, 597

Babbitt, Milton. Book reviews, 84, 141; The function of set structure in the twelve-tone system, 138; An introduction to the music [Moses und Aron], 442; Some aspects of twelve-tone composition, 157; Twelve-tone invariants as compositional determinants, 175b; Who cares if you listen? 232

Bach, David Joseph. New music by Berg, Webern, Krenek, 526; A note on Arnold Schoenberg, 358

Bachmann, Claus-Henning. Ein Wechsel auf die Zukunft, 438
Badings, Henk. Electronic music, 281; Electronic music: its development in the Netherlands, 266
Ballif, Claude. Introduction à la métatonalité, 159
Ballo, Ferdinando. Le musiche chorali di Dallapiccola, 646
Barraqué, Jean. Rythme et développement, 618
Barrault, Jean Louis. Pierre Boulez, 30
Bartlett, K. W. Henze, Hans Werner, 704
Baruch, Gerth-Wolfgang. Anton von Webern, 568
Basart, Ann P. The twelve-tone compositions of Luigi Dallapiccola, 654
Bauer, Marion. Schoenberg and his innovation, 297; Twentieth century music, 297
Becerra, Gustavo. ¿Que es la música electrónica? 261
Bekker, Paul. Kritische Zeitbilder, 309; Schönberg: 'Erwartung,' 288
Bentzon, Johan. Musik er mere end musik, 54
Bentzon, Niels Viggo. Omkring Arnold Schønberg, 347; Tolvtoneteknik, 147
Berg, Alban. A propos des formes employées dans Wozzeck, 509; Arnold Schönberg: Kammersymphonie, op. 9, 436; Che cosa significa atonale? in Rognoni, 94; Credo, 509; Ecrits, 509; [Essays], 492; Glauben, Hoffnung und Liebe (poem), 293; Indications pratiques pour l'étude de Wozzeck, 509; Lecture on Wozzeck, 496; Lettera aperta ad Arnold Schönberg, 94; Lettre ouverte à Schoenberg, 509; The musical form in Wozzeck, 552; Offener Brief an Arnold Schönberg, 492; Open forum: variations on a theme, 15; Pourquoi la musique de Schoenberg est-elle si difficile a comprendre? 509; La société viennoise d'exécutions privées, 509; Die Stimme in der Oper, 451; La voce nell' opera, 94; Warum ist Schöbergs Musik so schwer verständlich? 288, 492; Was ist Atonal? 4; What is atonality? 4; Why is Schoenberg's music so hard to understand? 470; Zwei Feuilletons, 508
Berichte/Analysen (Die Reihe, 5), 67, 173, 269, 283, 628, 772
Berio, Luciano. Aspetti di artigiano formale, 606; Musik und Dichtung, 174; Note sulla musica elettronica, 259; Poesie e musica, 609; Prospettive nella musica, 246; Sur la musique electronique, 230
Beyer, Robert. Elektronische Musik, 223; Die Klangwelt der elektronischen Musik, 222; Zur Geschichte der elektronischen Musik, 235; Zur Situation der elektronischen Musik, 224
Birke, Joachim. Richard Dehmel und Arnold Schönberg: ein Briefwechsel, 375
Blanks, Fred. Arnold Schoenberg, 354
Der blaue Reiter, 74
Blaukopf, Kurt. Current chronicle: Austria, 714; New light on Wozzeck, 555
Blyme, Anker. Efter Stockhausen, 776
Borri, Biancamaria. Catalogo generale delle opere di Igor Strawinsky, 780
Boucourechliev, André. La fin et les moyens, 267
Boulez, Pierre. Alban Berg heute gesehen, 498a; Alea, 170; At the ends of the fruitful land, 275; Auprès et au loin, 30; Einsichten und Aussichten, 38; Eventuellement, 146; Incidences actuelles de Berg, 503; Propositions, 208; Schoenberg is dead, 332; Son, verbe, synthèse, 233; Tendances de la musique récente, 253; The threshold, 570; Trajectories: Ravel, Stravinsky, Schoenberg, 464
Bouquet, Fritz. Alban Bergs 'Lyrische Suite,' 536
Brainard, Paul. A study of the twelve-tone technique, 144

Brauner, Rudolph Franz. Von Dreiklang zum Zwölftonakkord, 188
Brindle, Reginald Smith, see Smith Brindle, Reginald
Briner, Andreas. Guillaume de Machaut 1958/59, oder Strawinskys 'Movements for piano and orchestra,' 809c
Broch, Hermann. Irrationale Erkenntnis in der Musik, 293
Bruno, Anthony. Two American twelve-tone composers: Milton Babbitt and Ben Weber, 602
Bruyn, J. W. de. Electronic music, 281
Bücken, Ernst. Führer und Probleme der neuen Musik, 310
Burkhard, Willy. Versuch einer kritischen Auseinandersetzung mit der Zwölftontechnik, 31
Burnier, Lucien. Réflexions sur la dodécaphonie, 16
Burt, Francis. An antithesis, 348
Busoni, Ferrucio Benvenuto. Entwurf einer neuen Ästhetik der Tonkunst, 1

Cage, John. Experimental music, 635; To describe the process of composition used in 'Music for piano 21-52,' 166; Zur Geschichte der experimentellen Musik in den Vereinigten Staaten, 174
Calvocoressi, M. D. The classicism of Arnold Schönberg, 308
The Canon [Schoenberg Jubilee issue], 300
Carner, Mosco. Alban Berg, 522; Mátyás Seiber and his Ulysses, 766; Technique of twelve-note music, 120
Les carnets critiques, 611
Carsalade du Pont, Henri de. La musique dodécaphoniste, 102
Castiglioni, Niccolò. Sul rapporto tra parola e musica nella seconda Cantata di Webern, 594; Il valore del silenzio e della durata, 58
Catalogue des oeuvres d'Arnold Schoenberg, 406
Cecci, César. Qué es la dodecafonía, 125

Chailley, Jacques. Malentendus sur le mot 'atonalité,' 23; Traité historique d'analyse musicale, 145
Chambure, Alaine de. Infrastructure technique, 267
Chase, Gilbert. America's music, 99a
Citkowitz, Israel. Stravinsky and Schoenberg, 343
Clarke, Henry Leland. The abuse of the semitone in twelve-tone music, 175
Collaer, Paul. Le cas Schoenberg, 314; La musique moderne, 1905-1955, 100; Une nouvelle oeuvre d'Alban Berg: Loulou, 525
Colucci, Matthew Joseph. A comparative study of contemporary musical theories in selected writings of Piston, Krenek, and Hindemith, 725
Cort Van den Linden, R. Arnold Schoenberg, 312
Costarelli, Nicola. Nota sulla dodecafonia, 119
Costère, Edmond. Entre l'harmonie classique et les harmonies contemporaines, 193
Cowell, Henry. Current chronicle: New York (Jan 1949), 456; ____ (Jan 1952), 617, 632
Craft, Robert. Anton Webern, 591; Bach-Strawinsky, 780; Ein Ballett für zwölf Tänzer, 789; Boulez and Stockhausen, 621; Il 'Canticum sacrum,' 780; A concert for Saint Mark, 799; Discoveries and convictions, 576; Reihenkompositionen: vom 'Septett' zum 'Agon,' 778; Schoenberg's Erwartung, 429
Curjel, Hans. Cage oder das wohlpräparierte Klavier, 634

Dace, Wallace. The dramatic structure of Schönberg's Erwartung, 430
Dahlhaus, Carl. Eine 'dritte Epoche' der Musik? 227
Dallapiccola, Luigi. A propos d'un trait 'expressionniste' de Mozart, 141; Contemporary composers on

their experiences of composition with twelve notes, 151; The genesis of the Canti di prigionia and Il prigioniero, 670; In memoria di Anton Webern, 567; Notes sur mon opéra, 647; On the twelve-note road, 640; Sulla strada della dodecafonia, 640

Dallin, Leon. Techniques of twentieth century composition, 165

d'Amico, Fedele, see Amico, Fedele d'

Dangel, Arthur. Wolfgang Fortner [Impromptus], 684a

Dansk Musiktidsskrift [twelve-tone and electronic issue], 54

Darmstädter Beiträge zur neuen Musik, 170, 174

Dean, Winton. Schoenberg's ideas, 143

del Mar, Norman. Gerhard as an orchestral composer, 691

Demuth, Norman. French piano music, 627; Musical trends in the twentieth century, 403

de Paoli, Domenico, see Paoli, Domenico de

Deutsch, Leonhard. Das Problem der Atonalität und des Zwölftonprinzip, 183; Zur Einführung in die Harmonik der Zeitgenössischen Klavierliteratur, 457

Deutsch, Max. Les cinq Pièces pour Orchestre d'Arnold Schönberg, 455; Le Concerto de chambre d'Alban Berg, 520

Il diapason [twelve-tone issue], 25

Dorian, Frederick Deutsch. Webern als Lehrer, 580a

Drew, David. The arts and entertainment: Dallapiccola, 658; Modern French music, 105; Roberto Gerhard, 687

Driesch, Kurt. Wolfgang Fortner, 680

Duhamel, Antoine. Arnold Schoenberg, la critique, et le monde musical contemporain, 331

du Pont, Henri de Carsalade, see Carsalade du Pont, Henri de

Eco, Umberto. L'opera in movimento e la coscienza dell'epoca, 71

Eimert, Herbert. Arnold Schönberg, der Fünfundsiebzig-Jährige, 322; Atonale Musiklehre, 128; A change of focus, 570; The composer's freedom of choice, 166; Die drei Shakespeare-Lieder, 778; Elektronische Musik, 237; Hauer, Josef Matthias, 700; Intermezzo II: Adorno und Kotschenreuther, 168; Interval proportions: String quartet [Webern], 570; Ist Zwölftonmusik lehrbar? 18; Lehrbuch der Zwölftontechnik, 142; Manuale di tecnica dodecafonia, 142; Möglichkeiten und Grenzen der elektronischen Musik, 236; Musique électronique, 253; Von der Entscheidungsfreiheit des Komponisten; Was ist elektronische Musik? 234; What is electronic music? 275; Zum Kapitel: atonale Musik, 128

Eisenmann, Will. Zur Sache Hauer, 697

Eisler, Hanns. Arnold Schönberg, 344

Electronic music (Die Reihe, 1), 275

Elektronische Musik in Italien, 256

Elston, Arnold. Some rhythmic practices in contemporary music, 599

Engel, Carl. Dischords mingled, 463; Schönberg Lunaire, 463

Engelmann, Hans Ulrich. Dodekaphonie und Musikgeschichte, 26; Fortners Phantasie über B-A-C-H, 684

Enkel, Fritz. Die Grundlagen der neuen Musik, 277

Erickson, Robert. Křeneks amerikanische Texte, 737; Krenek's later music (1930-1947), 733; The structure of music, 154

Erpf, Hermann Robert. Studien zur Harmonie- und Klangtechnik der neueren Musik, 181

Eschman, Karl. Changing forms in modern music, 137

Evangelisti, Franco. Towards electronic composition, 70; Verso una composizione elettronica, 70

Evans, Edwin. Krenek, Ernst, 746; Webern, Anton von, 587

Author Index

Experiences musicales: musiques concrète, electronique, exotique, 267

Fano, Michel. Pourvoirs transmis, 30; Wozzeck ou le nouvel opéra, 554
Felber, Erwin. Arnold Schönberg und die Oper, 450
Feldman, Harry Allen. Futurism—Arnold Schoenberg, 315; Music and the listener, 315
Ferrari, Luc. Les étapes de la production, 267; Les étapes de la vision, 267
Fiebig, Kurt. Was ist Zwölftonmusik? 124
Fiechtner, Helmut A. Ernst Krenek, 736; Hanns Jelinek, 711
Fleischer, Herbert. La musica contemporanea, 80
Forneberg, Erich. Der Geist der neuen Musik, 200
Forte, Allen. Composing with electrons in Cologne, 251; Contemporary tone structures, 432
Fortner, Wolfgang. Bluthochzeit nach Federico Garcia Lorca, 681; Kranichsteiner Aspekte, 170
Foss, Hubert. Schoenberg, 1874-1951, 365
Frid, Géza. Twaalf contra twaalf, 202, 203
Friedländer, Walther. Moderner Kompositionsunterricht, 678
25 [i.e., Fünf und zwanzig] Jahre neue Musik, 76, 381
Füssl, Karl Heinz. Selbstbesinnung am Beispiel Strawinskys, 788

Gardner, John. The Duenna, 692
Gatti, Guido M. Current chronicle: Italy, 665; Dallapiccola, Luigi, 643
Gavazzeni, Gianandrea. Musicisti d'Europa, 649
Gerhard, Roberto. Apropos Mr. Stadlen, 59; Contemporary composers on their experiences of composition with twelve notes, 151; Developments in twelve-tone technique, 163; Letters of Webern and Schoenberg, 581; Die Reihentechnik des Diatonikers, 787; Reply to George Perle, 195; Tonality in twelve-tone music, 191; Twelve-note technique in Stravinsky, 783; Wozzeck, 551
Gindele, Father Corbinian. Von cis nach c, 219
Glanville-Hicks, Peggy. Cage, John, 633
Glock, William. The arts and entertainment: Stravinsky's Threni, 818; Comment, 333
Godet, Robert. Après une audition de 'Pierrot Lunaire,' 462
Goehr, Alexander. Arnold Schoenberg's development towards the twelve-tone system, 105
Goehr, Walter. Arnold Schoenberg's development towards the twelve-tone system, 105; Musica-Umschau: Schönbergs Aussöhnung mit der Tonalität, 480
Goeyvaerts, Karol. The sound material of electronic music, 275
Goldbeck, Fred E. Boulez, Pierre, 612; Current chronicle: France, 610; Séries et hérésies, 51; The strange case of Schönberg, 334
Goldman, Richard F. Current chronicle: New York (Jul 1951), 669; ___ (Apr 1956), 809; ___ (Apr 1960), 809b
Goléa, Antoine. Deux portraits: Luigi Nono—Karlheinz Stockhausen, 30; Esthétique de la musique contemporaine, 29; Recontres avec Pierre Boulez, 615; Tendances de la musique concrète, 253
Gorer, Richard. An interim report on Humphrey Searle's muisc, 755
Gottlieb, Louis. Brandeis festival album, 603
Gottschalk, Nathan. Twelve note music as developed by Arnold Schoenberg, 103
Gould, Glenn. The dodecaphonist's dilemma, 199
Gradenwitz, Peter. The idiom and development in Schoenberg's quartets, 466; Reihenkomposition in Orient, 111; The religious

works of Arnold Schönberg, 413; Schönbergs religiöse Werke, 413
Graf, Max. Legend of a musical city, 318; Modern music, 319; Modern music in Vienna, 318; The path of Arnold Schoenberg, 319
Gravesano: Musik, Raumgestaltung, Elektroakustic, 239
Gray, Cecil. Arnold Schoenberg, 291; Arnold Schönberg, a critical study, 287; Atonalism, 9; Predicaments, 9; A survey of contemporary music, 291
Gredinger, Paul. Serial technique, 275
Greissle, Felix. Die formalen Grundlagen des Bläserquintetts von Arnold Schönberg, 474
Grout, Donald Jay. Opera between two wars, 539; A short history of opera, 539
Guàccero, Domenico. Problemi di sintassi musicale, 70; Problems of musical syntax, 70
Guenther, Siegfried. Der Kurs in Ernst Kreneks jungstem Schaffen, 732; Das trochäische Prinzip in Arnold Schoenbergs op. 13, 414

Hába, Alois. Neue Harmonielehre, 182; Schönberg und die weiteren Möglichkeiten der Musikentwicklung, 293
Hall, Richard. Twelve-tone music and tradition, 20
Hamel, Fred. Arnold Schönbergs Bekenntniswerk, 439
Hamilton, Iain. Alban Berg and Anton Webern, 105
Hampton, Christopher. Anton Webern and the consciousness of time, 579
Harrison, Lou. Homage to Schönberg: the late works, 398
Hartmann, Thomas von. Über Anarchie in der Musik, 74
Hartog, Howard. European music in the twentieth century, 105; German contemporary music, 105
Hauer, Josef Matthias. Atonale Musik, 127; Offener Brief [an Herbert Eimert], 128; Die Tropen und ihre Spannungen zum Dreiklang, 178; Über die Klangfarben, 126; Vom Wesen des Musikalischen, 126; Von Melos zur Pauke, 129; Zwölftontechnik, die Lehre von den Tropen, 130
Heck, Ludwig. Klänge in Schmelztiegel, 624
Heiss, Herman. Elemente der musikalischen Komposition, 140
Helm, Everett. Current chronicle: France, 777; ____: Germany (Apr 1951), 683; ____ (Oct 1952), 682; ____ (Oct 1955), 765; ____ (Jan 1959), 751; ____ (Apr 1959), 707; Operas by Egk, Klebe and Fortner, 718; Six modern German composers, 679
Henderson, Robert L. Schönberg and 'expressionism,' 117
Henze, Hans Werner. Contemporary composers on their experiences of composition with twelve notes, 151; Wo stehen wir Heute? 170
Herz, Gerhard. Current chronicle: Louisville, Kentucky, 674
Herzfeld, Friedrich. Musica nova, 93; Der Reiz des Krebses, 212
Hijman, Julius. Nieuwe oostenrijkse musiek, 81
Hill, Ralph. The concerto, 522
Hill, Richard S. Annual reports on acquisitions: music, 374; Book reviews, 151, 156; Music reviews: Arnold Schoenberg: De Profundis, 419; ____: Phantasy for violin, 431; ____: String trio, op. 45, 482; ____: Survivor from Warsaw, 479; Reviews of records: Berg: Lulu, 532; Schoenberg's tonerows and the tonal system of the future, 386
Hiller, Lejaren Arthur. Experimental music, 268
Hodeir, Andre. The young French music, 614
Holländer, Hans. Alban Berg, 500
Hübner, Herbert. Berg, Alban, 494
Humplik, Josef. Dem Freunde, 564
Hymanson, William. Schoenberg's String trio, 481

Inventaire des techniques rédactionelles, 207, 618
Isaacson, Leonard M. Experimental music, 268

Jachino, Carlo. Tecnica dodecafonica, 139
Jalowetz, Heinrich. On the spontaneity of Schoenberg's music, 388
Jelinek, Hanns. Anleitung zur Zwölftonkomposition nebst allerlei Paralipomena, 190, 215; Contemporary composers on their experiences of composition with twelve notes, 151; Versuch über der Sinn der Verwendung von Zwölftonreihen, 189
Joachim, Heinz. Current chronicle: Germany, 744; Ernst Krenek, 739
Johnson, Martha. A study of linear design in Gregorian chant and music written in the twelve-tone technique, 206
Jone, Hildegard. A cantata, 570
Jouve, Pierre Jean. Wozzeck d'Alban Berg, 563; Wozzeck ou le nouvel opéra, 554
Junge Komponisten (Die Reihe, 4), 168

Kaefer, Johannes. Essenza della dodecafonia, 25
Kagel, Mauricio. Ton-Cluster, Anschäge, Übergänge, 173
Kandinsky, Wassily. Über die Formfrage, 74
Katz, Adele T. Challenge to musical tradition, 389
Keller, Hans. The audibility of serial technique, 40; The B.B.C.'s victory over Schoenberg, 335; Concert and opera: Schoenberg memorial concert, 405; Dodecaphoneys, 41; First performances: (Feb 1952), 758; ___ (Nov 1952), 426; ___: the eclecticism of Wozzeck, 550; ___: their pre- and reviews, 486; ___: Schönbergians and Stravinskyians, 811; First performances and their reviews, 28; The half-year's new music [on Dallapiccola's Quaderno musicale], 673; ___ [on Schoenberg's op. 50a], 418; In Memoriam Dylan Thomas: Stravinsky's Schoenbergian technique, 806; ___: Strawinskys schönbergische Technik, 778; The 'lucky' hand and other errors, 434; Mátyás Seiber, 763; Moses, Freud, and Schönberg, 353; The new in review: Schoenberg I: the problem of performance, 350; ___: Schoenberg II: the last work, 422; ___: Schoenberg III: Moses und Aron, 448; New music: two Schoenberg problems, 433; Schoenberg, 400; Schoenberg's comic opera, 490; A serial masterpiece, 808; Serial octave transpositions, 198; Stravinsky as serialist, 807; Strict serial technique in classical music, 158; XIII Maggio Musicale Fiorentino, 667; Unpublished Schoenberg letters, 373
Keller, Wilhelm. Elektronische Musik und musique concrète, 226
Kelterborn, Rudolf. Gegensätzliche Formprinzipien in der Zeitgenössichen Musik, 167; Stilistisch gegensätzliche Entwicklungen auf der Basis der Zwölftontecnik, 46
Kerman, Joseph. Opera as drama, 558; Terror and self-pity: Alban Berg's Wozzeck, 557; Wozzeck and the Rake's progress, 558
Kessler, Hubert. Some problems of tonality in relation to Schönberg's twelve-tone technique, 187
Ketting, Otto. Arnold Schönberg in Amerika, 372.
Kirchmeyer, Helmut. Igor Strawinsky, 786
Klammer, Armin. Webern's Piano variations, op. 27, 570
Klangstruktur der Musik, 240
Klebe, Giselher. First practical work, 275; Über meine Oper 'Die Räuber,' 717
Klein, Fritz Heinrich. Die Grenze der Halbtonwelt, 179
Kloppenburg, W. C. M. Het thema

van Schoenbergs Variationen für Orchester, 485

Koechlin, Charles. Quelques réflexions au sujet de la musique atonale, 14

Koegler, Horst. The international scene: Germany (Apr 1957), 750; ____ (Feb 1958), 409; ____ Hamburg, 743

Köhler, Siegfried. Was ist Zwölftonmusik? 221

Koenig, Gottfried Michael. Bo Nilsson, 168; Henri Pousseur, 168; Studio techniques, 275; Studium in studio, 283

Kolisch, Rudolf. Nonos Varianti, 752; Über die Krise der Streiche, 170

Koperberg-Van Wermeskerken, A. Bij een pianostuk van Schoenberg, 460

Korn, Peter Jona. Apropos Zwangsjacke, 56

Koster, Ernst. Kinderkrankheiten der elektrogenen Musik, 242

Krenek, Ernst. Alban Berg, 492; Alban Bergs 'Lulu,' 535; Alle spalle dei giovani, 50; Arnold Schoenberg, 295; Bericht über Versuche in total determinierter Musik, 170; Book reviews, 190, 496, 712; Ein Brief zur Zwölftontechnik, 33; Cadential formations in twelve-tone music, 135; Contemporary composers on their experiences of composition with twelve notes, 151; De rebus prius factus, 54; Extents and limits of serial technique, 739a; Freiheit und Verantwortung, 564; A glance over the shoulders of the young, 275; Homage to Schönberg, 387; Is the twelve-tone technique on the decline? 150; Kurzer Rechenschaftsbericht, 735; Lydteorier, 54; Music here and now, 11; Der musikalische Fortschnitt, 720; New developments in electronic music, 244; New developments of the twelve-tone technique, 136; The same stone, 570; Selbstdarstellung, 720; Self-analysis, 723; Sestina, 747; Studies in counterpoint, 209; Technique de douze sons et classicisme, 141; Über neue Musik, 10; Versuch einer Sebstanalyse, 721; Was ist Reihenmusik? 172; Zu meinem Kammermusikwerken, 1936-1950, 738; Zur Sprache gebracht, 535; Zwölfton-Kontrapunkt-Studien, 209; Die Zwölftonmusik als Lehre, 17

Krüger, Walther. Zwölftonmusik und Gegenwart, 19

Kulbin, N. Die freie Musik, 74

Laaff, Ernst. Wolfgang Fortner, 677

Lang, Paul Henry. Editorial [Musical quarterly], 65

Laux, Karl. Die moderne Musik ist tot, 345

Le Caine, Hugh. Electronic music, 276

Leibowitz, René. Alban Berg et l'essence de l'opéra, 538; Alban Berg's Five orchestral songs, 541; Arnold Schoenberg's recent tonal works and the synthesis of tonality, 300; Arnold Schoenberg's 'Survivor from Warsaw,' 478; Aspects récents de la technique de douze sons, 141; Besuch bei Arnold Schönberg, 363; Innovation and tradition in contemporary music: I, the traditional significance of the music of Arnold Schoenberg, 320; ____: II, the tragic art of Anton Webern, 575; ____: III, Alban Berg, 502; Introduction à la musique de douze sons, 484; Music chronicle: two composers, 360; La musique: Anton Webern, 565; Les oeuvres d'Arnold Schoenberg ou la conscience du drame futur, 452; Open forum: variations on a theme, 15; Qu'est-ce que la musique de douze sons? 595; Schoenberg and his school, 84; Schoenberg et son école, 84; Schönbergs Klavierkonzert, 424

Leichtentritt, Hugo. Arnold Schoenberg: opus 11 and opus 19, 459; Musical form, 459

Lesure, François. Profili di musicisti contemporanei, 616
Lewinsky, Wolf-Eberhard von. Giselher Klebe, 168; Junge Komponisten, 168
Lewkovitch, Bernhard. Agon: Ballet for 12 dansere, 792; Stravinskijs klagensange, 823
Ligeti, György. Pierre Boulez, 168; Zur III. Klaviersonate von Boulez, 628
Lindlar, Heinrich. Cantata, 778; Elektronische Musik im Kölner Funkhaus, 274; Igor Strawinskys sakraler Gesang, 779; Mir fehlt die grosse Freude, 504; Der Sakralkomponist, 787; Strawinskys sakraler Gesang, 796
Lissa, Zofja. Geschichtliche Vorform der Zwölftontechnik, 8
List, Kurt. Anton von Webern, 574; Homage to Schönberg: Ode to Napoleon, 449; Lulu, after the première, 529
Lockspeiser, Edward. Humphrey Searle, 757
Luening, Otto. Karlheinz Stockhausen, 770

Macchi, Egisto. The composer, the listener, and the new music, 70; Produzione e consumo della nuova musica, 70
Machabey, Armand. La singulière figure de Jean-Mathias Hauer, 694
Mâche, François-Bernard. Connaissance des structures sonores, 267
Maclean, Charles. London notes, 355; Schönberg—a short sketch of his life, 356
Maegaard, Jan. Dodekafoni—et resumé, 54; Karlheinz Stockhausen, 768
Magnani, Luigi. Book review, 84; Le frontiere della musica, 305; Schönberg e il simbolismo, 25
Magni Dufflocq, Enrico. La musica contemporanea, 79
Mahler, Fritz. Zu Alban Bergs Oper Wozzeck, 561

Malipiero, Riccardo. La dodecafonia come tecnica, 149
Mangeot, André. Schoenberg's Fourth quartet, 472
Mann, Robert W. Vita musicale: Stoccolma, 716
Mantelli, Alberto. Elenco delle opere di Berg, 518; Note su Alban Berg, 491
Manzoni, Giacomo. Breve introduzione alla musica elettronica, 262; Bruno Maderna, 168; Profili di musicisti contemporanei: Karlheinz Stockhausen, 769
Mar, Norman del, see del Mar, Norman
Marcel, Luc-André. Arnold Schoenberg, 324
Maren, Roger. Electronic music, 255; The music of Anton Webern, 577; The musical numbers game, 636
Martenot, Maurice. Lutherie électronique, 30
Martin, Frank. Schoenberg and ourselves, 336; Schoenberg et nous, 141
Mason, Colin. Dallapiccola and the twelve-note method, 672; Dodecaphoneys: a reply, 44; Gerhard, Roberto, 683; Die Kammermusik, 787; New music, 593; Reviews of music (Jul 1955), 774; ____ (Apr 1958), 620; Searle, Humphrey, 756; A Spanish composer in exile, 690; Stravinsky's contribution to chamber music, 781; Stravinsky's newest works, 809a; Webern's later chamber music, 592
Masullo, Aldo. La 'struttura' nell'evoluzione dei linguaggi scientifici, 70
Mayer, Harry. Een blik achter de werkwijze van Arnold Schoenberg, 461; De liedkunst van Anton Webern, 601; Twaalf contra twaalf, 203; Twee toneelwerken van Arnold Schoenberg, 453
Melichar, Alois. Musik in der Zwangsjacke, 56
Mellers, Wilfred Howard. Recent trends in British music, 91; Ro-

manticism and the twentieth century, 349; Schoenberg and Hindemith, 349
Menasce, Jacques. Berg and Bartók, 501
Mersmann, Hans. Die moderne Musik seit der Romantik, 292; Die tonsprache der neuen Musik, 131
Messiaen, Olivier. Préface, 267
Metzger, Heinz-Klaus. Analysis of the Sacred song, op. 15, no. 4 [Webern], 570; Gescheiterte Begriffe in Theorie und Kritik der Musik, 67; Hommage à Edgard Varèse, 174; Intermezzo I: das Alten der Philosophie der neuen Musik, 168; John Cage o della liberazione, 637; Nochmals 'Wider die Natur,' 229; Webern and Schönberg, 570
Meyer-Eppler, Werner. Elektronische Kompositionstechnik, 273; Elektronische Musik, 238; Gravesano, 239; Statistic and psychologic problems of sound, 275
Middleton, Robert E. Abt, 68
Mila, Massimo. Book review, 94; Dallapiccola, Luigi, 641; La dodecafonia e la sua offensiva, 25; L'incontro Heine-Dallapiccola, 655; Lettera da Venezia, 699; 'Il prigioniero' di Luigi Dallapiccola, 668; Vita musicale: Venezia (Jul 1956), 795; ___ (Sept 1958), 815
Milhaud, Darius. Begegnungen mit Schönberg, 370; Erinnerungen am Arnold Schönberg, 371; Konstruierte Musik, 162; Open forum: variations on a theme, 15; To Arnold Schoenberg on his 70th birthday, 359
Milner, Anthony. English contemporary music, 105; The lunatic fringe combed, 49; Melody in Stravinsky's music, 785; The vocal element in melody, 45
Mitchell, Donald. Bartók, Stravinsky, and Schoenberg, 341; The character of Lulu, 534; The emancipation of the dissonance, 88; Schoenberg the traditionalist, 321; Summer festivals: Von Heute auf Morgen and Erwartung, 454

Moles, Abraham André. Instrumentation électronique et musiques expérimentales, 267; Machines à musique, 253

Morton, Lawrence. Current chronicle: Los Angeles, 790; Los Angeles letter (Nov 1952), 626; ___ (Feb 1953), 660

Musical craftsmanship (Die Reihe, 3), 166

Le musiche religiose di Igor Strawinsky, 780

Un musicien d'aujourd'hui: Luigi Dallapiccola, 647

Un musicien d'aujourd'hui: René Leibowitz, 141

Musikalisches Handwerk (Die Reihe, 3), 166

La musique et ses problèmes contemporains, 30

Myers, Rollo H. Music in France in the post-war decade, 98; Some personalities and trends in contemporary French music, 613

Myhill, John. Musical theory and musical practice, 42

Nathan, Hans. The twelve-tone compositions of Luigi Dallapiccola, 653; The Viennese Lied, 132

Neighbor, Oliver W. Dodecaphony in Schoenberg's String trio, 483; The evolution of twelve-note music, 99; In defense of Schönberg, 330; A talk on Schoenberg for Composers' Concourse, 473

Nettel, Reginald. Electronic music, 258

Neumann, Friedrich. Tonalität und Atonalität, 197

Newlin, Dika. Arnold Schönberg in Amerika, 368; Bruckner, Mahler, Schoenberg, 298; Music reviews: Anton von Webern, Quintet, 600; Schönberg in America, 1933-1948, 361; Schoenberg's new 'Fantasy,' 300

Newman, Ernest. A propos of Schönberg's Five orchestral pieces, 307; Wozzeck, 559

Nono, Luigi. Die Entwicklung der Reihentechnik, 170; Gitterstäbe am Himmel der Freiheit, 73b; The historical reality of music today, 73b; Vorword zum Kranichsteiner Kompositions-Studio 1958, 174
Norman, Gertrude. Letters of composers, 390

Oesch, Hans. Einführung in die elektronische Musik, 248
L'oeuvre du XXe siècle, 331, 563
Oeuvres d'Alban Berg, 519
Oeuvres d'Anton Webern, 589
Ogdon, Wilbur Lee. Series and structure, 155; The twelve-tone series and cantus firmus, 745
Open forum: variations on a theme, 15
Oper im XX. Jahrhundert, 556, 671
Opera news [issue on Wozzeck], 562
Ordini; studi sulla nuova musica, 70

Pacque, Désiré. L'atonalité, ou mode chromatique unique, 5
Pade, Else Marie. Efter Stockhausen, 776; Lydprofetier? 54
Pannain, Guido. L'Internationale Musikgesellschaft für Neue Musik, 475; Origine e significato della musica dodecafonica, 97; Schönberg e la 'Filosofia della musica nuova,' 342
Paoli, Domenico de. Chroniques et notes: Italie, Luigi Dallapiccola, 644
Pauli, Hansjörg. Hans Werner Henze's Italian music, 708; On Stravinsky's 'Threni,' 814; Zur seriallen Struktur von Igor Stravinsky's 'Threni,' 814
Payne, Elsie. The theme and variation in modern music, 171
Perle, George. Atonality and the twelve-note system in the United States, 118b; Book review, 156; Evolution of the tone row, 134; The harmonic problem in twelve-tone music, 196; The possible chords in twelve-tone music, 194; Schönberg's late style, 392; Serial composition and atonality, 160; Theory and practice in twelve-tone music, 69
Pestalozza, Luigi. I compositori milanesi del dopoguerra, 106; L'ultima avanguardia, 250; Vita musicale: musiche nuovissime, 629
Pfaundler, Geertruy von. De jongste werken van Igor Strawinsky (uit de jaren 1952-1957), 782
Pfrogner, Hermann. Elektronik—Lust am Untergang? 231; Die Zwölfordnung der Töne, 27
Philippot, Michel. Espace vital, 267; Musique et acoustique, 30
Pijper, Willem. Alban Berg, 499
Pincherle, Marc. Aspects de Schoenberg, 340
Piovesan, Alessandro. Catalogo generale delle opere di Igor Stravinsky, 780; Promesso, 780
Pisk, Paul Amadeus. Arnold Schoenberg—the influence of my musical youth, 300; Schoenberg's twelve-tone opera, 295, 488; The tonal era draws to a close, 180
Piston, Walter. More views on serialism, 60
Pizzetti, Ildebrando. Internationale Musik? 34
Polnauer, Josef. Briefe [by Anton Webern], 582; Schönbergs 'Verbundenheit,' 293
Pont, Henri de Carsalade du, see Carsalade du Pont, Henri de
Porena, Boris. L'avanguardia musicale di Darmstadt, 63
Poulenc, Francis. Open forum: variations on a theme, 15
Poullin, Jacques. L'orielle et le malentendu, 267; Son et espace, 253
Pousseur, Henri. Da Schoenberg a Webern: una mutazione, 586; Domaines à venir, 30; Ecrits [Alban Berg], 509; Forma e pratica musicale, 73; Formal elements in a new compositional material, 275; Outline of a method, 166; Scambi, 754; Theorie und Praxis in der neuesten Musik, 174; Webern und die

Theorie, 170; Webern's organic chromaticism, 570; Zur Methodik, 166
Preussner, Eberhard. Ernst Krenek, 729
Prieberg, Fred K. Erste elektronische Partitur, 279; Italiens elektronische Musik, 265; Lexikon der neuen Musik, 112; Musica ex machina, 283a; Musik im technischen Zeitalters, 247; Musik: Töne aus der Elektronröhre, 260

<u>The progress of science: electronic music</u>, 263

Prosperi, Carlo. L'atonalità nella musica contemporanea, 201

Radiodiffusion Télévision Française. Groupe de récherches musicales. Experiences musicales, 267
Randolph, David. A new music made with a machine, 270
Rankle, Karl. Arnold Schönberg, 404
Rebling, Eberhard. Arnold Schönbergs Lebensbekenntnis, 446
Reck, Albert von. Gestaltzusammenhänge in 'Canticum Sacrum' von Strawinsky, 804
Redlich, Hans Ferdinand. Alban Berg, the man and his music, 496; Alban Berg: Versuch einer Würdigung, 496; Alban Bergs Violinkonzert, 496, 524; Alle guten Dingen, 496, 512; Arnold Schönberg, 402; Gerhard, Roberto, 686; Hanns Jelinek, 713a; Hauer, Josef (Matthias), 698; Heimat und Freiheit; zur Ideologie der jüngsten Werken Ernst Kreneks, 730; Křenek, Ernst, 724; New music: a critical interim report, 812; Wozzeck: Dramaturgie und musikalische Form, 560
Reich, Willi. Alban Berg (1930), 515; ____ (1941), 493; Alban Berg als Apologet Arnold Schönbergs, 508; Alban Berg: Bildnis im Wort, 509a; Alban Berg: mit Bergs eigenem Schriften, 492; Alban Berg: 'Wozzeck,' 556; Alban Berg's Lulu, 528; Alban Berg's 'Wozzeck,' a guide to the text and music, 548; An der Seite von Alban Berg, 535b; Anton von Webern, 588; Arnold Schönberg, 327; Arnold Schönbergs Oper 'Moses und Aron,' 445; Aus Alban Bergs Jugendzeit, 513; Aus unbekannten Briefen von Alban Berg, 511; Berg, Alban, 495; Berg's new work, 'Der Wein,' 543; Berichte aus dem Ausland: Schönberg-Premier, 489; Ein Briefwechsel über 'Moses und Aron,' 444; Les dernières oeuvres d'Alban Berg, 517; Deutsche Première nach 15 Jahren, 531; Erinnerung an Alban Berg, 506; Ernst Krenek als Musikschriftsteller, 722; Ernst Křeneks Arbeit in der Zwölftontechnik, 734; Freiwillige für Schoenberg, 328; Grenzgebiete der neuen Töne, 6; Josef Matthias Hauer, 695; Lieber Freund Doktor Ploderer, 564; Lulu, the text and music, 527; Musica-Bericht: Krenek und Martinu, 741; Schönberg's new Männerchor, 417; Versuch einer Geschichte der Zwölftonmusik, 89; Weberns Musik, 564; Weberns Vorträge, 564

<u>Die Reihe</u>. (1) Electronic music, 275; (2) Anton Webern, 570; (3) Musical craftsmanship, 166; (4) Junge Komponisten, 168; (5) Berichte/Analysen, 67, 173, 269, 283, 628, 772
Reti, Rudolf Richard. Tonality, atonality, pantonality, 169
Ringger, Rolf Urs. Zur formbildenden Kraft des vertonten Wortes, 542
Robbins, Michela. A Schoenberg seminar, 367
Rochberg, George. The harmonic tendency of the hexachord, 204a; The hexachord and its relation to the twelve-tone row, 156; Indeterminacy in the new music, 73a; Music reviews: Milton Babbitt, Woodwind quartet, 604; Tradition and 12-tone music, 43

Rössler, Ernst Karl. Zeitgenössische Kirchenmusik, 52
Rognoni, Luigi. Espressionismo e dodecafonia, 94; Die Frage der Technik in der elektronischen Musik, 228; La musica 'elettronica' e il problema della tecnica, 228; Musik der jungen Generation: Kompositions und Interpretations-Probleme, 228
Rondi, Brunello. Il cammino della musica d'oggi e l'esperienza elettronica, 268a; La dodecafonia e il messaggio dell'ordine, 25
Roosenfeld, Paul. Musical portraits, 285; Schoenberg, 285
Roostal, Max. Berg's Violin concerto: a revision, 523
Rostand, Claude. Canticum Sacrum d'Igor Stravinsky, 800; Dodécaphonisme, 122; French music today, 90; L'Italie musicale actuelle, 109; König Hirsch de H. Werner Henze, 709; La musique de scène de Pierre Boulez, 623; La musique française contemporaine, 90; Note sommaire sur le système dodécaphonique et la méthode sérielle, 301; Zwölfton-Manierismus, 53
Rubin, Louis. The idiom of the violin in twentieth century music, 425
Rubin, Marcel. Alban Berg und die Zukunft der Schönberg Schule, 505; Was bedeutet und Schönberg? 346
Rubsamen, Walter H. Schoenberg in America, 366
Rufer, Josef. Arnold Schönbergs Nachlass, 411; Composition with twelve notes, 151; Dokumente einer Freundschaft, 514; Intorno alla genesi del Moses und Aaron di Schoenberg, 441; Die Komposition mit zwölf Tönen, 151; Luigi Dallapiccola: Il prigioniero, 671; A talk on Arnold Schoenberg, 410; Was ist Zwölftonmusik? 166a; Das Werk Arnold Schönbergs, 412
Ruppel, K. H. Berichte aus dem Ausland: Strawinskys neues Werk, 816

Ruwet, Nicholas. Contraddizioni del linguaggio seriale, 72
Le rythme musical, 208, 503

Saathen, Friedrich. Ernst Křeneks Botschaft im Wort, 727; Le Marteau sans maître von Pierre Boulez, 619
Sabin, Robert. Alban Berg's Wozzeck, 549
Saby, Bernard. Un aspect des problèmes de la thématique sérielle, 141
Sackville-West, Edward. Atonalism: second thoughts, 12
Saerchinger, César. The truth about Schoenberg, 295
Salazar, Adolfo. Arnold Schoenberg post-mortem, 325; Music in our time, 82
San, Hermann Van, see Van San, Hermann
Santi, Piero. Conseguenze e inconseguenze, 55; Luciano Berio, 168
Schaeffer, Pierre. Le Groupe de recherches musicales, 267; Situation actuelle de la musique expérimentale, 267; Vers une musique expérimentale, 253
Schaeffner, André. Chroniques et commentaires, 465
Schatz, Hilmar. Theoretiker des Zufalls, 110
Scherchen, Hermann. Depassement de l'orchestre, 253; Stockhausen und die Zeit, 775
Schilling, Hans Ludwig. Zur Instrumentation in Igor Strawinskys Spätwerk, 813
Schindler, Kurt. Arnold Schönberg's Quartet in D minor, 468
Schlee, Alfred. Vienna since the Anschluss, 83
Schmale, Erich. Die Zwölftonmusik von Josef Matthias Hauer, 696
Schmidt-Garre, Helmut. Berg als Lehrer, 507; Zwölftonmusik—Ende einer Entwicklung, 21
Schnebel, Dieter. Karlheinz Stockhausen, 168
Schneider, J. Marius. Ernst Krenek, 731

Schnippering, H. Atonalität und temperierte Stimmung, 218; Von der Logik der Zwölftonmusik, 220

Schoenberg, Arnold. Apollonian evaluation of a Dionysian epoch, 152; Aus Briefen Arnold Schönbergs, 378; Briefe, 376; Briefe aus vier Jahrzehnten, 377; La composition à douze sons, 141; Composition with twelve tones, 143; Foreword to Webern's Six bagatelles, op. 6, 570; Further to the Schoenberg-Mann controversy, 362; Gesinnung oder Erkenntnis? 76; [Letter to Nicolas Slonimsky], 390; [Letters to Roberto Gerhard], 581; Mein Publikum, 357; Mia evolución, 364; My evolution, 364; Open forum: variations on a theme, 15; The orchestral variations, op. 31, 485a; Problems of harmony, 184, 295; A self-analysis, 369; Structural functions of harmony, 152; Style and idea, 143; Tonality and form, 185, 295; Über Alban Berg, 510; Ein unbekannter Brief von Arnold Schönberg an Alban Berg, 379; Unpublished Schoenberg letters, 373; Das Verhältnis zum Text, 74

Schubert, Reinhold. Bernd Alois Zimmermann, 168

Schuh, Willi. Strukturanalyse eines Fragments aus Strawinskys 'Threni,' 819; Uraufführungen neuer Kirchenmusik, 798; Zu Ernst Kreneks Invention, 740

Schweizer, Gottfried. Komponistenporträt: Mátyás Seiber 50 Jahre, 761; Zwischen Bartók und Schönberg: das Bild Mátyás Seibers, 762

Schweizerische Musikzeitung [Ernst Krenek Heft], 738, 740

Schwieger, Johannes. Josef Matthias Hauer, 701

Score [Roberto Gerhard issue], 163, 687-689, 691-692

Scriabine, Marina. Athématisme et fonction thématique dans la musique contemporaine, 207; Pierre Boulez et la musique concrète, 611

Searle, Humphrey. Atonal and serial music, 113; Book review, 143; Contemporary composers on their experiences of composition with twelve notes, 151; Conversations with Webern, 580; Leibowitz, René, 748; Luigi Dallapiccola, 638; A new kind of music, 108; Notes of the day, 326; Open forum: variations on a theme, 15; Schoenberg and the future, 302; Schoenberg, Arnold, 304; Twelve-note music, 153; Twentieth century counterpoint, 211; Webern, Anton, 569

Seiber, Mátyás. Composing with twelve notes, 123; Contemporary composers on their experiences of composition with twelve notes, 151; A note on 'Ulysses,' 767

Sessions, Roger. Book review, 10; Music in crisis, 7, 295; Some notes on Schönberg and the 'method of composition with twelve tones,' 337; Song and pattern in music today, 48; To the editor [Score], 61

Shawe-Taylor, Desmond. The arts and entertainment: Stravinsky as serialist, 807

Simbriger, Heinrich. Die heutige Situation der Zwölftonmusik, 114; Die Situation der Zwölftonmusik, 164

Simpson, Robert Wilfred. Guide to modern music on records, 113

Skrebkow, S. Gegen die Atonalität Schönbergs, für Prokofjew, 351

Skulsky, Abraham. After Webern, who? 622; Dallapiccola felt impelled to introduce a new romantic era, 639; Opera, 1954, 663

Slonimsky, Nicolas. Music since 1900, 4; The plurality of melodic and harmonic systems, 133; A Schoenberg chronology, 295

Smith, Moses. Alban Berg—Finale: a requiem, 521

Smith, Robert. Nichtsmusik, 62

Smith Brindle, Reginald. Current chronicle: Italy (Oct 1955), 666; ____ (Apr 1957), 657; ____ (Jan 1958), 608; ____ (Jul 1959), 749;

Italian contemporary music, 105; The lunatic fringe: I. electronic music, 249; ____: III. computational composition, 161; The origins of Italian dodecaphony, 104; Reports from abroad: Italy, the R. A. I. Studio, 264; ____: Venice contemporary music festival, 817; The symbolism in Berg's 'Lyric suite,' 537
Sollertinskii, Ivan I. Arnold Schoenberg, 294
Somigli, Carlo. Il modus operandi di Arnold Schoenberg, 380
Sonner, Rudolf. Elektronische Musik, 243
Spinner, Leopold. Analysis of a period: Concerto for nine instruments [Webern], 570; A short introduction to the technique of twelve-tone composition, 175a
Stadlen, Peter. Book review, 570; Kritik am Seriellen, 57; No real casualties? 66; Serialism reconsidered, 57
Stefan, Paul. Arnold Schoenberg, 296; Schoenberg's operas, 295, 428
Stefan-Gruenfeldt, Paul. Arnold Schönberg, 289
Stein, Erwin. Anton Webern, 583; ____: obituary, 303, 566; Die Behandlung der Sprechstimme in Pierrot Lunaire, 303; Berg's opera Lulu in Zurich, 303; Einige Bemerkungen zu Schoenbergs Zwölftonreihen, 382; Das gedankliche Prinzip in Beethovens Musik, 383; The Gurrelieder, 303; Idées d'Arnold Schönberg sur la musique, 313; Igor Stravinsky: Canticum Sacrum, 794; Mahler, Reger, Strauss, and Schoenberg, 303; Mahler, Reger, Strauss, und Schönberg, 303, 381; Musical thought: Beethoven and Schoenberg, 303; Neue Chöre von Schönberg, 415; Neue Formenprinzipien, 288; New formal principles, 303; Orpheus in new guises, 303; Performing Schoenberg's music, 303; Schoenberg, 303; Schoenberg and the German line, 311; Schönberg's new structural form, 471; Schoenberg's position today, 316; Some observations on Schoenberg's twelve-note rows, 303; Stravinsky's Septet (1953), 810; The treatment of the speaking voice in Pierrot Lunaire, 303; Über den Vortrag von Schönbergs Musik, 303; Wozzeck, 303, 553; Zu Schoenbergs neuer Suite, op. 29, 477
Steinecke, Wolfgang, ed. Darmstädter Beiträge zur neuen Musik, 170, 174
Steinhard, Erich. Bemerkungen zum Expressionismus, 75
Stephan, Rudolf. Anton von Webern, 585; Eine 'dritte Epoche' der Musik? 227; Gegenwärtiges Komponieren, 675; Hans Werner Henze, 168; Neue Musik, 170a; Über einige geistliche Kompositionen Anton von Weberns, 590; Unorthodoxe Musik, 401
Steuermann, Eduard. The piano music of Schoenberg, 295
Stockhausen, Karlheinz. A proposito di musica elettronica, 252; Actualia, 275; Elektronische und instrumentale Musik, 269; Une expérience électronique, 30; For the 15th of September, 1955, 570; How time passes, 166; Musik in Raum, 174, 771, 772; Sprache und Musik, 170; Structure and experimental time, 570; Weberns Konzert für 9 Instrumente, 596; Wie die Zeit vergeht, 166
Stravinsky, Igor. Answers to 34 questions, 784; 35 Antworten auf 35 Fragen, 784
Strawinsky in Amerika, 778
Strawinsky: Wirklichkeit und Wirkung, 787
Stuckenschmidt, Hans Heinz. Alban Berg, 115; Anton von Webern, 115; Anton Webern, 571; Arnold Schoenberg, 301; Entwicklung oder Experiment? 170; German musical life, 107; Hans Werner Henze, 115, 706; Henze, Hans Werner, 705; Igor Strawinsky, 115; Josef Matthias Hauer, 693;

Author Index

König Hirsch (Re Cervo) di Hans Werner Henze, 710; Luigi Dallapiccola, 115; Moderne Psalmen von Arnold Schönberg, 420; Il mondo della sonorità ignote, 257; Neue Musik, 86; Schönbergs religiöse Werke, 407; Schöpfer der neuen Musik, 115; Sitten und Gebräuche der Neutöner, 118; Stil und Ästhetik Schoenbergs, 115, 306; Synthesis and new experiments, 703; The third stage, 275; Vocal style in the twentieth century, 205; Das Zwölftonsystem, 77

Suder, Alexander L. Die überflüssige Windmaschine, 225

Swarowsky, Hans. Canticum Sacrum, 797

Symkins, L. O. Arnold Schoenberg's new world of dodecaphonic music, 121

Le système dodécaphonique, 141

Tall, Joel. Music without musicians, 254

Tardieu, Jean. Décade de musique expérimentale, 253

Taylor, Noel Heath. Arnold Schoenberg: music in motion, 317; The Schoenberg concept, 186

Tenschert, Roland. Hanns Jelinek: zu seinem 'Zwölftonwerk,' 715

Le théâtre musical, 452, 647

Thilman, Johannes Paul. Die Kompositionsweise mit zwölf Tönen, 47; Probleme der neuen Polyphonie, 210

Thomas, Ernst. Ein 'Allelujah' aus dem Jahre 1956, 607

Thompson, Oscar. Great modern composers, 296, 493

Thomson, Virgil. The art of judging music, 24; Atonality today, 87; Music right and left, 87; Reflections, 24

Thoresby, Christina. Lulu d'Alban Berg au théâtre, 530

Thybo, Lief. Menneske-Maskine, 54

Tiessen, Heinz. Zur Geschichte der jüngsten Musik (1913-1928), 2

Titone, Antonio. Order and quadridimensionality, 70; Ordine e quadridimensionalità, 70

Truscott, Harold. The real atonalism, 204

Turchi, Guido. Critica, esegesi e dodecafonia, 32; Lettere critiche: Igor Strawinsky, 805

Tuttle, T. Temple. Schönberg's compositions for piano solo, 458

Unger, Udo. Die Klavierfuge im zwanzigsten Jahrhundert, 213; Luigi Nono, 168

Ussachevsky, Vladimir. La 'tape music' aux Etats-Unis, 253

Valentin, Erich. Klassiker aus antikem Geist: Luigi Dallapiccola, 650

Vandella, Romuald. Musique exotique et musique expérimentale, 267

Van den Linden, R. Cort, see Cort Van den Linden, R.

Van San, Hermann. Einheitswissenschaft und Musik, 280

Van Wermeskerken, A. Koperberg, see Koperberg-Van Wermeskerken, A.

Vellekoop, Gerrit. De 'Lamentatio Jeremiae Prophetae' van Ernst Krsjenek, 742

Vers une musique expérimentale, 253

Viebig, Ernst. Berg's 'Wozzeck,' 544

Viertel, Berthold. Schoenberg's Jakobsleiter, 295

Vlad, Roman. Anton von Webern e la composizione atematica, 584; Aspetti metafisici della poetica dodecafonica, 116; Dallapiccola, 35, 651; Elementi metafisici nella poetica dodecafonia, 25, 35; Igor Strawinskys 'Threni,' 821; Luigi Dallapiccola, 116, 648, 652; Moderne Psalmen von Arnold Schönberg, 423; Modernità e tradizione nella musica contemporanea, 35; Le musiche religiose di Strawinsky, 780; My

first impressions of Roberto
Gerhard's music, 689; Note
sulla dodecafonia, 35; Poetica
e tecnica della dodecafonia, 22;
Il prigioniero, 35; Recensioni:
Pierre Boulez, Structures, 630;
Die Reihe and electronic music,
245; Storia della dodecafonia,
116; L'ultimo Schoenberg, 35,
399; Vita musicale: Roma (Mar
1957), 656; ___ (Dec 1957), 791
Voci aggiunte a un dizionario dei
musicisti italiani contemporanei:
Luigi Dallapiccola, 645
Vogelsang, Konrad. Alban Berg,
Leben und Werk, 498
von Lewinsky, Wolf-Eberhard, see
Lewinsky, Wolf-Eberhard von
von Pfaundler, Geertruy, see
Pfaundler, Geertruy von
von Reck, Albert, see Reck, Albert
von
von Webern, Anton, see Webern,
Anton

Walker, Alan. Back to Schönberg,
175c; Schönberg's classical
background, 394
Walter, Arnold. Music and electronics, 272
Walter, Franz. A l'écoute des musiciens d'avant-garde, 64
Walters, Willard Gibson. Technical
problems in modern violin music,
427
Webern, Anton. Aus Schönbergs
Schriften, 293; Briefe an Hildegard Jone und Josef Humplik,
582; Choralis constantinus, 570;
Homage to Arnold Schoenberg,
570; [Letters to Roberto Gerhard],
581; Schönbergs Musik, 284; Der
Schönbergschüler, 564
Weiss, Adolf. The lyceum of Schönberg, 385; The twelve-tone series,
295
Weissmann, Adolph. Ernst Krenek,
728
Weissmann, John S. Current chronicle: Italy (Jan 1957), 801; ___
(Jan 1959), 820; Mátyás Seiber,
759; The new in review: Venice
1958, 822; Seiber, Mátyás
(György), 760; Die Streichquartette von Mátyás Seiber,
764
Wellesz, Egon. Arnold Schönberg
[article], 467; ___ [book], 286;
Arnold Schönberg et son oeuvre,
396; Arnold Schönberg: la doctrine, 290; ___: la voie nouvelle,
290; The origins of Schönberg's
twelve-tone system, 393; Reviews of music: Webern, Anton,
String Quartet, 598; Schönberg
and beyond, 395; Schoenberg,
Arnold, 397
Werker, Gerard. Alban Berg en
zijn opera Lulu, 533
Werner, Eric. Current chronicle:
France, 437
Westphal, Kurt. Arnold Schoenbergs
Weg zur Zwölftonmusik, 384
White, Eric Walter. Stravinsky, 105
Wiedman, Robert William. Expressionism in music, 101
Wiesengrund Adorno, Theodor, see
Adorno, Theodor Wiesengrund
Wildberger, Jacques. Dallapiccolas
'Cinque canti,' 661
Wildgans, Friedrich. Anton von
Webern, 578; Jelinek, Hanns,
712; Josef Matthias Hauer zum
75. Geburtstag, 702
Wilkinson, Mark. Pierre Boulez's
'Structure 1a,' 631; Two months
in the 'Studio di fonologia,' 282
Winckel, Fritz. Die Komposition
mit elektroakustischen Mitteln,
271
Wind, Hans E. Die Endkrise der
bürglichen Musik, 78
Winkler, Hans. Georg Büchners
'Woyzeck,' 546
Winter, Carl. Canticum Sancti
Marci, 802
Wirtz, Warren. The problem of
notation in the twelve-tone technique, 217
Wörner, Karl H. Arnold Schönberg:
zu seinem 75. Geburtstag, 323;
Current chronicle: Germany (Jul
1954), 440; ___ (Apr 1959), 625,
773; ___ (Jan 1960), 719; Dallapiccola's 'Job,' 662; Expression-

ismus, 96; Gotteswort und Magie, 448a; Krenek (Křenek), Ernst, 726; Musik der Gegenwart, 299; Neue Musik in der Entscheidung, 95; Neue Musik 1946-1958, 174; Die 39 Schlusstakte von Schönbergs 'Moses und Aron,' 447; Der unbekannte Schönberg, 338; 'Und trotzdem bete ich': Arnold Schönbergs letztes Werk, 421; Wolfgang Fortner in seinen Werken seit 1945, 676

Wolff, Helmut Christian. Movement, 570; Palestrina und Schönberg, 352

Wood, Ralph W. Concerning 'Sprechgesang,' 391

Wouters, Jos. Nieuwe balletmuziek van Stravinsky, 793

Xénakis, Yannis [Janis]. La crise de la musique sérielle, 39; Notes sur un 'Geste électronique,' 267; Wahrscheinlichkeitstheorie und Musik, 278

Yasser, Joseph. A letter from Arnold Schoenberg, 192

Zeiger, Jean Wilson. Early expressionistic songs, 476

Zenk, Ludwig. Mein Lehrer, 564

Zillig, Winfried. Notes on Arnold Schoenberg's unfinished oratorio, 'Die Jakobsleiter,' 435; Schoenbergs Moses und Aron, 443; Variationen über neue Musik, 118a

SUBJECT INDEX

Underlined items are main subject entries.

Acoustics, 30 (Phillippot), 239, 240, 253 (Poullin), 275 (Meyer-Eppler), 771, 772
Adler, Oscar, 373
Adorno, Theodor Wiesengrund, 168 (Eimert)
Aleatory composition see Indeterminacy in musical composition
All-interval rows see Row (twelve-tone)—structure
American twelve-tone music see United States—twelve-tone composition
Apostel, Hans Erich, 112
Athematicism, 207, 584
Atonality, 5, 9, 11, 12, 14, 15, 20, 23, 42, 46, 76, 79, 82, 88, 100, 112, 118b, 127, 128, 144, 145, 149, 159, 160, 169, 176, 177, 179, 180, 183, 185, 197, 201, 204, 218, 299, 317, 325, 351, 380, 387, 389, 499. See also Expressionism in music
Audibility of serial structure, 3, 28, 31, 40, 49, 57, 175c, 809
Avant garde, musical see Darmstadt, Germany. Summer School of new music; Experimental music; Indeterminacy in musical composition; Musique concrète; Post-Webern school; Totally determined serial music

Babbitt, Milton, 602-604
Badings, Henk, 112; Cain and Abel (ballet), 281
Bartòk, Bèla, 99, 160, 341, 501, 762

Beethoven, Ludwig van, 158, 303, 346, 383, 394
Berg, Alban, 491-563
Berio, Luciano, 605-609
Bibliographies and literature surveys: Berg, Alban, 94, 494, 496, 498; Dallapiccola, Luigi, 641, 645, 647; electronic music, 235, 237, 239, 247, 248, 267, 276, 277, 280; expressionism, 94, 96; Hauer, J. M., 696, 698, 700; Jelinek,. Hanns, 713; Krenek, Ernst, 724; Schoenberg, Arnold, 94, 151, 289, 386, 406, 412; Seiber, Mátyás, 761; Stravinsky, Igor, 780, 786; twelve-tone music 17, 22, 32, 81, 86, 88, 94, 95, 103, 144, 153; Webern, Anton, 94, 569, 570, 589
Blacher, Boris, 151, 703
Der blaue Reiter, 86
Blom, Eric, 28
Boubourechliev, André, 267
Boulez, Pierre, 610-631
Brazil—twelve-tone composers, 85
Bruckner, Anton, 298
Büchner, Georg, 562; Woyzeck, 546, 560
Busoni, Ferrucio B., 231

Cadences, 135
Cage, John, 632-637
Cantus firmus, 745
Chance music see Indeterminacy in musical composition
Chart music see Indeterminacy in musical composition
Chords in twelve-tone music, 178,

[147]

179, 182, 183, 191, 194, 195
Chromaticism see Expressionism; Harmony
Chronologies: Berg, Alban, 81, 509; Dallapiccola, Luigi, 647; Darmstadt, Germany. Summer School of new music, 170, 174; electronic music, 770; Schoenberg, 81, 286, 295 (Slonimsky), 301, 356, 412
Church music and the twelve-tone technique see Religious music
Classical music and serialism, 43, 141 (Krenek, Dallapiccola), 158, 308, 394
Cologne, Germany. N.W.D.R. Electronic studios see Germany: electronic music
Combinatoriality see Hexachordal division of the row; Row (twelve-tone)—structure
Composers: electronic music see entry under a specific country, e.g., Italy—electronic music; twelve-tone see entry under a specific country, e.g., Japan—twelve-tone composition
Compositional techniques, 119-175; Boulez, Pierre, 610-631; electronic music, 273-283; Schoenberg, Arnold, 380-394; Webern, Anton, 585-586
Computer music, 268
Concrete music see Musique concrète
Correspondence: Berg, Alban, 511-514; Schoenberg, Arnold, 373-379; Webern, Anton, 581-582
Counterpoint, 209-216

Dallapiccola, Luigi, 638-674
Darmstadt, Germany. Summer School of new music, 63, 110, 170, 174, 228, 263, 772
Debussy, Claude, 99, 160
Declamation, text see Text setting
Discographies and record reviews: Berg, Alban, 496, 498, 532; electronic music, 113, 267; Krenek, Ernst, 723; Schoenberg, Arnold, 301; Seiber, Mátyás, 763; twelve-tone music, 81, 84, 86, 113, 622; Webern, Anton, 577
Donatoni, Franco, 161
Duration see Rhythm

Egk, Werner, 718
Eisler, Hanns, 112, 345, 346
Electronic music: compositional techniques, 273-283; description and history, 234-272; philosophy and criticism, 222-233
Engelmann, Hans Ulrich, 112
Europe—twelve-tone composers, 88, 105
  See also France, Germany, Great Britain, Italy, and Spain
Experimental music, 49, 56, 63, 64, 70, 168, 170, 174, 232, 242, 250, 253, 267, 268, 270, 615.
  See also Darmstadt, Germany; Electronic music; Indeterminacy in musical composition; Musique concrète; Post-Webern school; Totally determined serial music
Expressionism in music, 2, 13, 74, 75, 80, 82, 94, 96, 100, 101, 117, 177, 310, 476.
  See also Atonality

Far East—twelve-tone composition, 111
Feldman, Morton, 632
Fortner, Wolfgang, 675-684
France: electronic music, 98, 262; Radiodiffusion Télévision Française. Groupe de Recherches Musicales see Musique concrète; twelve-tone composition, 90, 98, 105 (Drew), 613, 614, 627
Freud, Sigmund, 353
Functions of the row see Row (twelve-tone)—functions

Garcia Lorca, Federico, 681
Genzmer, Harald, 118a
Gerhard, Roberto, 685-692
Germany: electronic music, 251, 262, 272, 274, 276, 770; twelve-tone composition, 56, 105 (Hartog), 107, 118a

Golyshev, Lev, 99, 112, 160
Gravesano see Switzerland—electronic music
Great Britain—twelve-tone composers, 88, 91, 105 (Milner)

Harmony, 176-204
Hauer, Josef M., 693-702.
    See also Tropes
Heine, Heinrich, 655
Henze, Hans Werner, 703-710
Hexachordal division of the row, 43, 133, 136, 150, 156, 157, 199, 204a, 431, 482, 734, 742.
    See also Tropes
Hindemith, Paul, 349, 725
History of twelve-tone music, 74-118
Hoffmann, Richard, 151; —Tripartita for violin, 103
Humplick, Josef, 582

Incontri musicali (concerts) see Milan: Incontri musicali
Indeterminacy in musical composition, 71, 73a, 73b, 170, 636, 637, 739a
Instrumentation, 540, 813
International Society for Contemporary Music, 118, 230, 475
Internationale Ferienkurse für neue Musik, Darmstadt see Darmstadt, Germany
Interpretation see Performance of twelve-tone music
Israel—twelve-tone composition, 111
Italy—electronic music, 241, 246, 256, 262, 264, 265, 282; twelve-tone composition, 104, 105 (Smith Brindle), 106, 109, 116, 118a, 671

Janáček, Leos, 346
Japan—twelve-tone composition, 111
Jelinek, Hanns, 711-715
Jone, Hildegard, 582
Joyce, James, 640; _____, Ulysses, 609, 766, 767

Klangfarbenmusik, 222, 223, 224, 231
Klebe, Giselher, 716-719
Kranichsteiner Musikinstitut see Darmstadt, Germany
Krenek, Ernst, 720-747

Landvai, Ernö, 202, 203
Letters see Correspondence
Leibowitz, René, 748
Liebermann, Rolf, 151
Lieder see Songs; Vocal writing
Liszt, Kurt, 99a
Lutyens, Elizabeth, 112

Maderna, Bruno, 749
Maegaard, Jan, 112
Mahler, Fritz, 549
Mahler, Gustav, 132, 298, 303, 318
Malipiero, Riccardo, 112
Mann, Thomas—Doktor Faustus, 362
Martinů, Bohuslav, 741
Marxist criticisms of twelve-tone music, 345, 346, 351, 446, 505
Mathematics and serial music, 3, 10, 278, 280.
    See also Totally determined serial music
Melody, 205-207
Messiaen, Olivier, 54 (Pade), 253 (Boulez)
Milan: Incontri musicali (concerts), 629; Primo Congresso per la Musica Dodecafonica, 1949, 149; Studio di Fonologia Musicale see Italy—electronic music; twelve-tone composers see Italy—twelve-tone composition
Modal functions of the row see Row (twelve-tone): functions
Modes (Krenek) see Hexachordal division of the row
Moses, 353
Mozart, W. A., 141 (Dallapiccola), 158, 394
Musique concrète, 226, 236, 237, 254, 255, 267, 268, 270, 276, 611

Netherlands—electronic music, 266

150 Subject Index

Nielsen, Riccardo, 112
Nilsson, Bo, 168 (Koenig)
Nono, Luigi, 750-752
Notation, 217-221

Octave transpositions, equivalence of in twelve-tone music, 57, 59, 61, 66, 69, 175, 198
Orchestration see Instrumentation

Palestrina, Giovanni P. da, 352
Pedagogy see Teaching methods
Pepping, Ernst, 118a
Peragallo, Mario, 109, 112
Perameters see Totally determined serial music
Performance of twelve-tone music, 57, 59, 103, 228, 303, 350, 425, 427, 627
Perle, George, 28, 99a
Permutation of serial elements, 127, 150, 167, 170 (Nono), 191, 739a, 752
Piano music, 213, 295 (Steuermann), 457, 458, 627
Piston, Walter, 725
"Pointillism" in music see Post-Webern school
Politics and music, 478.
  See also Marxist criticisms of twelve-tone music
Post-Webern school, 38, 41, 46, 53, 62, 72, 108, 110, 118, 165, 199, 250, 332
Pousseur, Henri, 753-754
Practice and theory of twelve-tone music, relation between see Theory and practice of twelve-tone music
Pre-compositional techniques see Totally determined serial music
Primo Congresso per la Musica Dodecafonica (Milan, 1949) see Milan: Primo Congresso per la Musica Dodecafonica, 1949
Princeton Seminar in Advanced Musical Studies, 175b, 739a
Prokofiev, Sergei, 351
Prosperi, Carlo, 109
Proust, Marcel, 640

Radiodiffusion Télévision Française. Groupe de Recherches Musicales see France: electronic music; Musique concrète
Ravel, Maurice, 464
Reger, Max, 303
Religious music: and the twelve-tone technique, 52, 164; Schoenberg, Arnold, 52, 118a, 354, 407, 413, 423, 448a; Stravinsky, Igor, 779, 780, 798, 802; Webern, Anton, 52, 590
Repetition of tones, 133
Rhythm, 208
Riegger, Wallingford, 99a, 112
Roslavetz, Nikolai, 160
Rotation of serial elements see Permutation of serial elements
Row (twelve-tone): division into hexachords see Hexachordal division of the row; function, 134, 135, 136, 138, 143, 144, 155, 157, 160; structure, 10, 136, 138, 142, 143, 157, 160, 163, 175, 196, 386, 392, 398, 442, 471, 543, 606, 631, 654.
See also Hexachordal division of the row

Scelsi, Giacento, 112
Schaeffer, Pierre, 250
Schenker, Heinrich—system of analysis, 389, 432
Schoenberg, Arnold, 284-490
Schubert, Franz, 346
Scriabine, Alexander, 8, 99, 160
Searle, Humphrey, 373, 755-758
Secondary series see Row (twelve-tone): function
Seiber, Mátyás, 759-767
Series, twelve-tone see Row
Set, twelve-tone see Row
Silence, 58
Six-note division of the row see Hexachordal division of the row
Songs, 132, 476, 542, 601.
  See also Text setting; Vocal writing
Spain—twelve-tone composers see Gerhard, Roberto
Sprechstimme, 303, 391, 433, 559
Stein, Erwin, 373

Subject Index 151

Stockhausen, Karlheinz, 768-777
Strauss, Richard, 303, 318
Stravinsky, Igor, 778-823
Studio di Fonologia Musicale, Milano see Italy—electronic music
Switzerland—electronic music, 239
Symbolism in music, 251 (Magnani), 520, 537
Symmetrical row structure see Hexachordal division of the row; Row: structure

Tape-recorder music, 253 (Ussachevsky), 254, 268, 270
Teaching methods: electronic compositional techniques, 283; twelve-tone technique, 17, 18, 367, 507, 580a, 678
Terminology, 23, 67, 236, 242, 251, 282
Text setting, 74 (Schoenberg), 132, 233, 476, 594, 609, 623, 655, 737
Theory and practice of twelve-tone music, relation between, 42, 57, 59, 61, 66, 69, 72, 73, 73a, 174 (Pousseur), 775.
See also Audibility of serial structure; Totally determined serial music
Togni, Camillo, 112, 161
Tonality in twelve-tone music, 142, 175, 191, 202, 203, 300 (Leibowitz), 330, 449, 484, 505, 787 (Gerhard)
Totally determined serial music, 39, 46, 48, 50, 55, 68, 73a, 146, 150, 157, 161, 162, 163, 170 (Krenek), 172, 272, 608, 610, 775

Tropes, 129, 130, 140, 178.
See also Hauer, J. M.

United States—tape-recorder music see Tape-recorder music; twelve-tone composition, 99a, 118b, 157, 174 (Cage)

Varèse, Edgard, 174 (Metzger), 253 (Boulez)
Variation technique, 171, 460, 484
Vienna, 83, 117, 318, 509
Violin music, 103, 170 (Kolisch), 425, 427
Vlad, Roman, 109, 112
Vocal writing, 45, 170 (Stockhausen), 205, 229, 303, 451.
See also Sprechstimme; Text setting
Von Webern, Anton see Webern, Anton

Wagner, Richard, 450
Wagner-Régeny, Rudolf, 151
Weber, Ben, 99a, 602
Webern, Anton, 564-601
Wedekind, Frank—Lulu, 534
Weiss, Adolph, 99a
Werndorff, Marietta, 373
Wolf, Hugo, 542
Wolpe, Stefan, 99a

Zillig, Winfried, 151
Zimmermann, Bernd Alois, 168 (Schubert)

www.ingramcontent.com/pod-product-compliance
Lightning Source LLC
Chambersburg PA
CBHW021711230426
43668CB00008B/796